Wings of Valor

Wings of Valor

of

Honoring America's Fighter Aces

Nick Del Calzo
and Peter Collier

Naval Institute Press
Annapolis, Maryland

This book has been brought to publication with the generous assistance of the American Fighter Aces Association.

Naval Institute Press
291 Wood Road
Annapolis, MD 21402

Library of Congress Cataloging-in-Publication Data
Names: Del Calzo, Nick, author. | Collier, Peter, date, author.
Title: Wings of valor : honoring America's fighter aces / Nick Del Calzo and Peter Collier.
Other titles: Honoring America's fighter aces
Description: Annapolis, Maryland : Naval Institute Press, [2016] | Includes bibliographical references.
Identifiers: LCCN 2016032781 (print) | LCCN 2016033636 (ebook) | ISBN 9781591146414 (hbk. : alk. paper) | ISBN 9781682471555 (ePDF) | ISBN 9781682471555 (ePub) | ISBN 9781682471555 (mobi)
Subjects: LCSH: Fighter pilots—United States—Biography.
Classification: LCC UG626 .D45 2016 (print) | LCC UG626 (ebook) | DDC 358.40092/273—dc23
LC record available at https://lccn.loc.gov/2016032781

♾ Print editions meet the requirements of ANSI/NISO z39.48-1992 (Permanence of Paper).
Printed in the United States of America.

24 23 22 21 20 19 18 17 16   9 8 7 6 5 4 3 2 1
First printing

Contents

Acknowledgments   ix

Introduction   1

Benjamin C. Amsden ★ LIEUTENANT (JG), USNR   3

Clarence E. Anderson ★ COLONEL, USAF   6

Abner M. Aust Jr. ★ COLONEL, USAF   9

Raymond M. Bank ★ MAJOR, USAF   12

Richard S. Becker ★ MAJOR, USAF   15

Richard L. Bertelson ★ LIEUTENANT, USNR   18

Stephen J. Bonner Jr. ★ MAJOR, USAF   21

Clarence A. Borley ★ COMMANDER, USN   24

James L. Brooks ★ CAPTAIN, USAF   27

Henry Buttelmann ★ LIEUTENANT COLONEL, USAF   30

Richard G. Candelaria ★ COLONEL, USAFR   33

Robert B. Carlson ★ LIEUTENANT COMMANDER, USNR   36

Dean Caswell ★ COLONEL, USMC   39

Lawrence A. Clark ★ LIEUTENANT COMMANDER, USN   42

Robert A. Clark ★ LIEUTENANT COMMANDER, USN   45

Charles G. Cleveland ★ LIEUTENANT GENERAL, USAF   48

John T. Crosby ★ COMMANDER, USN   51

Perry J. Dahl ★ COLONEL, USAF   **54**

Barrie S. Davis ★ MAJOR, USAAFR | COLONEL, ANG (NCANG)   **57**

Jefferson J. DeBlanc ★ COLONEL, USMCR   **60**

James E. Duffy ★ LIEUTENANT COMMANDER, USNR   **63**

Fred L. Dungan ★ LIEUTENANT COMMANDER, USN   **66**

Clyde B. East ★ LIEUTENANT COLONEL, USAF   **69**

Billy G. Edens ★ COLONEL, USAF   **72**

Robert P. Fash ★ LIEUTENANT, USNR   **75**

Edward L. Feightner ★ REAR ADMIRAL, USN   **78**

Arthur C. Fiedler ★ COLONEL, USAF   **81**

Richard H. Fleischer ★ CAPTAIN, USAAF   **84**

Joseph J. Foss ★ CAPTAIN, USMCR | BRIGADIER GENERAL, ANG   **87**

Cecil G. Foster ★ LIEUTENANT COLONEL, USAF   **90**

Frank L. Gailer Jr. ★ BRIGADIER GENERAL, USAF   **93**

Robert E. Galer ★ BRIGADIER GENERAL, USMC   **96**

Clayton K. Gross ★ CAPTAIN, USAAF   **99**

Willis E. Hardy ★ COMMANDER, USN   **102**

Charles D. Hauver ★ MAJOR, USAF   **105**

Frank D. Hurlbut ★ LIEUTENANT COLONEL, USAF   **108**

Arthur F. Jeffrey ★ COLONEL, USAF   **111**

Lynn F. Jones ★ CAPTAIN, USAAF   **114**

Philip L. Kirkwood ★ COMMANDER, USNR   **117**

Dean S. Laird ★ COMMANDER, USN   **120**

Kenneth B. Lake ★ CAPTAIN, USN   **123**

Jack Lenox ★ LIEUTENANT COLONEL, USAF   **126**

George G. Loving ★ LIEUTENANT GENERAL, USAF   **129**

James F. Low ★ MAJOR, USAF   **132**

James F. Luma ★ FLYING OFFICER, RCAF | FIRST LIEUTENANT, USAAF **135**

Winton W. Marshall ★ LIEUTENANT GENERAL, USAF **138**

W. Robert Maxwell ★ COMMANDER, USNR **141**

Frank E. McCauley ★ MAJOR, USAF **144**

Joseph D. McGraw ★ CAPTAIN, USN **147**

Donald M. McPherson ★ ENSIGN, USNR **150**

Henry Meigs II ★ FIRST LIEUTENANT, USAAF | COLONEL, ANG (KANG) **153**

Robert C. Milliken ★ LIEUTENANT, USAAF **156**

Sanford K. Moats ★ LIEUTENANT GENERAL, USAF **159**

George P. Novotny ★ FIRST LIEUTENANT, USAAF **162**

Fred F. Ohr ★ MAJOR, USAAF **165**

Jeremiah J. O'Keefe Sr. ★ FIRST LIEUTENANT, USMC **168**

Ralph S. Parr ★ COLONEL, USAF **171**

Frederick R. Payne ★ BRIGADIER GENERAL, USMC **174**

Steve N. Pisanos ★ PILOT OFFICER, RAF | COLONEL, USAF **177**

Tilman E. Pool ★ LIEUTENANT, USN **180**

Ralston M. Pound ★ COMMANDER, USNR **183**

Luther D. Prater ★ CAPTAIN, USN **186**

Donald L. Quigley ★ LIEUTENANT COLONEL, USAAFR **189**

Alden P. Rigby ★ MAJOR, USAF **192**

R. Stephen Ritchie ★ BRIGADIER GENERAL, USAFR **195**

LeRoy W. Robinson ★ COMMANDER, USNR **198**

George I. Ruddell ★ COLONEL, USAF **201**

Leslie C. Smith ★ BRIGADIER GENERAL, USAF **204**

Donald J. Strait ★ MAJOR GENERAL, USAF **207**

James E. Swett ★ COLONEL, USMCR **210**

David F. Thwaites ★ LIEUTENANT COLONEL, USAF **213**

Alexander Vraciu ★ COMMANDER, USN   **216**

Ralph H. Wandrey ★ MAJOR, USAAF   **219**

Charles E. Watts ★ LIEUTENANT COMMANDER, USN   **222**

Darrell G. Welch ★ COLONEL, USAF   **225**

William H. Wescott ★ LIEUTENANT COLONEL, USAFR   **228**

David C. Wilhelm ★ CAPTAIN, USAAF   **231**

Bruce W. Williams ★ LIEUTENANT, USNR   **234**

John T. Wolf ★ LIEUTENANT (JG), USNR   **237**

John A. Zink ★ LIEUTENANT (JG), USN   **240**

William H. Allen ★ MAJOR, USAF   **243**

Robert A. Karr ★ LIEUTENANT COLONEL, USAF   **244**

Author's Note   **245**

Selected Bibliography   **249**

Acknowledgments

OUR GOAL WAS TO PAY HOMAGE TO and immortalize America's Fighter Aces and their aerial combat achievements, which represent a significant historical period in military aviation history. The culmination of this project is the result of contributions of numerous individuals.

Foremost among them is Gen. Charles C. Cleveland, an Ace and president of the American Fighter Aces Association (AFAA). From the first day that the photographic process began in August 2012, General Cleveland's insights, diligence, and resourcefulness have been invaluable. His steadfast commitment to see this project to completion has been an inspiration to me. He was involved in its creation, as well as its purpose to perpetuate the legacy of these amazing pilots, sharing the vision that author Peter Collier and I had for this body of work.

In addition, I wish to extend a special acknowledgment to members of the AFAA Board of Directors, and in particular: Dr. Frank Olynyk, Dr. Gregg Wagner (who provided most of the archival images), Phil Schasker, Dean Wolff, and Scott Thomas. Most importantly, I want to thank all of the Aces who participated as well as their family members and friends who assisted in coordinating the photographic process.

The photographic challenge to complete this project was a race against time because of the high mortality rate of the Aces, most of whom are now in their nineties. Although my original intent was to personally photograph all of the Aces, it was far more important to ensure that as many Aces as possible would be included in the book. Consequently, I recruited photographers throughout the country to assist in creating the portraits. Without their participation, the book could not have been completed. Their meaningful portraits add immeasurable value to this telling of the Aces' stories. Credit lines appear with the portraits they contributed.

The photographers are: Alan Abramowitz, Andrew Achong, Amber Barker, Mark R. Bertelson, Chandler Crowell, Tom Dubanowich, Ariel Fried, Marco Garcia, Marc Glassman, Gabe Hernandez, Dominik Huber, David Jaffe, Athena Lonsdale, Alex McKnight, August Miller, Eric Muetterties, Frank Olynyk, Peter Panayiotou, Anna Reed, Rich Saal, Mark Skalny, Michael Schoenholtz, John Slemp, Jimmy Williams, and Todd A. Yarrington.

This important work also was made possible with the contributions of numerous individuals who helped in their own way, by offering their time, talents, interest, and financial support to transform this historical vision into a reality. Among them are: Tom Allee, Gregg Aretakis, Jan Baker, Ward Boyce, Arlene Boyer, Amanda Campbell, Matthew Cavarra, Paula Clark, Gloria Clinton, Dean Del Calzo, Sue DeNure, Nadja de Sa`, Patricia Germek, Jim Gunlock, Matt Hayes, Dominik Huber, Doug King, Ron Landucci, Gen. Sanford K. Moats, Scott Nickell, Linda Raper, Harold Rubin, Scott Schmehl, Richard Schneider, Tom Wilkerson, J. D. Wyneken, Harry Ziegler, and Frontier Airlines.

Finally, I wish to recognize the contributions, talents, and gifts of author Peter Collier. Our first joint book project (*Medal of Honor: Portraits of Valor Beyond the Call of Duty*) featured a two-page format of a Medal of Honor recipient, with a portrait on one page and a six-hundred-word narrative on the opposite page. However, due to the Ace designation qualification of at least five enemy air combat "kills," this word count restriction was too limiting. The reader would not experience Peter's masterful ability to craft the Ace's combat actions into a compelling story. Therefore, as the lead photographer, I elected to change the two-page format noted above to one in which the action-packed and personal accounts of the Aces dominate, in order to provide the reader a better understanding and appreciation of the heroics of these men. Aces are listed along with their rank and service branch at the time of retirement or separation from military service. ⭐

—NICK DEL CALZO

I am indebted to Gen. Charles Cleveland, who helped this book come to be. Thanks also to Frank Olynyk, one-man encyclopedia about the Aces and author of what is rightly regarded as the "bible" of their actions: *Stars and Bars: A Tribute to the American Fighter Ace 1920–1973*; to military historian Jon Guttman; to Arthur Bednar of the Museum of Flight in Seattle; and finally to Doris Y. Collier (1914–86), one of American Airlines' first and most beautiful stewardesses, who made flight a central part of her family's story. ⭐

—PETER COLLIER

Introduction

THE CONCEPT OF THE ACE, a combat aviator of exceptional skill and daring in confronting the enemy, was born in the skies over western Europe in World War I, the first conflict in which aircraft played a major role. At the onset of this war, airplanes were used primarily for reconnaissance and observation, along with rudimentary bombing runs at low altitudes in which explosives were dropped by hand out of an open cockpit. As they became effective in locating an enemy force and passing information about its size and disposition to the high command below, airplanes were targeted for destruction by ground fire and increasingly by rival aircraft. In the first days of the war in 1914, pilots used pistols, hunting rifles, grenades, and even grappling hooks in clumsy efforts to bring each other down. As air superiority became a major objective of the warring armies, the technology of aerial combat advanced rapidly. By the midpoint of the conflict fighter planes had become precision instruments of death as a result of machine guns, which were mounted on their noses and synchronized to fire through the arcs of their propellers without striking and shredding the blades.

Unlike the impersonal carnage taking place in the trenches below, the air war was fought by men who became public personalities and acquired mass followings. The term "Ace" was first applied to Frenchman Adolphe Pégoud by Parisian newspapers when he shot down five German planes. It was soon applied to all pilots who had met this standard. Then and ever after, "Ace" was a status coveted by every pilot who climbed into the cockpit of a fighter plane.

Rules evolved to guarantee that someone called an Ace had earned the honor. A "kill" had to be physically confirmed by sighting of the wreckage or witnessed by an independent observer. By World War II, the use of gun cameras would make the confirmation process more objective and definitive. It was also in World War II that fractions of a kill were awarded when more than one aircraft brought down an enemy, and that the term "probable" (not counted in determining Ace status) was coined to describe a victory claim that was likely but not able to be proven with certainty.

The Aces of World War I were regarded as knights of the sky, obeying an unwritten code of noblesse oblige. (Indeed, there were several instances in which an army sent planes to drop a wreath on the wreckage of a rival pilot who had fought well before falling in battle.) The romance of flight still clung to the Aces of World War II, but they had a different and more decisive mission. Less figures of chivalry now than their predecessors, they were hunters trying to survive in the jungle warfare of the skies, stoic heroes asking no quarter of the enemy and giving none as they scored the five kills that made them a special breed. (How special was never in doubt: Aces, an estimated 5 percent of all combat pilots, were responsible for about one-third of air victories in this conflict.)

Unlike the ground forces they protected, the Aces of World War II—flying Hellcats, Thunderbolts, Mustangs, and other iconic fighter planes off aircraft carriers and sometimes off hastily constructed airfields that just weeks earlier had been enemy territory—were on their own, relying on their individual skills, determination, and daring to prevail in engagements that were the aerial equivalent of a bare-knuckle brawl. The stakes—control of the skies over the Pacific and western Europe, where the battles were fought that would determine the course of history—couldn't have been higher. It was little wonder that Gregory "Pappy" Boyington, "Butch" O'Hare, Dick Bong, "Gabby" Gabreski, and other Aces from this war became household names with a strong and durable hold on the American imagination.

In Korea U.S. pilots became Aces in jets flying close to the speed of sound. Engaged in an ambiguous "police action" with restrictive rules of engagement about where and how combat would take place that often prevented them from seeking final victory, these pilots controlled the skies of Korea and dared the enemy to come up and fight.

In Vietnam the rules of engagement were even more stringent. Combat was an aerial chess match involving a handful of aircraft rather than multiple squadrons, and was fought for the most part with guided missiles rather than staccato bursts of machine-gun fire, but achieving status as an Ace was still a shining ideal for the U.S. pilots who served there.

But if the Ace has become an honored, even mythic, figure as a result of the wars the United States has fought over the last one hundred years, he is today also an endangered species. American air superiority has become so complete and the technology of unmanned aircraft so crucial to military strategy that it is hard to imagine a future air war that will produce a new generation of Aces.

Of the approximately 60,000 pilots who flew in combat for the United States in World War I, World War II, Korea, and Vietnam, 1,447 became Aces. On May 19, 2015, 76 remained when the U.S. Congress awarded a Congressional Gold Medal to all U.S. Aces. As of this writing, there are fewer still. They are likely to be the last of their breed. The men and women who sit behind computers operating the joysticks of drones will play a crucial role in our future national defense, but it is hard to imagine that they will ever face the challenges or have the emotional claim on our imagination that the fighter Ace has had.

Wings of Valor takes a last look at these larger-than-life heroes—quite literally in formal photographic portraits that show the content of their character. It enters the drama of their dogfights one final time, and listens to the lessons each of them learned from his rendezvous with destiny. The things they achieved saved lives, shortened wars, and left an indelible imprint on our national history. The stories they tell will never grow old and never die. ★

Benjamin C. Amsden

LIEUTENANT (JG), USNR

October 10, 1922–December 10, 2014

"AS A GOOD CATHOLIC BOY," BEN AMSDEN later said to military historian Jon Guttman in an interview about his days as a Navy flyer in World War II, "I had my rosary and did a lap around the beads every night, praying for two things—that I would come back alive and that I would get five planes to become an Ace. And I got my fifth on the second-to-last day before our air group was relieved. So I guess someone up there was looking out for me."

Amsden, a native of Buffalo, New York, was not quite twenty years old when he joined the Navy as an aviation cadet on September 22, 1942. He got his wings at Naval Air Station Pensacola on February 1, 1944, and served in a training squadron until August. Then he was assigned to VF-22 on board the USS *Cowpens*, an *Independence*–class light carrier named for a Revolutionary War battle that took place near Cowpens, South Carolina.

By mid-September Amsden was flying his first combat missions against Japanese positions in the Palau Islands and on Luzon. He immediately learned to trust his F6F Grumman Hellcat for its sturdiness and firepower. As he later described the plane's assets to Guttman: "Each Hellcat had six .50-caliber machine guns firing 75 rounds a second. . . . In three seconds they could put 22 1/2 pounds of lead in an enemy plane . . . and also carry a 500-pound bomb for land missions. What really made the Hellcat stand out, though, was that it could take tremendous abuse and still fly. It was a sponge for punishment."

On October 12, Amsden and seven other Hellcat pilots were staging a rocket attack on an enemy airfield on Formosa when they were attacked by fourteen Japanese fighters. In the fierce action that followed, Amsden got his first kill—a Mitsubishi A6M5 Zero.

Over the next few days, Japanese torpedo planes retaliated with a series of fierce attacks on the American fleet. The heavy cruiser USS *Canberra* and the light cruiser USS *Houston* were disabled. The *Cowpens* was assigned, along

Alex McKnight /AM Photo Inc.

with the USS *Cabot*, to protect the two cruisers as they were towed toward the Navy's staging area at Ulithi Atoll in the Caroline Islands. The enemy smelled blood, and, as Amsden later said, "For the next several days, we were under constant attack, day and night."

On October 15, while fighting off this onslaught, he had what he called his "most memorable mission of the war." Shortly before noon eight G4M "Betty" (in the Allied classification code for Japanese aircraft) bombers appeared to administer the coup de grâce to the wounded ships. Amsden and seven other Hellcats flying a combat air patrol immediately attacked. Picking out a pair of the bombers, he opened fire and "hit the cockpit of the first causing it to plunge into the ocean." As the second Betty dropped down to the wave tops in the hope of evading him, Amsden realized that if he dove on it he risked overshooting and hitting the water

himself, so he sped a mile ahead of the bomber and then came around and approached it from the side. After taking out the plane's waist gunner on his first pass, he came around again and "was able to get a good shot at the pilot's cabin and finished him off, fifteen feet above the water."

Once the *Canberra* and *Houston* had made it to safety at Ulithi, the *Cowpens* rejoined Navy Task Force 38, which was then moving to support Gen. Douglas MacArthur's long-promised return to the Philippines. Amsden was up with three other Hellcats on October 22, just days after MacArthur waded ashore at Leyte. The U.S. planes saw a Japanese troop ship docking to land soldiers for a counteroffensive against the Americans. "The four of us came down strafing," he later recalled. "The first pass must have killed a hundred of them. It was a lot of damage caused by a few pilots."

In mid-December, the *Cowpens* passed through Typhoon Cobra in the South China Sea along with the rest of Task Force 38—an event that the men who experienced it always regarded as almost as bad as the battles they survived. Three U.S. destroyers sank in the storm with a loss of nearly eight hundred men. Nine ships were badly damaged, including the *Cowpens* itself, which docked at Ulithi for over a week of repair.

At the beginning of 1945 the carrier was back in combat, once more launching raids on Formosa. On January 3, Amsden was part of a flight of eight Hellcats on a mission over the island when they encountered fourteen enemy planes. He picked out a Nakajima J1N1 "Irving," Japan's frontline night fighter, and shot it down with relative ease. ("Maybe the sun was in his eyes," Amsden later quipped about the pilot.)

On January 21, on another raid against Formosa, all that "telling" of the rosary beads finally paid off when Amsden shot down a Nakajima Ki-43 "Oscar" fighter and became an Ace.

A few days later VF-22 was replaced on board the *Cowpens* and Amsden was sent home. By March he was flying the F4U Corsair as part of VF-74 at Otis Field, Massachusetts, for what he later said was an "enjoyable" three months. "There were also some German POWs staying there," he later recounted to Jon Guttman. "The authorities actually let them go out under supervised conditions. Well, to give you an idea of how cocky fighter pilots could be, I befriended a waitress at Coonamessett Inn on Cape Cod. She'd tell me when the Germans would be there. That night I'd buzz the inn—and they'd dive under the tables."

Ben Amsden never went back to the war zone. He left the Navy in September 1945, earned a degree from Cornell in hotel management, and went on to work for Sheraton and Holiday Inn for more than twenty years, finishing his career as the manager of private country clubs. ★

Clarence E. Anderson

COLONEL, USAF

January 13, 1922–

"BUD" ANDERSON (HE WAS BORN CLARENCE EMIL and regarded the nickname he was given in infancy as an act of mercy) always remembered the 1929 crash landing of a Boeing Model 80 Trimotor in a field near his family's home when he was seven years old. It was a major event: people from all around came to gawk at the plane. Bud and his best friend rushed to the crash site and spent the day climbing through the cabin and sitting in the cockpit, imagining themselves airborne and in command.

Growing up on a large fruit-tree farm near the small California foothills town of Newcastle, a few miles north of Sacramento at the gateway to the High Sierra, Anderson was five years old when Charles Lindbergh crossed the Atlantic. This event helped him fall in love with flight, and his father deepened the romance soon after by driving him to a little dirt airfield in Sacramento for a ride in a biplane. After this, as Anderson later wrote in his memoir *To Fly and Fight*, the walls of his bedroom were papered with photos torn out of the pages of *Popular Aviation*, squadrons of model planes hung by strings from his ceiling, and he had at least a vague sense that flying was in his future.

After graduating from high school in 1939, Anderson took stock of what was required to get into the Army Air Corps—be single, twenty years old, and have two years of college. He enrolled in Sacramento Junior College Technical Institute for Aeronautics (later joking that the entrance exam was being able to remember the name) and also entered the Civilian Pilot Training Program, which meant he could learn to fly for free while pursuing his studies. He had just graduated from the junior college, had a few hours' flight time in a Piper Cub, and was working as an aircraft mechanic at the Sacramento Air Depot when the Japanese bombed Pearl Harbor. Less than a month later, Anderson turned twenty and immediately enlisted; he was sent to Lindbergh Field in San Diego for flight training.

Not long after receiving his wings in September 1942, he was checked out in the P-39 Airacobra at Hamilton Army Air Field in Northern California and then assigned to the newly formed 357th Fighter Group. In the spring of 1943, the pilots of the 357th were sent to the gunnery range in Tonopah, Nevada, to learn combat tactics. One of the men he would meet there was Chuck Yeager, who would become Bud Anderson's longtime good friend. Among the things that the two men had in common was 20/10 vision: they could spot planes when they were still only specks in the air, invisible to men with only average good vision.

The 357th sailed for England in November 1943 on board the *Queen Elizabeth*, and was assigned the new P-51 Mustang when it settled into the RAF base at Leiston, sixty miles north of London. (Anderson had "Old Crow" in the whiskey-maker's lettering painted on his fuselage.)

The 357th would become one of the most lethal of all the U.S. fighter groups, scoring 658 victories against 128 losses while going up against the Germans' best pilots and planes. "We weren't like other people," Anderson later said, "at least not in our own minds. We were bolder, braver, smarter, more spirited." Yet he also saw that only the fittest survived.

Of the twenty-eight original pilots in Anderson's squadron, sixteen would either die in combat or be shot down and captured. (Yeager was shot down over France but managed to make his way to Spain and returned to the unit.)

As the engine of his Mustang idled heavily while he waited to take off on his first mission, Anderson was "more afraid of screwing up than of dying." But he didn't even see an enemy aircraft in his first few missions over France because the Germans had concentrated their air defense closer to home. Then he had all the action he wanted as his squadron began flying escort for the bombers, which were beginning to pound aircraft factories and other targets in the German homeland.

The German fighters would come at the B-17s and B-24s head-on, trying to scatter the formation. They would fire long bursts, roll down, then circle around to get ahead of the bomber stream and attack again. Before the 357th arrived, the bomber losses were fearsome, with up to a 4 percent casualty rate being regarded as acceptable by the Allied High Command. The arrival of the Mustangs improved the bombers' odds so dramatically that the minimum number of missions for a crew was raised from twenty-five to thirty-five.

On March 8, 1944, Anderson got his first kill when he fired a Hail Mary burst at a Messerschmitt Me 109 after engaging it in a series of tight turns to get inside position, which caused the German pilot to fly directly into his gunnery pattern. Over the next two months, he got three more. On May 12, Anderson became an Ace without firing a shot when he closed on an Me 109 and the German pilot, panicking at his approach, preemptively bailed out of the plane.

In late May, Old Crow and the other Mustangs got a new paint job—black and white stripes on their wings—so that Allied gunners wouldn't target them during the Normandy invasion. By the end of June, after supporting the landing, the 357th was back to escorting missions that at times involved as many as 1,300 U.S. bombers and 1,100 fighters. On June 29, Anderson's biggest day of combat, he shot down three Focke-Wulf 190s.

By mid-January 1945, Anderson had flown 116 missions, completed two tours of combat, and was a triple Ace with 16.25 kills. Amazingly, his plane had never even suffered a hit in all the dogfights he had experienced. On January 14, he and Yeager flew their last missions of the war, the two of them flying as "spares" to back up the main force of Mustangs heading toward Germany. Since they were not needed for combat that day, they took a sightseeing tour of the Alps.

After the war Bud Anderson worked as a test pilot and reluctantly spent time at the Pentagon. He did a tour in Southeast Asia during the Vietnam War in command of the 355th Tactical Fighter Wing, and flew combat missions in F-105s against enemy supply lines. While he was there, his son Jim, just out of flight school, was flying O-2s over the jungle as part of a Special Operations project. Bud made a surprise visit to Jim's base and accompanied him as copilot on one of their missions.

Bud Anderson retired from the Air Force as a colonel in 1972. In 1988, he and Chuck Yeager climbed into refurbished Mustangs like those they had flown over forty years earlier (even with the same paint job) and went up together at Troy, Alabama, disproving the old adage that "there are old pilots and bold pilots, but no old bold pilots." ⭐

Abner M. Aust Jr.

COLONEL, USAF

October 7, 1921–

ABNER AUST GREW UP AS A WALKING EMBODIMENT of the truth in Mark Twain's famous observation that "it's not the size of the dog in the fight that counts, but the size of the fight in the dog."

Born at home in the tiny Mississippi town of Scooba on October 7, 1921, Aust grew up in Belzoni. He had family throughout Mississippi, Alabama, and Texas—some of them in America since before the Revolution. He was named Abner after one of Saul's generals in the Old Testament Book of Samuel, by his father, whose own name, Absolom, was taken from the same book.

Aust reached his full height of five feet six inches before he was in high school. He was shy but also self-assured, a competitive boxer who won most of his matches by knockout. In the Air Force he would say, "I might be short on the ground, but in the air I'm the biggest guy up there."

Aust became interested in aviation at the age of seven when his was living in Lawton, Oklahoma, and he watched planes practicing bombing techniques at nearby Fort Sill. In the fall of 1941, attending Mississippi Delta Community College, he entered the Civilian Air Patrol Cadet Program and to pay expenses helped build a runway at the college. He was a natural flier and after six flights with his instructor was allowed to solo.

After completing the primary phase of forty hours of flight time he drove to the state capitol of Jackson with the other men in the program to get his pilot's license. Asked for his birth certificate, he replied that he didn't have one because he had been born at home. With the help of school records and information on the fly leaf of the family Bible, his birth date was confirmed.

In June 1942, Aust and fifteen other student pilot graduates drove to Greenville Army Air Base in South Carolina to take the aviation exam. Afterward, the recruiting sergeant asked the men how soon they could leave for cadet training. All the others named a future date within the month. Aust said, "I'm

ready to leave this afternoon." Within two weeks he received his orders to report to the air base in Santa Anna, California.

After basic training there, he transferred in October 1942 to primary flying school. He and four other cadets were assigned to an instructor who had been a crop duster and who never soloed any of the five. Aust later said that because he could fly the P-17 better than this instructor, he was reassigned to fly with the squadron operations officer and commander.

In March 1943, Aust and his group of cadets were transferred to Luke Air Base in Arizona and volunteered to fly the somewhat outmoded P-40s, similar to those used by the Flying Tigers in China. After advanced training, he was assigned to the 43rd Fighter Group at Fort Myers, Florida, a place known as "Mosquito Heaven." Aust got a reputation as a daredevil because of his aerobatics and

speed passes, some at fifty feet above the ground. As a result of these stunts, he was once grounded and assigned to duty as runway control officer for two months.

Early in 1945, Aust was assigned to the 457th Fighter Squadron flying brand new P-51s off a grass strip on Tinian originally built for Japanese fighters. After some missions against the Japanese island Chichi Jima, the 457th was assigned to a new base on the northeast corner of Iwo Jima in April 1945. Aust got a sense of the ferocity of the battle being waged there when he stepped out of his plane and saw the bodies of Japanese soldiers strewn around the airfield, most of them missing teeth, valuable for their gold fillings. "The Marines had accomplished a lot of dental work on the bodies," he later said. "I could have traded a bottle of Mission whiskey for a large marble-sized ball of gold."

On June 1, Aust had to take his turn as command pilot on one of the B-29s that navigated for the P-51s on their way from Iwo Jima to the coast of Japan. He was in the last of the twelve bombers escorting 144 P-51s. Halfway to target they encountered heavy squalls that went from sea level to above 25,000 feet. The Mustangs tried to fly in formation through the weather, but Aust and his B-29 pilot poured on the power and broke out above 25,000 feet. He saw eleven P-51 pilots who had also been lucky enough to get above the turbulence and escorted them back to Iwo Jima. When the mission, known as "Black Friday" by the Air Force, was over, twenty-seven pilots and twenty-nine planes had been lost.

On July 16, Aust, leading two flights of P-51s, spotted six enemy Nakajima Ki-84 "Frank" fighters approaching head-on. He called for the American pilots to drop their fuel tanks and then selected the leader of the enemy flight and shot him down immediately. He then destroyed a second "Frank." "As I pulled up another was almost in front of me," he later said. "I finished him with a burst into the cockpit that I believe killed the pilot."

Aust was firing on one of the last enemy planes when another Mustang also dived down to attack it. He felt his plane take hits on the left wing and headed back to base. After he landed, his crew chief pointed out a circle of bullet holes about a foot in diameter just behind the cockpit, damage caused by friendly fire from the other P-51. Aust marched over to the operations hut of the 462nd, the other Mustang squadron, and told the pilots there: "You guys are walking on dangerous ground when you mess with me!"

On August 10, four days after the bombing of Hiroshima, Aust shot down two Japanese Zeros in a swirling dogfight near Tokyo. These were the last Japanese fighters shot down in the Pacific and Aust became the last American Ace of World War II.

On August 14, Aust's squadron escorted B-29s on their last mission against the Japanese. The following day Emperor Hirohito announced his country's surrender.

Abner Aust remained in the Air Force for the next twenty-seven years, serving in Korea and Vietnam, where he flew three hundred combat missions in the F-4 and F-100 and commanded the 3rd, 31st, and 33rd Tactical Fighter Wings. He retired as a colonel in 1972. ★

Raymond M. Bank

MAJOR, USAF

March 15, 1924–

WHEN RAYMOND BANK'S FATHER LOST HIS FARM, located near the small town of Kendall, Michigan, during the Depression, he moved with his children to Chicago so he could find work. Raymond's mother had died in 1927 when he was three years old, and his father was hard-pressed to care for him and his six brothers and sisters by himself. Yet there was one bright childhood memory for Raymond amidst the hard times: sitting on the veranda of the local hospital while recuperating from a tonsillectomy and witnessing the thrilling spectacle of a large number of Army airplanes passing overhead in formation.

That image stayed with Banks and was one reason why he decided to enlist in the Army Air Corps soon after graduating from high school in 1942. He received his wings in August 1943 and hoped to go directly into combat but was instead made an instructor at Laughlin Air Field in Texas. Over the next year he constantly pestered the operations officer when they ran into each other: "Don't forget. If you need a combat pilot, I'm your boy."

In August 1944 Bank finally got his wish when he shipped out for England to join the 357th Fighter Group. Flying a P-51 Mustang he named "Fireball," Bank had completed several fairly routine missions escorting bombers into Germany when he went up on Christmas Eve day. In the middle of Germany, he broke into clear sky and saw a group of aircraft dead ahead. As he later recalled, "I reported, 'Bogies at 12 o'clock.' Ten seconds later I recognized them as Bf 109s. We broke to the left, so hard that my aircraft stalled." Recovering, he fired a short burst and hit a Messerschmitt in the aft fuselage. "I said to myself, 'That's no good,' and readjusted so that the next burst hit the cockpit. The 109 began to tumble ass over tea kettle. I followed him down and gave him another burst for good measure before he hit the ground."

Three weeks later, on January 14, 1945, Bank's squadron was escorting the lead formation of a group of B-17s bombers toward a suburb of Berlin when he saw several puffs of black smoke in concentrated patterns. At first he

Tom Dubanowich

thought it must be explosions of flak from 40-mm guns. But then he realized that it was cannon fire from one of the revolutionary new German Me 262 jet fighters, "a wondrous sight to behold as it whizzed by." Bank fired a quick burst, but the speeding jet was already gone when his bullets arrived in the spot where it had been—"a small speck in the distance."

Just then he saw several Focke-Wulf 190s dropping down to attack another Mustang. He called for a hard break to the left, which put him in behind one of them, and fired a short burst that set it on fire. As he rolled to avoid colliding with it, he saw another Fw 190 directly ahead. He opened fire and saw flames erupt from this Fw's engine as well. Again he rolled to avoid a collision and again he found himself on the tail of another 190. "This time my adversary tried a series of violent right and left turns to try and spoil my aim," Bank later wrote. The German headed straight down "in a 90-degree dive" and Bank followed. When the 190 pulled out of the dive, he did too, the 7 g maneuver inflating his anti-g suit. He was finally able to fire a short burst that set the Focke-Wulf on fire and gave him his third kill in a matter of minutes. He was amazed to find that his "total ammunition expenditure was 690 rounds for the entire battle!"

On March 2, Bank shot down a Messerschmitt Me 109 southeast of the German city of Magdeburg and became an Ace. Not long after, he and other Mustangs were strafing an airfield when he saw one of them hit by ground fire. He radioed the pilot that he would escort him back to base, but when he dropped his flaps to slow down for the other P-51, nothing happened and he realized that he too had been hit during the strafing run and had no hydraulics. Next he saw the coolant temperature hit the red on the gauge and realized that his engine would soon seize and blow up. Seeing an open field below he hooked his shoulder harness for a crash landing. Next, he felt the prop lock and the plane's scoop dig into the ground on impact and he bashed his forehead against the gun sight.

Emerging from the plane, he thought to run toward a stand of pines nearby, but German soldiers were already running toward him. "At 10:30 in the morning I crashed," Bank later remarked. "At 10:31, I was a POW."

He was marched to the small town of Zerbst and from there shipped to Frankfurt Am Main. After being interrogated, he was put on the road with other U.S. airmen, marched to Munich, and put in a prison camp. On the morning of April 29, after he had spent a couple of weeks there, he noticed that the guards had vanished. It was because Gen. George Patton's army had arrived.

After the war's end, Bank was released because of the "reduction in force," and entered the University of Illinois to study veterinary medicine. He had not finished his degree when war broke out in Korea and he was recalled—not as a fighter pilot but flying B-29 bombers.

Later on, Bank served in the Strategic Air Command and during the 1960s was stationed with his family in Japan, flying C-130s into and out of Vietnam on hazardous missions for the 315th Tactical Airlift Squadron. He retired from the Air Force as a major in 1970. ★

Richard S. Becker

MAJOR, USAF

December 4, 1926–January 5, 2015

RICHARD BECKER, WHO WAS CALLED "MiG Wrecker Becker" by the other pilots in his squadron, also carried the label of "Second Ace of the Korean War" with him most of his life. It was only after the opening of the official records of the former Soviet Union, whose best pilots Becker had gone up against in dogfights over North Korea in 1951, that he discovered that one of his "probables" might a have been a kill and therefore that he actually could have been the first Ace of the war. But by then, as Becker often said, such distinctions had long since ceased to matter. He only wished that he had been able to fly more combat missions in Korea and take down more enemy planes.

Becker first entered the Army Air Forces as an enlisted man in 1944 after graduating from high school in his hometown of Fleetwood, Pennsylvania. He served in Italy in the last months of World War II as a member of a ground crew and decided that some day he would be a pilot himself. After being discharged at the end of the war, he entered the newly established U.S. Air Force in 1948 as a cadet and was commissioned as a second lieutenant a year later.

He went through training at the advanced gunnery school at Nellis Air Force Base in Nevada and was assigned to the 334th Fighter-Interceptor Squadron. He started off flying the F-80 Shooting Star, the Air Force's first jet fighter, but by the time the 334th was sent to Korea in December 1950, it had been assigned the new F-86 Sabre jet, the sharpest weapon in the U.S. air arsenal. Becker had the name "Miss Behaving" painted on the side of his plane.

In the first days of the war, North Korean pilots, flying World War II–era Soviet YAK-9 fighters, had quickly established superiority against South Korea's tiny air force. Then the United States arrived at the head of the UN force with its first generation of jets—the F-80 and F-84—and had the upper hand until the Russians, in support of the Chinese (who entered the war in October 1950), introduced the new MiG-15 fighter into combat. Fast and heavily armed, the MiG-15 controlled the skies for several weeks until the

Alex McKnight /AM Photo Inc.

United States answered with the F-86, setting up the contest between the two second-generation jet fighters that would define the air war in Korea.

The USSR denied that experienced Soviet pilots were flying the "Chinese" MiGs and did everything to disguise their identity—ordering them to wear Chinese uniforms, to play the role of "tourists" when not on duty, to speak only Chinese or Korean and not to stray from the Chinese border so that if they were shot down they would not be captured. (In fact, some of the dogfights in "MiG Alley," the narrow section of North Korea on the Chinese border where most combat took place, took place fifty or sixty miles south of the Yalu.) But U.S. pilots sometimes reported catching glimpses of them in the cockpit, and the U.S. ground intercept stations heard them blurt out sentences in Russian over the radio during the chaos of dogfights. It was no mystery who the enemy was.

The United States was at a numerical disadvantage in the early part of the air war. As Becker later said, "We never had more than sixteen aircraft in the air at the beginning. . . . It was not unusual for a flight of four Sabres to take on thirty to forty MiGs." Moreover, U.S. pilots had to fly about two hundred miles to get to MiG Alley, while the MiGs were always within sight of their bases in China just over the Yalu River. They could climb to altitude over friendly territory and then dive on the Americans when they appeared. They could also see how many of the F-86s they were facing and quickly send up more of their own planes in what Becker and the other U.S. pilots called "MiG trains"— twenty-four MiGs followed by another twenty-four and then a third twenty-four. Moreover, the MiGs could break off the fight whenever they wanted and head back over the Yalu, knowing that the Sabres had been ordered not to pursue them over the border. The F-86s, on the other hand, sometimes had to fight their way back home, their fuel so low that often they were forced to glide the last few miles to their base and make dead-stick landings. "It was a fight to the death," Becker later recalled. "It was also a short fight. Sometimes during an entire day, combat lasted only four or five minutes, but it was so violent that we were exhausted when we landed."

On December 30, 1950, Becker was part of a flight of eight F-86s flying a sweep over MiG Alley. When they spotted "a huge gaggle" of twenty or more MiGs, the flight leader ordered the Americans to drop their auxiliary fuel tanks and attack. Becker's left tank didn't release. According to combat protocols, he should have returned to base, but he wanted to get into the fight and wrenched his plane to get a MiG in his sights. As he fired a long burst, the MiG began to smoke and went into a spin. He followed it down but had to break off before seeing it hit the ground because he was being attacked by other MiGs. Back at the base, he claimed a kill, but was only given a "probable." In fact, as writer Diego Zampini has shown, Soviet archives opened in the 1990s confirmed that the MiG did indeed crash and

that the Soviet pilot—named Savinow—was killed. (If credited with this kill, Becker, rather than his fellow pilot Captain James Jabara, would have been the first American Ace of the Korean air war.)

On April 22, 1951, Becker was flying wing to his flight leader when they jumped a group of MiGs below. He hit one of them with a short burst and put it in a death spin. On July 8, he shot down another MiG while covering a B-29 raid against the North Korean capital of Pyongyang: "I started at 40,000 feet and fought with him for at least ten minutes. We ended up on the deck, flying between mountains. I finally got him and he crashed into a mountain within a mile of the Yalu."

His big day came on August 19, when he was one of four Sabres that ran into eight MiGs. "We climbed behind them and they didn't see us." Becker got within five hundred feet of the enemy flight leader and opened fire; the MiG rolled over and the pilot bailed out. Then he went after the next MiG. "I hit him hard and he blew up in my face." Pieces of the disintegrating fighter smashed into Becker's windscreen and canopy and he had to struggle with his plane's falling hydraulic pressure on the way back home.

On September 9, Becker got his fifth MiG (sixth, if the first "probable" had been included). Within an hour of landing back at the base, he received a telegram from the secretary of the Air Force ordering him to return to the United States. He complained bitterly that he only had eighty-two missions, not the one hundred that usually comprised a tour. But his commanding officers had decided that because of his Ace status, he would be a propaganda asset to the enemy if shot down and captured, and his appeals were denied.

Richard Becker continued flying fighters until 1955, when he lost an eye in an accident. He retired from the Air Force as a major in 1970. ★

Richard L. Bertelson

LIEUTENANT, USNR

March 14, 1923–May 2, 2015

AS A BOY GROWING UP IN MINNEAPOLIS IN THE 1930S, Richard Bertelson ran home every day to listen to the radio serial *Jack Armstrong, All-American Boy*. Athlete, adventurer, scourge of America's enemies, Jack sometimes traveled in the Silver Albatross, a plane flown by his friend Billy Fairfield's uncle Jim. The scenes that took place in the plane were so realistic and exciting to Bertelson that they made him vow to someday be a pilot himself.

He got his chance years later, in August 1942, when he joined the Navy as an aviation cadet after studying for a year at the University of Minnesota. Midway through training he summoned the courage to inform his instructors that he would settle for nothing less than an assignment in a carrier-based fighter plane and used his high scores in gunnery tests to support his argument. He was commissioned on February 1, 1942, and assigned to the newly formed VF-19 Squadron of F6F Hellcats stationed in Hawaii.

Bertelson wanted to get into combat and chafed at what seemed to him the protracted training VF-29 was forced to undergo. But when the squadron was finally assigned to the USS *Cabot* in October 1944, Bertelson got all the action he wanted. Four days after arriving on board the carrier, he was on patrol when he saw a Japanese G4M bomber below him. He dived on it and made two passes as the "Betty" (as Allied intelligence called it) dipped lower and lower to evade him. It was just feet above the water when he fired a long burst on his third pass and the bomber hit the water and broke up.

On November 25, the *Cabot* was in the Leyte Gulf supporting the U.S. invasion of the Philippines when Japanese kamikazes swarmed the ship. It had fought off several attacks when one of the enemy planes, already a fire-bomb as a result of direct hits by the *Cabot*'s guns, smashed into the deck, spreading flames and shrapnel that killed thirty-five crew members.

Bertelson was in the air flying cover for the ship when the kamikaze struck, and had engaged a Japanese B6N "Jill" torpedo bomber that was part

Mark R. Bertelson

of the assault. The plane had tried to run from him and Bertelson had chased it at full throttle. When he caught up with it, he had triggered a short burst that sent the plane rolling into the water. But the chase had spent Bertelson's fuel and his gauge showed empty as he headed home. With the *Cabot* under attack, he approached the first U.S. carrier he saw and landed even though the landing signal officer on deck below tried frantically to wave him off.

On April 5, 1945, the *Cabot* was near Okinawa, its planes striking Japanese positions on the island as U.S. ground forces tried to consolidate their beachhead. That morning Bertelson was part of a flight of ten Hellcats assigned to bomb enemy Japanese airfields in the northern part of the island. There

were no enemy planes on the ground, as they had expected, so half of the American pilots strafed the field while the other half, Bertelson among them, flew cover for the operation.

He suddenly understood why there had been no Japanese fighters on the runway as more than a dozen Zeros dove down out of the sun. "It seemed just like a Hollywood movie with planes milling all around each other," Bertelson later said. He attacked the last plane in the long string, knocking it out of the air immediately. In the swirling chaos of the dogfight that ensued, he shot down two more of the Japanese fighters in the space of a few minutes, becoming an Ace.

The Hellcats had shot down ten of the enemy aircraft. But two of their pilots were down. One of them was being carried by the current toward land and looked as though he would make it. (Picked up by native Okinawans, he did, indeed, survive.) As the other floated in a life raft, Bertelson saw a small boat headed toward him. He thought it might be manned by the enemy and considered strafing it, but then decided not to in case the craft was friendly and on a rescue mission. It turned out to be a Japanese boat that captured the American pilot and imprisoned and ultimately executed him. This outcome continued to haunt Richard Bertelson long after he left the Navy at the end of the war and reentered civilian life. ★

Stephen J. Bonner Jr.

MAJOR, USAF

January 16, 1918–

WHEN STEPHEN BONNER WAS GROWING UP in western Oklahoma in the 1920s, few airplanes visited the prairies around him. So when he heard that a local pilot hired to fly for the U.S. Air Mail was going to train at a makeshift airport near his hometown of Guymon, Bonner spent long days there simply watching him take off and land. As he later told military historian Jon Guttman, in a profile for the *American Fighter Aces and Family Bulletin*, he also read all the pulp fiction about Eddie Rickenbacker and the other World War I Aces he could get his hands on, dreaming of becoming an Ace himself someday. He didn't sense that his dream might someday come true until the spring of 1942 when he left his studies at Oklahoma's Panhandle Agricultural and Mechanical College to join the Army Air Forces.

After receiving his wings in February 1943, Bonner was assigned to the 76th Squadron of the 23rd Fighter Group in China. This unit was the successor of the famed Flying Tigers, a group of volunteer pilots attached to the beleaguered Chinese air force that had been fighting against the Imperial Japanese Air Force since late 1941. As the United States tried to recover from Pearl Harbor in the summer of 1942, the Flying Tigers were absorbed into the regular Army Air Forces. But the P-40 Warhawks of the 76th Squadron retained the distinctive shark noses of that group, its élan, and also the larger-than-life presence of the legendary Claire Chennault, who had become a national hero leading the old American Volunteer Group and was now put in charge of the U.S. Army air units operating in China and Burma.

When Bonner arrived in China in June 1943, Chennault was no longer fighting an outnumbered rearguard action against overwhelmingly superior numbers of enemy aircraft. Rather, he was exchanging body blows with the air forces of the Japanese army in an equal fight. On July 23, 1943, Bonner got his first taste of action when the Japanese sent heavy bombers, escorted by Zero fighters, against U.S. bases in Lingling and the 76th Squadron scrambled

Rich Saal/Rich Saal Photography

to intercept them. In the air battle that followed, he got his first kill when a Zero more or less blundered into his path, a maneuver so careless that Bonner concluded that the pilot was a "greenhorn." But the experience, nothing like the heroic notion of air combat he had imagined as a boy reading the pulp fiction of World War I, left a stale taste. As Bonner later told John Reynolds of the Illinois *State Journal Register*: "The pilot of this plane flew in front of me and I fired. I saw the bullets go into the cockpit.

After I fired, I said to myself, 'You killed that guy.' I didn't think of any glory or anything like that. I just thought that I had killed some guy."

The Japanese sent another raid against Lingling later that day and in several more minutes of hectic action, Bonner believed that he got two more Zeros, although his claims could not be confirmed and he was credited only with "probables." The anxiety he first felt about going into action began to disappear. "Once you started your engine on the ground to take off," he told Reynolds, "some of your fear left you. I don't know why. It happened to everybody."

On September 10, when U.S. bombers attacked the Japanese base at Hankow, Bonner was flying cover and took down another Zero. On December 27, soon after the 76th moved to a new base at Suichwan, Ki-48 "Lily" (in the Allied identification code) bombers attacked the base, and Bonner was part of a flight of fourteen American fighters that engaged the Zeros escorting them. He shot down two, but one was counted as a probable. Two weeks later, in an hour of action during another Japanese raid on the American airfield, he poured fire into the engine of a Lily bomber until it went down in flames.

On May 12, Suichwan was struck again as part of the continuing drama of strike and counterstrike between U.S. and Japanese air forces. Bonner led a flight of P-40s to attack the enemy bombers' escort.

In half an hour of concentrated action he shot down an "Oscar" (as the Allies called the nimble and deadly Ki-43 Japanese army fighters) and was given credit for another probable and two more damaged.

He was now an Ace, but once again the experience was not what he had expected: "When I got the fifth, I didn't feel like it was anything tremendously great. Even though I had dreams of becoming an Ace when I was young, it didn't seem like such a wonderful thing."

Bonner remained in the Air Force until 1950, but decided against making the military his career. Instead, he earned a degree at the University of Illinois and eventually worked as the division president of a manufacturing company in Urbana until his retirement.

In 2005, along with other pilots who had served there, Stephen Bonner returned to China where he was given a hero's welcome by the government and followed everywhere by large numbers of citizens who remembered the Americans who had defended their country in the planes with the snarling shark noses. Ten years later, on May 20, 2015, Bonner had an even more significant honor when he journeyed to Washington, D.C., and joined thirty-three other living Aces to receive the Congressional Gold Medal awarded to the 1,447 U.S. pilots who had achieved the status of Ace since World War II. Joined by thirty members of his family, he was, at ninety-seven, the oldest member of the group. ★

Clarence A. Borley

COMMANDER, USN

July 17, 1924–

ON HIS FOURTH DAY ADRIFT IN THE PACIFIC after being shot down, Clarence Borley, who at the age of twenty had just become the Navy's youngest Ace, was overcome by the hopelessness of his situation. Utterly alone in a flimsy raft, hallucinating from lack of food and water, he pulled out his service revolver to end it all. "I thought that before I shot myself I'd better make sure it was working all right," he later said of a potentially tragic moment that suddenly turned comic. "So I popped off a shot in the air. The shock of the noise brought me back to sanity." Borley quickly decided that continuing to try to survive was preferable to death.

A gangly young man, Borley grew up in Yakima, Washington. Then seventeen years old, he had worked with his father on the family farm all day on December 7, 1941, and didn't find out about the attack on Pearl Harbor until late in the evening when a neighbor told him what had happened. What Borley told aviation writer Tom Cleaver years afterward summed up the feelings of his entire generation on that day of infamy: "I knew my life had changed forever, though I wasn't sure how."

He had been interested in flying since seeing *Dive Bomber*, an Errol Flynn film released a few months before the attack. He thought that he would never be able to satisfy the requirement of two years of college to enter flight training, but in the spring of 1942, he learned that naval aviation was now accepting high school graduates who could pass a test showing college-level knowledge. Borley hopped a bus to Seattle right after his eighteenth birthday in July, took the test, passed it, and waited impatiently for orders. When they finally arrived the week of Thanksgiving, he thought to himself, "This is the best Christmas present ever."

He reported first to Pensacola where he qualified for fighters and acquired the nickname "Spike." He was assigned to air group VF-15, which called itself "Satan's Playmates." In early April 1944, VF-15 was ordered to the USS *Essex*.

His first aerial combat came on June 19 as a part of a flight of four Hellcats launched to protect the task force. They launched at 5 a.m. into total darkness and climbed to 26,000 feet. "The sunrise was spectacular," Borley later told aviation writer James Oleson. "It lit up scattered cumulous clouds in a variety of colors and reflected off the ever-changing white-capped seas."

But this poetic mood disappeared when the Hellcats were suddenly summoned back to the carrier. When Borley landed his operations officer ran up with a map showing a position where a mass of enemy planes had been spotted. As seamen were yelling, "The Japs are coming!" the officer ordered him and the other Hellcat pilots back into the cockpit. Soon Borley was airborne for the second time that morning.

They soon saw thirty enemy dive-bombers and twenty fighters three thousand feet below them. "With an altitude advantage," Borley later told Oleson, "we dove into the enemy fighters and all hell broke loose. . . . Planes were blowing up and falling into the sea below. The white-capped ocean framed several parachutes."

Borley was in the middle of what would become known, because of the large number of enemy planes destroyed, as the Great Marianas Turkey Shoot. But his part in the engagement was over as quickly as it had begun when the enemy planes were suddenly recalled, and he found himself alone in an empty sky. He headed back to the carrier and saw his exultant squadron mates congregated on the deck of the carrier, nearly all of them having shot down at least one Japanese aircraft. Borley was chagrined: "I had to confess to my utter shame that I had not fired a single shot. . . . In the excitement and confusion of my first aerial combat, I had forgotten to charge my guns!"

At daybreak on October 10, his plane was part of a flight of fourteen F6F Hellcats that took off for Okinawa. Later that day, after destroying several Japanese aircraft on the ground, Borley spotted five Zeros. He got on the tail of the leader of the group, squeezed the trigger and fanned his rudders to spread the shot pattern from one wing tip of the enemy plane to the other. The Zero caught fire and rolled over, hitting the cane fields below.

"It gives you a feeling of great exhilaration when you overcome somebody in combat," Borley recalled of his first kill five decades later. "You're fighting for your life."

Two days later, as the *Essex* approached the island of Formosa, Borley felt a vague sense of apprehension as he took off with three other Hellcats just before dawn. Two of the planes soon experienced engine problems and were forced to return to the carrier. Borley and his flight leader continued on. As Formosa loomed up in the sunrise, they saw several Japanese fighters. Almost without encountering resistance, Borley shot down four of them in quick succession and became an Ace.

As the remaining enemy aircraft fled, Borley and his flight leader turned back to the ship. Spotting more Japanese planes taking off from an airfield below, they went in for a strafing run. Antiaircraft fire bloomed in the air all around them. Borley felt his plane shudder from a hit and saw fire coming out of the engine. He didn't want to go down over enemy territory and decided to try to glide to the ocean about five miles away. He had just cleared the shoreline when his plane stalled, smacked down into the water, and broke apart. His Mae West life preserver brought him to the surface. Seeing that the current was taking him back to land, he started swimming toward open water.

Borley popped open a container of dye so that the U.S. planes would see him. As a Japanese patrol boat headed in his direction, a Hellcat dropped down to destroy it. The pilot spotted Borley and came around again, lowered his landing gear to slow his air speed, and dropped a raft that saved Borley's life.

Over the next three days the wind continued to increase and the waves became rougher and higher. The water canteen and provisions that had been stored in the life raft were lost in one of the many times it overturned, and he had nothing to eat or drink. On the fourth night—one of terror—he passed through the eye of a typhoon and the raft overturned repeatedly; if it had not been connected to him by the eight-foot lanyard he had tied to his waist, the raft would have floated away.

By October 15, he was a speck adrift in the Taiwan Straits, suffering from sunburn, hunger, thirst, exhaustion, and desperation. Fearing that if captured he might be tortured into giving up details of the coming invasion of the Philippines, he thought about taking his own life.

Later that day, after the pistol shot made him decide to carry on, Borley saw a submarine rise up out of the water beside him. He thought it was Japanese and again drew his pistol, but then a voice yelled through a bullhorn: "Put down that gun!" It was the USS *Sawfish*. The sub was actually looking for another pilot and happened by accident onto Borley, who was seventy-five miles from where he first went down. Two sailors came down to help him on board.

The second day after his rescue, the *Sawfish* was attacked by a Japanese convoy and depth charged for over an hour. Borley considered the irony: he had survived being shot down, had been hammered by a typhoon, and had come close to suicide only to be crushed in the ocean depths. But the *Sawfish* survived and finally put ashore on November 9.

After the war Clarence Borley decided to make the Navy a career, retiring as a commander in 1968. ★

James L. Brooks

CAPTAIN, USAF

January 8, 1921–

PROWLING THE SKIES OVER EUROPE in his P-51 Mustang in early 1944, James Brooks never once lost sight of the fact the air war was deadly serious. "You might win one day," he said later on, "but you might lose everything the next." Yet despite the high stakes there were a few funny moments. On July 25, a day in which he got three of his 13.5 kills (the .5 for a victory shared with another U.S. pilot), Brooks was chasing a German Ju 87 Stuka dive-bomber. It was the plane that had put fear into the hearts of civilian populations from Madrid to Moscow as it dived down out of the sky with the distinctive whine that signaled destruction. But when not in a dive, the Stuka, with its fixed landing gear, was slow and ponderous. In this engagement, as Brooks used his flaps to slow down and get the Ju 87 in his gun sights, he saw its canopy pop off. Then the goggled faces of the pilot and tail gunner stared at him for a moment with looks of comical panic before both men gave a shrug and bailed out. Brooks had not even fired a shot. He couldn't help but break out in laughter as the enemy plane flipped over and headed down alongside the two open parachutes.

Southeastern Poland, where this engagement took place, was a long way from Vinton, a small town near Roanoke in the middle of Virginia's farm country where Brooks had grown up. His father worked for the railroad most of his life, and got Brooks a job after he graduated from high school in 1940 delivering packages, which had been shipped by train, on a Harley Davidson motorcycle. He had joined the National Guard when he was seventeen, in part because the one dollar a week he received for attending drills was enough to take a girl to the movies and buy her a milk shake afterward. With the coming of war some of his friends signed up for flight training and when they returned on leave from Pensacola, he was awed by their dress uniforms. Wanting to wear one himself, he joined the Army Air Corps in the spring of 1942.

After getting his wings in May 1943, Brooks was sent to the Panama Canal where Army Chief of Staff Gen. George Marshall feared the Japanese might strike in order to force U.S. ships to travel around Cape Horn to get to the Pacific. After patrolling the Canal Zone for six months in a P-39, Brooks was assigned to the 307th Fighter Squadron in San Severino, Italy. At first he was checked out in a Spitfire, which, because of its limited range, he later described as "a cute little plane, although I wouldn't want to go to war in it." Then his squadron was given P-51s, which he immediately decided was "a man-sized plane."

Brooks named his Mustang "January" because it was his birth month, and began flying missions escorting bombers deep into Europe and the Balkans. The bombers especially targeted the oil fields in Ploesti, Romania, which were key to the German war effort. He got his first kill on May 18, 1944, over Câmpina when, flying as wingman for his flight leader, he encountered a Fiat G-50. His flight leader couldn't get the proper angle on the G-50 and radioed, "You take him, Jim." The Italian fighter, which had made its debut fighting on the Fascist side in the Spanish Civil War, was no match for the Mustang and went down after Brooks had fired two sustained bursts into it.

A week later, while on a mission escorting U.S. bombers to Vienna, he shot down a Messerschmitt Me 109. And on May 29, when Brooks' squadron was attacked by sixty Me 109s during another mission to Vienna, he got credit for one of the seven enemy planes the Mustangs shot down in the fight that followed.

When another U.S. pilot flying "January" was forced to ditch in the Adriatic, Brooks got a new Mustang, which he christened "February." He had four kills on July 18 when he shot down a Macchi C.205, Italy's best fighter, while on a mission escorting U.S. B-17s over Germany, and became an Ace.

The most peculiar of Brooks' thirteen victories came not long after when he was in a dogfight close to ground level with an Me 109. As the enemy plane got on his tail, Brooks headed for a mountain range at full throttle. At the last minute he pulled up, just clearing a peak. The pilot of the Messerschmitt hesitated for an instant and then slammed into the mountain. Back at base he at first refused to take credit for the kill, telling his superior officer, "I didn't shoot him down. He killed himself!" The officer insisted, "A kill is a kill."

On July 25, Brooks was on a mission over eastern Poland when he saw a strange sight on the horizon. It was a group of nearly forty German Ju 87s fleeing Soviet ground fire. "Good God, they're Stukas!" he radioed the other Americans. The Stukas might be fearsome in dive-bombing runs, but they were awkward and vulnerable in level flight. The Mustangs quickly destroyed twenty-seven of them in the next few minutes, with Brooks getting two, including the one whose pilot and tail gunner pre-emptively left the plane before he could open fire. After the war, Brooks found out that he had been decorated by the Soviet Army for his participation in this engagement.

He had 11.5 kills on August 29: he was part of a flight escorting B-17s on a bombing run over Czechoslovakia when the bombers were suddenly jumped by fifteen Me 109s. The German fighters managed to get into the bomber formations before the Mustangs could react, but in the dogfight that followed, Brooks shot down two of the 109s.

Soon afterwards, he was promoted to captain and sent home for the duration of the war. He transferred to the Air Force after its creation in 1947. He became jet qualified, and was sent to Korea soon after war broke out there. Flying an F-86 Sabre jet, he participated in the first large-scale all-jet battle between U.S. and Communist planes over the Yalu River on December 22, 1950. A few months later, after fifteen combat missions, he came home, resigned from the Air Force, and became a test pilot for North American Aviation, a job that he held for the next twenty-five years. ★

Henry Buttelmann

LIEUTENANT COLONEL, USAF

June 26, 1929–

THE WAR IN KOREA WAS A "FORGOTTEN WAR" for the American public, even while it was taking place, but for Henry Buttelmann it would always be a vivid and emotional experience, filled with intense friendships, good times, and the life-and-death drama of aerial combat in a remote place called "MiG Alley." As he later said, "Fighters were aircraft with a mission that bound guys closely together. For most people I know who went to Korea, it was the high point of their lives."

Born in Corona, New York, in 1929, Buttelmann was finishing his second year at the University of Bridgeport in Connecticut in 1950 when the Communist forces of North Korea attacked the fragile government of the South. Buttelmann, already in the Air National Guard, was called to active duty and applied for pilot training. After receiving his wings, he completed basic at Greenwich Air Force Base and was sent to Nellis Air Force Base in southern Nevada for advanced gunnery school. There he was integrated into an elite group of pilots. His instructors primarily emphasized air-to-ground combat, although some of them talked about aerial engagements with Russian and Chinese pilots in Korea in late-night bull sessions at the officers' club.

Assigned to the 25th Fighter Squadron, Buttelmann arrived at the Suwon Air Base, about twenty miles south of the South Korean capital of Seoul, on December 23, 1952, and flew his first mission about two weeks later. At this time, the fierce urgency of the first years of the war had been replaced by a sense of stalemate. Buttelmann's squadron flew almost daily patrols over MiG Alley, the area on North Korea's border with China that had been the site of such intense combat in the first years of the conflict, often without any evidence of the enemy, although the Communist airfields were only minutes away. In his first five months Buttelmann would only see MiGs twice—both times while flying as wingman supporting the flight leader. But he was confident that when his time came, he would be ready and so would his plane.

"The MiG-15 had certain advantages—it flew higher and was lighter—but the F-86 hit Mach [the speed of sound] faster and our pilots were better trained." The kill ratio between the two planes bore him out: 818 MiGs and 56 F-86s were downed in air action during the war.

Looking a little like Ernest Hemingway with his brush mustache and bottom-heavy face, Buttelmann had fifty missions under his belt in the beginning of June 1953 when his commanding officer told him he was being moved from wingman to "a shooting position." He later recalled what came next: "On June 19, we were in MiG Alley on a normal patrol, when I noticed a flight of MiGs. They were very low. After we punched our [extra fuel] tanks off, I saw [them] heading for home. . . . I slid in behind one MiG. I gave several short bursts when his canopy flew off. . . . I gave him two more short bursts and the pilot ejected. . . . The guy never even made a single turn. It was an easy kill."

With negotiations for an armistice nearing a conclusion, the enemy was once again sending up swarms of fighters. (In May 1953 U.S. flyers would record fifty-six kills, with seventy-seven more in June and thirty-two in July, the last month of the war.) Buttelmann was busy, scoring four more kills over the next two weeks, becoming, four days after his twenty-fourth birthday, the youngest Ace of the Korean War.

One of these missions involved a near miss. Buttelmann had just shot down a MiG when he looked over his shoulder and saw another one firing at him. He was hit under the fuselage and immediately saw two warning lights on his display panel. He pulled back on his power and the attacking MiG shot by him. "I was extremely fortunate because there were thunderstorms in the area," he remembers. "I got into the weather and stayed there. That saved me. I was able to work my way home."

He called it his "most difficult mission," but it didn't make him less anxious for action. "I was desperate to get more MiGs," he later admitted. This compulsion to engage was typical of the best flyers. In Korea, a study later revealed, 5 percent of the U.S. pilots were responsible for 37 percent of the kills, an indication that a small number driven to excel did most of the damage against the enemy.

Henry Buttelmann shot down two more MiGs in July, the last one on the twenty-second, five days before the war ended. He came home to work as an air combat instructor in the program at Nellis, whose demanding curriculum he credited with his success in Korea. A later assignment involved working with the air force of Taiwan. He did two tours in Vietnam, the first flying forty-seven missions in the F-105 and the second flying 234 missions in the F-100. He retired from the Air Force in 1979 as a lieutenant colonel. ★

Richard G. Candelaria

COLONEL, USAFR

July 14, 1922–

RICHARD CANDELARIA REMEMBERS RIDING HIS BIKE from his home in Pasadena to the top of the Hollywood Hills in the late 1930s to look down at the sleek new Lockheed P-38s taking off from the Burbank airport. Coming from a family that had emigrated from Mexico to America a hundred years before California statehood, he was like the other boys in his neighborhood in every way except for one. While they read comics about superheroes, he haunted the local library in search of books about Eddie Rickenbacker and the other Aces of World War I. By the time he was a teenager he was certain that he, too, would someday be a fighter pilot.

After the attack on Pearl Harbor Candelaria tried to join the Army Air Corps but was told that pilots had to have a college degree. He enrolled at USC. After he had studied there for almost three years, the Air Corps dropped the college requirement and Candelaria immediately enlisted. Finally in the fall of 1944 he was sent to England and assigned to a squadron of P-51 Mustangs operating out of the Royal Air Force base in Ipswich.

His group's primary mission was supporting the U.S. bombers flying through heavy flak and swarms of Luftwaffe interceptors to pound the German homeland. Along with others in his squadron, he engaged in sarcastic banter with the bomber pilots, ribbing them as "bus drivers." But as he watched them take their B-24s up day after day knowing that they would suffer huge losses, he developed a deep respect for their stoical bravery.

On January 4, 1945, "Candy," as the other pilots called him, was flying as wingman to the flight leader on a mission northwest of Berlin when his squadron ran into eighty enemy fighters sent up by the German high command in a desperate effort to stop the B-24s. The Mustangs immediately attacked. Candelaria's flight leader was on the tail of one Focke-Wulf Fw 190 when three other enemy fighters swooped down on him and opened fire. Candelaria singled out the lead plane and engaged it in an acrobatic, high-speed dogfight

that ended with the Fw 190 spiraling downward in flames. He shot down another Fw 190 before the German interceptors scattered.

On April 7, Candelaria was taxiing for takeoff as a leader of his section when he got a call from the control tower informing him that his rear tire was flat. The ground crew quickly appeared to put on a new one, but by the time he got airborne the rest of the flight element had disappeared. Taking shortcuts to the location where the Mustangs were supposed to rendezvous with the bombers they were escorting to the target over Berlin, he arrived early. He saw two Me 262s—the revolutionary new jets the Luftwaffe had just introduced—waiting to attack the B-24s. He had caught glimpses of the advanced aircraft before—unmistakable even from far away because of their stark white color and the polka dots adorning their fuselage, as well as their blazing speed—but had never been this close to them.

He headed directly toward the oncoming jets. When they dipped to go below him, he dropped his fuel tanks, hoping that he might get lucky and hit one of them. This didn't happen, but the tanks did distract the two German pilots. As they began to circle, Candelaria pulled his Mustang to get inside their wide turn. He hit the trigger and the first of the German jets in effect ran into his machine-gun fire. It began to smoke and rolled over. Candelaria was following it down to confirm the kill when he saw orange, tennis-ball-sized, 30-mm cannon rounds whizz by his cockpit and realized that the other jet was attacking him. As he turned to engage, the other Me 262 unaccountably broke off and headed away. He was credited with a "probable" for the first one.

The U.S. bombers appeared on the scene and almost immediately set off flares to indicate that they were under attack. Looking up, Candelaria saw several Messerschmitt Me 109s getting ready to feast on the B-24s. He radioed the rest of his squadron, "Get here quick. I've got fifteen 109s cornered." He then singled out the leader, hoping that engaging him would disrupt the Germans' disciplined attack on the bombers. After shooting down the lead Me 109, Candelaria went after the remaining German fighters and shot down three more of them before the rest of his squadron finally arrived and the German planes vanished. He was now an Ace.

A few days later, Candelaria led an attack on a German airfield. In his first strafing run he destroyed a gun position along with four parked aircraft. Then he "got greedy" and went back for a second run. As he dove down, the German antiaircraft fire "lit up the sky like a Christmas tree" and shredded the fuselage of his plane.

Candelaria headed the damaged Mustang back in the direction of Allied lines, but after a few minutes his engine caught fire and he was forced to bail out. After several days on the run, he was moving through an open field to get from one forested area to hide in another when two enemy soldiers appeared. Candelaria waved his bloodied white pilot's scarf, but the Germans ignored the effort to surrender and opened fire with their rifles. Scared in a way that he had never been in dogfights, Candelaria dove into a ditch. When the two soldiers came closer, he pulled his .45 pistol. Aiming at the belt buckle of the first, he hit him in the forehead; then he killed the second one with a shot to the chest.

After another two days, weakened from hunger and exposure, Candelaria found himself near a settlement and hid in a vacant cabin. But the locals had seen him. Soon a group of civilians approached the cabin along with a German army sergeant. The civilians wanted to lynch him on the spot because their village had recently been strafed by Allied planes. But the sergeant held them off until an officer arrived. "Don't worry," the officer said in perfect English as he escorted Candelaria away from the mob, "you're with the military now." Then he added incongruously, "And I have relatives in Wisconsin."

Candelaria was taken to a Luftwaffe command center, where other Allied pilots were also being held. On the way, the officer with relatives in Wisconsin pulled out a bottle of cognac and they drank it during the trip. Then the officer pulled out a raw onion and told Candelaria to eat so that the odor of alcohol on his breath would be masked. At the Luftwaffe center there was a distant camaraderie between the Allied pilots and their captors, who were also airmen. On some nights the Germans invited Candelaria and the other prisoners to sing with them. He learned the whole of "Lili Marlene."

After several weeks, Candelaria and two British officers managed to overpower a German captain inspecting the farmhouse where they were being kept. Taking the officer's pistol, they hustled him outside and seized the car of the local *burgermeister* (mayor). Holding the gun to the captain's side as they drove toward what they hoped was the U.S. Army, they forced him to reassure sentries at a series of checkpoints they had to pass through. Soon they had crossed over into Belgium, where they were surprised to learn that the war in Europe was over.

After the war, Richard Candelaria finished college and joined the Air National Guard. After retiring from the reserve as a colonel, he started a series of manufacturing businesses, including one that made parts for the X-15 experimental aircraft and the space program. But becoming an Ace remained the high point of his life. "It's the most exclusive club in the world," he says. "You can't buy your way in. You can't talk your way in. There's only one way in—through aerial combat." ⭐

Robert B. Carlson

LIEUTENANT COMMANDER, USNR

June 17, 1921–

GROWING UP IN BEAVER FALLS, a small town near Pittsburgh, Robert Carlson was about ten years old when some barnstormers landed a Ford Trimotor in a nearby grassy field. He and his father went up for a ride that took them up over the Beaver River and the green countryside around the family home. A year or two later Carlson remembers coming out of his house and standing transfixed in his back yard as a formation of thirty or so military aircraft roared overhead, heading toward Lake Erie and "making a noise like you've never heard." He watched until the last speck of the flight disappeared into the horizon.

But while these experiences were etched into his memory, Carlson always claimed that what really made him become a fighter pilot was "mud." His father had been an Army engineer in World War I and sometimes described the muddy nightmare in which the doughboys were forced to fight. "Another war was beginning," Carlson later said, "and I wasn't going to fight it slogging along in the mud."

He was in Riverside, California, living with his aunt and uncle and going to Riverside Junior College, when he came out of church on the morning of December 7, 1941, and heard that the Japanese had just bombed Pearl Harbor. The next day he went to the Navy recruitment office in Long Beach and signed up as an aviator.

Slightly built and weighing just 120 pounds, Carlson initially felt dwarfed by the planes in which he trained—first at Naval Air Station Los Alamitos in one of the yellow Stearman biplanes the flyers irreverently referred to as "the Yellow Peril," then in dive-bombers at Corpus Christi, and finally in F4F Wildcats when he did his carrier training in Norfolk.

In the late summer of 1943 his orders came to report to San Diego as part of VF-40 headed to the Pacific. After being introduced to their new F6F Hellcats, his unit boarded the USS *Long Island* to be ferried to Espiritu Santo and from there to Guadalcanal. Carlson's first kill came on January 1, 1944.

Dominik Huber

He was flying as wingman on an attack against a Japanese air base on southern Bougainville when enemy fighters suddenly appeared. In the chaos that followed he was concerned with only one thing—staying up with his flight leader. But then he saw the belly of a Zero flying straight up in front of him. "It was a total surprise to me," Carlson later said. "I pulled back hard on the stick to slow down and took a shot and he blew up and I flew through the debris."

Carlson was an Ace with five kills by January 23, 1944, and was rotated home in March at the end of his first tour.

After several months of stateside duty, he returned for his second tour in January 1945 as part of VF-30 on board the carrier USS *Belleau Wood*. Over the next few weeks, Japanese kamikaze activity increased and VF-30 tried to deflect the attacks. "They were sending down anything that would fly," Carlson recalled. "We did our best, but we couldn't keep them all from getting through."

One of the suicide planes that did penetrate the Hellcats' cover hit the USS *Franklin* on March 19. Carlson was in the air nearby. "The carrier was hit at the worst possible time. Its planes were on deck ready to launch, filled with gasoline and bombs. It was a terrible explosion." More than eight hundred sailors were killed. As the ship lay dead in the water, rescue operations got under way to recover the wounded. Carlson was part of a flight detailed to fly cover overhead to make sure that there were no further attacks. Miraculously, the *Franklin* managed to make the repairs that allowed her to limp back to Pearl Harbor.

Carlson was never hit by fire from an enemy aircraft, but he was hit by friendly fire. In April he had shot up a kamikaze from behind and thought it was a kill as the plane caught on fire. But then the fire went out and Carlson renewed the attack, concentrating so hard on getting the enemy plane that he came over the USS *Hornet*, which hit him with antiaircraft fire. Carlson barely managed to bring his Hellcat back in for a landing on the *Belleau Wood*. The plane was so mangled that crewmen immediately pushed it into the ocean.

Carlson had nine kills when the *Belleau Wood* headed back home at the beginning of June 1945. The ship was caught, along with the rest of the task force, in a typhoon that generated 120 mph winds. With other pilots, Carlson lay wedged into bunks below as 60-foot waves pounded the carrier. "It was designed to capsize at a 59-degree roll," he remembered, "and at one point it rolled 61 degrees but managed to come out of it. This was the scariest part of the war for me. In air combat you don't have time to worry. But during this typhoon we had to ride it out, hour after hour."

Carlson was at home in Riverside, enjoying a brief leave with his wife and new baby, when news came of the Japanese surrender. He thought of himself as a sober individual, but felt the occasion called for a moment of rowdiness. So he got in his car and drove to Riverside's main drag and set off a smoke bomb he had brought back from the war, snarling traffic for hours.

After leaving the Navy, Robert Carlson became a teacher and a missionary, serving in Nigeria, South Africa, and elsewhere around the world. ★

Dean Caswell

COLONEL, USMC

July 24, 1922–

IN 1940 DEAN CASWELL WAS A STRONG-WILLED eighteen-year-old from Blanco, Texas, who was tired of butting heads with his equally strong-willed father and decided it was time to leave home. He had already spent two years at Texas' Edinburg Junior College but had no idea of what he wanted to do with his life. He set out with thirty-five dollars in his pocket, his net worth at the time, and hitchhiked to Southern California. He enrolled at the Curtiss-Wright Technical Institute and was studying aircraft maintenance when he got his draft notice two months before Pearl Harbor. He immediately joined the Marines and was selected for aviation.

Upon finishing flight school Caswell had a disappointment when he was informed that he would be piloting dive-bombers. "There was this cute little Navy girl handing out orders," he later remembered. "I told her that I wanted to fly fighters, not dive-bombers. She said she didn't make the orders, but just handed them out. I didn't believe her and told her that the least she could do was go out for dinner with me that night. By the time our date was over, my orders had been changed to fighters."

Caswell was a standout in gunnery school. He always believed that his success went back to his years hunting birds with a .20-gauge shotgun in South Texas: "You learn how to lead the bird and fire from every angle. In combat I just pointed the nose of the plane at the enemy as if it were a shotgun and started firing."

He was assigned to Marine Fighter Squadron (VMF) 221, but it took a long time—too long, he felt—to get into combat because the unit had been trained to fly Corsairs and there was a shortage of these aircraft. Finally, in the fall of 1944, after Caswell had studied air combat with future Medal of Honor recipient Jim Swett, VMF 221 was sent to the USS *Bunker Hill*.

Caswell's first kill came in a mission over Tokyo in February 1945 in which Corsairs were flying cover for U.S. bombers. At 28,000 feet, they thought they

were too high to be attacked, but suddenly Japanese fighters swooped down on them. Caswell, who was flying wing, saw a Zero lining up for a shot on his flight leader and fired a long burst that set the plane on fire. (He was denied credit for the victory because his flight leader claimed it for himself.)

On March 18, Caswell's flight of eight Corsairs was flying cover for a bombing mission against Tom-itaka airfield near Kyushu when they were attacked by twenty-five Japanese fighters. "My guardian angel was with me that day," he remembers. In the wild melee that followed he took down three Zeros in less than five minutes.

On April 12, he shot down another Japanese fighter over Kikai Shima. Then, on April 28, he took off from the *Bunker Hill* with two other Corsairs and encountered twenty-five enemy fighters that were flying high cover for kamikazes. He lined up head-on against one of them and, ignoring his wing-man yelling over the radio, "There's a Zero on your tail!" as well as the tracer bullets flying all around him, continued to fire until the Japanese fighter exploded. Afterwards, he shot down two more Zeros.

Caswell ended the war with seven confirmed victories, making him the top scoring Marine carrier pilot in the Pacific. He believes that he had at least another seven kills that he did not get credit for because of malfunctions in his wing cameras recording the battle and other technical problems. But he was philosophical about this then and still is. "The big winners in air combat were lucky people— in the right place at the right time," he says. "It didn't matter how many planes they said you shot down. Most of us were glad just to do our part and get the hell out of there alive. We lost half of our squadron."

Dean Caswell remained in the Marines after the war, taking time off to fly Japanese fighters in the combat scenes of John Wayne's *Sands of Iwo Jima* and *Flying Leathernecks*. (As a result he met and dated Wayne's friend and frequent movie love interest, Maureen O'Hara.) He also flew for a time with the Blue Angels, the Navy's flight demonstration squadron. After two tours in Korea and one in Vietnam he retired from the Marine Corps as a colonel in 1968. He continued to be fascinated by planes, piloting fifty-six different aircraft during the following decades and making his last flight in 2002 at the age of eighty. ★

Lawrence A. Clark

LIEUTENANT COMMANDER, USN

February 8, 1923–

UNLIKE OTHER YOUNG MEN HIS AGE who saw the military as a place to get food and lodging, as well as a paycheck in hard times, Lawrence Clark did not suffer during the Depression. His family was not rich, but his father had a steady job in the oil industry and made enough money to buy several rental properties near the family home in Bell, California. Clark always remembered his father telling his tenants who came to him shamefaced at being unable to pay their rent, "Don't worry about it, we'll settle up when times get better."

Larry, as family and friends called him, grew up lean and muscular, a good athlete who was quarterback on his high school football team. But by his own admission, he was not a scholar, and after graduating in mid-1941 went to nearby Compton Junior College primarily to kill time while figuring out what came next. Then Pearl Harbor was attacked. Looking for revenge and adventure, Clark joined some of his friends in signing up for Navy flight training.

He did his primary training at Corpus Christi and then at Pensacola, where he got his wings late in 1943. He then married his high school sweetheart after she traveled alone by train from California to Florida.

Next came advanced training in Massachusetts, which Clark considered uneventful except for a trivial incident that stuck in his memory as a lesson in cultural relativity. He and his wife and another naval couple from Southern California, all of them weaned on the local Mexican food, decided one night that they had to have tacos. The women were dispatched to buy tortillas to make them but came home empty-handed after a long search. Clark was astonished to find that the local merchants not only didn't sell tortillas but in most cases had no idea what they were.

He was shipped to Hawaii in mid-1944 and used what turned out to be a long hiatus before he was assigned to a combat squadron to hone his skills in gunnery and close-formation flying. When he was finally taken by a C-46 transport plane to Guam to join the recently formed VF-83 on board the USS *Essex* in March 1945, he felt he was ready.

As part of Task Force 58 supporting the invasion of Okinawa, the *Essex* was facing fierce kamikaze attacks when Clark arrived. On his third mission on March 14, he saw an enemy dive-bomber vectored in on the USS *Bunker Hill*, flagship of Adm. Marc Mitscher, commander of the task force. Dodging heavy friendly fire to engage the enemy plane, Clark shot it down and was recommended for the Navy Cross by the grateful Mitscher.

On April 3, he shot down two more dive-bombers and a Ki-61 "Tony" fighter. He knew his Hellcat had taken some hits in the encounter, but he had no idea how badly it was damaged until he landed back on the *Essex* and watched crew members immediately strip out the plane's six .50-caliber machine guns and then push it overboard into the ocean. ("I *know* from personal experience that Grumman made really good planes," Clark said later on.)

On April 6, he became an Ace when he shot down a dive-bomber and a Zero on a raid against the Japanese mainland. He got his seventh and final kill on April 17, a twin-engine "Betty" bomber. Soon after this he had his closest call when he was strapped into his Hellcat lined up for takeoff and saw an enemy kamikaze streaking toward the *Essex* for what seemed a certain hit. Helpless, Clark braced himself for death. But at the last minute, with the kamikaze looming up larger than life in front of him, one of the carrier's guns scored a direct hit on the Japanese plane, sending it cartwheeling into the ocean just beyond the deck of the carrier.

Over the next four months, as Task Force 58 came closer to Japan, Clark flew bombing and strafing runs designed to soften up the enemy for an anticipated invasion. But then came Hiroshima and Nagasaki, and after completing a mission on August 15, Clark wrote in his logbook, "This is it. Today the Japs surrender. We were in the air just a few miles from Tokyo when they called us back." He added with incredulity, "We're still knocking Japs down over the fleet. They must be damned eager [to die.]" He was on patrol over the USS *Missouri* guarding against a "loose cannon" kamikaze when the surrender was signed on its deck on September 2.

After the war, Lawrence Clark started a family and an insurance business. When his son Steve once asked him how he had managed to survive the chaos of air combat, Clark laughed and said, "Adrenaline and bad judgment, I guess." ★

Robert A. Clark

LIEUTENANT COMMANDER, USN

July 17, 1922–January 21, 2015

BOB CLARK GREW UP AT THE LEAKE AND WATTS Episcopal Orphan House in Yonkers, New York. Located on a thirty-three-acre estate and known for its progressive attitudes toward child rearing, it was, as Clark often said later on to family and friends, "the place to be if you had to be in an orphanage." He thrived there, becoming valedictorian of his high school class in 1940 and choosing to continue to live at Leake and Watts for a year after graduating. But the question of why he had been sent there as a boy haunted him and he devoted long hours to trying to find the answer, going so far as to hire private investigators. The answer didn't come until after his death in 2015 when Clark's family finally found out that his single mother had been a showgirl and that New York City officials had placed him in the orphanage because they did not believe that she could take care of him.

A handsome young man (his wife of fifty-three years, Darlene, later said of Clark: "The ladies just lined up for him"), Clark moved confidently into the New York literary world, taking a job at *Look* magazine. He moved to the Alcoa company in Fairfield, Connecticut, after a few months because the pay was better, although he didn't lose his love of books and writing.

With the coming of war, Clark forgot about his career and entered the Navy as a cadet late in 1942. After sixteen months of flight training he was sent to Guam in late 1944, transferring to the USS *Hornet* as a Hellcat pilot on February 1, 1945. Within days, *Hornet* had joined Task Force 58 and was steaming toward Japan. On February 16, Clark participated in the first carrier air strike against the Japanese mainland since the Doolittle Raiders' attack three years earlier.

On March 19 Clark was part of an attack group of twenty Hellcats headed for Japan's Kure Naval Base. On the way, the group saw a flight of about sixty Japanese planes headed for the *Hornet*. They immediately engaged them. Clark headed toward a Kawanishi N1K "George," introduced late in

Chandler Crowell/Chandler Crowell Photography

the war and considered by some U.S. flyers the best of the Japanese fighters. He managed to maneuver his Hellcat into a firing position on the enemy's tail and opened fire. The "George" burst into flames and spiraled down toward the ocean.

But just as Clark was watching his first kill hit the water, he felt a jolt and heard a thumping sound. His plane had been hit by fire from a trailing Zero he hadn't seen. He rolled the Hellcat over and came around to attack the Zero broadside, shattering the plane's canopy with a burst from his guns and sending it down in flames. By now he was out of ammunition, as well as damaged, and headed back to the *Hornet*, managing to land in the middle of a kamikaze attack.

The *Hornet* next headed to Okinawa and Clark began flying missions against Japanese troop concentrations there, making strafing runs and dropping napalm in support of U.S. Marines. On April 7 he was flying one of a huge group of 360 American carrier planes that attacked the Japanese fleet off the island of Kyushu. In this raid he and the other Hellcat pilots protected the dive-bombers that attacked and sank the *Yamato*, the largest and most heavily armed battleship ever constructed and the symbol of Imperial Japan's naval power.

Five days later the *Hornet*'s Hellcats scrambled to intercept Japanese planes on the way to attack the task force. Clark engaged one of the stubby but highly maneuverable Mitsubishi J2M "Jack" fighters at five hundred feet and closing on the *Hornet*. He shot it down but took a hit from friendly fire that almost blew the tail off his plane. Once again he was barely able to bring the Hellcat in for a landing.

He got his fourth and fifth kills on April 14—Zeros he shot down during an exhausting ninety-minute dogfight—and his sixth one a day later. Over the next few weeks Clark flew missions against the Japanese homeland and its depleted air force.

After the war, Clark left the Navy and returned to civilian life. Still bookish and literary, despite the abilities he had displayed in combat, he earned a degree in English from Wesleyan College. Now a member of the Naval Reserve, he was called back to active duty when the Korean War erupted. Checked out for jets, he flew more than fifty combat missions in the F9F Panther on board the USS *Antietam*. He decided to make the Navy his career.

By 1961, Clark was commanding officer of VU-10, a fleet utility squadron at Guantanamo Bay, Cuba. With the start of the Cuban Missile Crisis on October 22, 1962, his squadron evacuated all U.S. dependents from the island, while flying continuous combat air patrols over the base.

Robert Clark retired in 1964 as a lieutenant commander and started a new career writing and directing documentary films, first as a Navy civilian employee and then as an independent producer. He bought an open-cockpit PT-23 trainer and until late in his life took his wife Darlene on jaunts, sometimes terrifying her by insisting on practicing his "touch and go" landings. ★

Charles G. Cleveland

LIEUTENANT GENERAL, USAF

November 13, 1927–

CHARLES CLEVELAND'S STORY AS A PILOT has a happy ending with an ironic twist: fifty-five years after he flew his last combat mission in an F-86 Sabre he finally was named an Ace, achieving this milestone with a direct assist from the former Soviet Union, whose planes he had flown against in combat in Korea.

Born in Honolulu in 1927, the year of Charles Lindbergh's epic flight, Cleveland was nicknamed "Chick" by his mother—a gesture of homage to the 19th Infantry in which Charles' father, Lt. Orestes Cleveland III, served. The regiment had been known as the "Rock of Chickamauga"—"Chicks" for short—since its heroic stand in that battle during the Civil War.

His father died when Chick was five years old. He and his older brother and sister prospered under their mother's strength and determination. She provided for the family and also maintained her Army connections—she had played bridge with Gen. Omar Bradley's wife—to help her sons in the military careers she envisioned for them.

A rangy six-footer, Charles was an outstanding high school basketball player and was offered a scholarship to Syracuse when he graduated in 1945. But he wanted to follow his brother John to West Point. John went directly into the combat engineers. Chick, who had read voraciously about World War I Aces when he was growing up, on graduation in 1949 decided to go with the Air Force, which had become a separate service two years earlier.

While he was going through flight training at Randolph Air Force Base, war broke out in Korea. With other top graduates of his class he was assigned to fighters and later was sent to the U.S. base at Kimpo, South Korea, in March 1952 as a member of the 4th Fighter Interceptor Wing.

He thought he would be flying the F-84 Thunderjet, America's workhorse fighter-bomber during the war. But the F-84 had been overmatched by the MiG-15s flown by Russian pilots when China entered the war. In response, the Air Force quickly deployed the F-86 Sabre jet, which was superior to the

MiGs in certain key respects—particularly in roll rate, the gun sight, and the ability to go supersonic in dives.

Cleveland joined the 334th Squadron and was soon flying one or two missions a day into "MiG Alley," the area south of the Yalu River where most air combat occurred. Feeling that they were better pilots flying a better plane, the U.S. flyers remorselessly hunted the enemy, constrained only by the rules of engagement, which forbade crossing the Yalu except when in "hot pursuit." The feeling of élan among them stretched to the ground crews.

"They engaged the enemy through us," Cleveland later recalled of his own crew. "They had bets on which pilot would get a kill on a mission. They knew that gun ports become blackened when the guns were fired, so when we came home they'd look for this and climb up to the cockpit to ask, 'Did you get one? Did you get one?'"

His first eighty missions as a wingman were fairly routine. Then, as a flight leader, on July 11 he sighted a lone MiG-15 and engaged it in a series of high g turns. He hit the MiG heavily and sent it into a steep dive, but it disappeared into the clouds so he didn't claim it as a kill, settling for a probable.

A month later he had his first confirmed victory when he saw a MiG near a Russian airfield. "I hit him with a burst from 1,200 feet. He tried to turn hard right and I hit him again from six hundred feet, and he ejected." Cleveland tried to catch sight of the pilot's face as the parachute started to blossom, but he couldn't.

September 1952 was a good month for the American pilots and a demonstration of the superiority of the F-86 (six lost) to the MiG-15 (thirty-seven shot down). It was also a good month for Cleveland. He got his second kill on September 15 and his third on the twenty-sixth—both quick and decisive engagements. He got his fourth two days later when he and his wingman saw three MiGs attacking F-84s that were on a strafing run against ground targets. Cleveland got behind the lead MiG, which was doing damage to an F-84, and hit it with sustained bursts. The pilot was slumped over dead in the cockpit as the plane crashed into the side of a hill.

But although it didn't seem so at the time, it was the kill he didn't claim that was most significant. It came on September 21, when he opened fire on a MiG-15, causing the plane to trail smoke and lose altitude. But he couldn't follow it down because of the appearance of two other MiGs coming down from 50,000 feet, and his wingman called a defensive break. When they landed back at the base his wingman said that it was a kill, but Cleveland refused to make the claim because he had not seen the pilot eject or the plane crash.

He had one hundred missions and could have come home, but he extended for twenty-five more to get a fifth confirmed kill. But weeks passed with no contact. "Sometimes you'd see them flying at 50,000 feet when you were at 40,000, but they wouldn't come down to fight," he later said. Cleveland had put in thirty-five additional missions before finally leaving Korea for the United States.

In the following decades, he had a full and interesting career, including service as Gen. William Westmoreland's executive officer during the Vietnam War, and later as commander of Air University. He retired in 1984 as a lieutenant general. The fact that he had just missed becoming an Ace had long since faded into memory in 1999 when he was talking to an old friend named D. D. Overton at a flyers' reunion and the subject of his two probables in Korea came up. Overton, himself an Ace, contacted Cleveland's wingman on his second probable who affirmed once again in a formal statement that it should have been considered an outright kill. The American Fighter Aces Association accepted the packet Overton assembled and gave Cleveland status as an Ace, but the Air Force Historical Research Agency, with more stringent standards, did not.

Staying on the case, Overton learned in 2004 that the Russian government, acting in the spirit of glasnost, had opened its Soviet-era Korean War records, which included documentation on every combat sortie flown there. This information was now available at the U.S. National Archives. Overton and Cleveland went there and found the Soviet combat records for September 21, 1952. With the help of a translator they determined that two MiGs had been lost that day, one of them matching exactly the time, the area, and the circumstances of Cleveland's engagement. They submitted their findings to the Air Force Board for the Correction of Military Records, which convened a hearing that involved extensive personal testimony. Soon after, Cleveland was informed that the secretary of the Air Force had officially made him the fortieth and last Ace of the Korean War. ★

John T. Crosby

COMMANDER, USN

July 30, 1920–January 24, 2014

ON APRIL 16, 1945, "TED" CROSBY and his friend Millard "Fuzzy" Wooley, along with their wingmen, were protecting a U.S. task force involved in the invasion of Okinawa against kamikaze attacks when they learned that a large formation of Japanese aircraft was approaching from the north. "Here we go, Ted," said Wooley, putting his Hellcat into a climb, "let's wipe these guys out." Crosby said, "I'm with you." Their wingmen were unable to follow because of mechanical difficulties as Crosby and Wooley rose to engage more than twenty Japanese aircraft. In the wild half hour that followed, Ted Crosby shot down five enemy planes, making him an "Ace in a day."

It was the combat action he had been seeking since December 7, 1941, when he was a carefree twenty-one-year-old commuting by ferry across San Francisco Bay from his home in Oakland every day to attend Marin Junior College, with money he had saved from working at the 1939 San Francisco World's Fair. After the Japanese attack on Pearl Harbor Crosby immediately enlisted in the U.S. Navy. He completed flight instruction at the naval air station in Corpus Christi, Texas, qualified for fighters at Opa-Locka, Florida, and then learned carrier landings on board the USS *Wolverine*, a training carrier stationed in the Great Lakes.

Arriving in San Diego by train for his next assignment, he was told by an assignment officer that he would be serving on board a "jeep carrier," one of the smaller and cheaper aircraft carriers built during the war to supplement the larger and more prestigious "fleet carriers." Crosby knew that these escort carriers were small and slow, and responded, "No, I want to be on one of the big guys." His confrontation with the officer became heated and was overheard by Jim Bellows, a hero of the Battle of Midway, who was putting together a big carrier squadron and immediately told the assignment officer he wanted Crosby.

The new squadron, VF-18, was ordered to sea on board the USS *Bunker Hill* in early November 1943. Crosby's first exposure to combat came in an attack on Rabaul, the heavily fortified Japanese naval installation in the Solomon Islands. On November 26, he and three other Hellcat pilots jumped a Japanese "Betty" bomber. The plane's tail gunner kept them at bay with effective fire for several minutes. Crosby later told Peter Hegarty of the *Oakland Tribune*, "I thought to myself, 'He's got to go.'" So he drew close to the bomber and fired a long burst that shattered the tail section and sent the tail gunner tumbling down into the ocean. Other U.S. planes were also attacking the enemy bomber and he got credit for one-quarter of a kill.

The *Bunker Hill* soon headed back to Hawaii for resupply and the VF-18 was out of action for several weeks. Then the squadron was sent to the Philippines, which had been recently reoccupied by U.S. forces. Renamed VF-17, Crosby's squadron was assigned to the USS *Hornet* in January 1945.

In April, as the U.S. Marines fought a fierce battle with Japanese troops dug in on Okinawa, naval aircraft tried to back them while also combating the waves of suicide attacks targeting the U.S. task force supporting the invasion. One of the vivid memories from these days that stayed with Crosby was of circling above the Japanese super battleship *Yamato* as the huge ship slowly sank off the coast of the island on April 7. As he later said, "You have to remind yourself that there's three thousand men on board that ship. . . . Things like that are not easy to forget."

Nine days later, on April 16, Crosby had his day of days when he and Millard Wooley attacked a group of twenty Japanese planes—dive-bombers and trainers in addition to fighters Crosby thought of as "kami-crazies"—all loaded with explosives to sink a U.S. ship. As the first enemy plane approached, he had a sense that this was a defining moment: "One of these guys turned to take me head-on as I caught up with their group. Thank God for those six .50-calibers in my wings. I opened up on him and the first thing I knew his engine was flying up over my cockpit. Those six .50s would just blow things to pieces."

In the next few minutes, he took down three more Japanese fighters and a dive-bomber. Later on, when he landed on the deck of the *Hornet*, his crew, learning that he had become an "Ace in a day," swarmed all over him with congratulations.

With Okinawa secured, the *Hornet's* mission was refocused on the Japanese mainland. It was during a raid on the coast, near Tokyo Bay, that Crosby had his closest call. As his flight of Hellcats was beginning strafing runs he looked up and saw a group of Zero fighters above. He pulled up to take on one of the enemy planes but pulled up too soon, lost air speed, and began to stall. As he fell off to one side, he felt a huge concussion and thought he had been hit by enemy fire. But he had collided with another Hellcat, whose propeller had torn into his tail section. Miraculously, both planes made it back to the *Hornet*.

Ted Crosby remained in the Navy after the war. He flew photo reconnaissance missions in Korea and retired as a commander in 1969. ★

Perry J. Dahl

COLONEL, USAF

February 18, 1923–

PERRY DAHL SHOT DOWN NINE JAPANESE PLANES in the Pacific during World War II. He also survived a crash landing and a midair collision. But one of his sharpest memories of the war is not about combat at all, but about a bizarre fishing trip with Charles Lindbergh.

The "Lone Eagle" had been sent to New Guinea by the U.S. government to help Dahl and the other P-38 pilots of the 475th Fighter Group stationed there learn techniques of better fuel conservation. He was not a gregarious man and so Dahl was a little surprised when Lindbergh asked him one afternoon if he wanted to go fishing. Dahl said yes and then Lindbergh led him to a beach where he had commandeered one of the large rafts carried for emergencies by B-25 bombers. They walked the raft out into the water and then jumped on board, paddling out beyond a coral reef. Dahl was about to ask how they would fish without poles when Lindbergh reached into his pack and pulled out a grenade, pulled the pin, and tossed it overboard. After the concussion sent up a spume of water, Lindbergh said, "Let's go fishing." He dived into the water, Dahl following, and they spent the next few minutes gathering the stunned fish floating toward the surface. That night the squadron had a fish fry.

Perry Dahl was seventeen when he enlisted in the Washington State National Guard in 1939, using the pay he received for attending weekend meetings to buy gas for his '32 Chevy. The unit was called to active duty early in 1941 and he had to complete his last year of high school at night. After marching back from infantry maneuvers in a driving rain at Fort Lewis one afternoon, he saw pilots standing under the wings of their planes laughing and smoking and, most important, dry. He applied for the Army Air Corps soon after and was accepted on September 6, 1942.

His unit at Williams Air Force Base was the first to train in P-38s and Dahl, like most of the other pilots who flew this plane, came to love the Lightning and was always ready to fiercely defend it against its detractors. His father

Alex McKnight/AM Photo Inc.

came to visit one afternoon and as four of the planes roared by overhead, he looked up in awe, and said, "23 Skidoo." That is what Dahl later named the P-38 he flew in the Pacific.

Just five feet five and 125 pounds (he had to sit on pillows to reach the controls), Dahl was assigned to the 475th Fighter Group in October 1943 as a replacement pilot along with another flyer whose hair was prematurely gray. When the commanding officer first saw them, he shook his head in despair and said, "My God, they're sending me old men and kids!"

Dahl was almost shot down on his fifth mission. "I was tail-end Charlie on a flight of eighteen planes," he remembers. "When the order came to drop tanks, I forgot to switch to internal tanks and as a consequence lost power. By the time my engines restarted, I'd been left behind." His flight leader radioed him to head back home. But on the way he saw an A6M Zero. As he went after it, a second enemy fighter suddenly appeared and opened fire. Dahl quickly rolled to the right and the shells, which would have shredded the cockpit of a single engine fighter, were absorbed by the tail boom of the P-38. Dahl limped back to base on one engine.

Dahl got his first kill—a Zero—on November 9, 1943, and his second—another Zero—over Wewak, capital of Papua New Guinea, three days before Christmas. In his next engagement, he was flying back to base after a reconnaissance mission to pinpoint the location of Japanese shipping when he saw a Zero dart into the clouds above him. He followed and when he came out, he saw the enemy plane just fifty meters ahead and opened fire. The Zero exploded and when Dahl flew through the debris, his landing gear was destroyed. He managed to get back to his base, where he walked away from a crash landing.

He became an Ace when he brought down a Zero and a Ki-43 "Oscar" on April 3, 1944.

By late summer, when his squadron moved to the Philippines, Dahl had six kills. On November 10, just after he shot down the leader of a flight of Ki-61 "Tonys" over the island of Ponson, another P-38 collided with "23 Skidoo." As the other plane crashed, Dahl saw that his tail section was badly damaged. Any thought that he might be able to make it back to base disappeared when his right engine fell off. The P-38 blew up just as Dahl managed to bail out, the explosion leaving flash burns on much of his body.

Over open water, he delayed pulling the ripcord as long as possible because the Japanese pilots often strafed American pilots in their parachutes. As he was about to hit the water, he opened the chute and prepared to slip out of the rigging. He popped his Mae West, came to the surface, and opened his one-man raft. As a Zero swooped down to open fire, Dahl flipped the raft over and hid under it. Soon after a Japanese destroyer headed toward him and was about to bring him on board when U.S. B-25s appeared and the destroyer began evasive maneuvers.

After several hours, Dahl managed to get to shore. He cached the raft, and began walking up a trail heading into the jungle. Hearing footsteps, he took out his .45 pistol. He saw someone in the heavy foliage a few feet away and pulled the trigger. The gun misfired and Dahl realized that the other man slashing at the bush between them with a machete was a Philippine guerrilla. Dahl shouted "Americano!" The guerrilla said angrily in perfect English, "Why the hell did you try to kill me?"

The guerrillas took him to an improvised medical clinic in the jungle where he was treated for his burns. Over the next month, he went from one guerrilla camp to another, one step ahead of Japanese patrols. Often subsisting on grub worms, Dahl weighed less than ninety pounds when a pair of U.S. scouts finally located him and called in a PBY seaplane to take him out.

After convalescence in a Sydney hospital, Dahl was back in combat in early spring 1945. In March he brought down a Japanese bomber and fighter, bringing his total enemy kills to nine.

After the war, he came home and earned degrees at the University of Washington and Colorado State University and was working at the *Seattle Post Intelligencer* when he was recalled to active duty in 1951. Deciding to make the Air Force his career, he eventually served as deputy chief of staff for the North American Air Defense Command and commanded the 56th Special Operations Wing. After flying two combat tours in Vietnam, Perry Dahl retired as a colonel in 1978. ★

Barrie S. Davis

MAJOR, USAAFR
COLONEL, ANG (NCANG)

December 22, 1923–August 19, 2014

IT WAS JUNE 6, 1944. BARRIE DAVIS KNEW it was D-day on the coast of Normandy. But the momentousness of the event hardly registered with him because of the strange circumstances in which he found himself. Four days earlier, he had taken off from a base in Italy in his P-51 Mustang as part of a group from the 317th Fighter Squadron. They were escorting U.S. B-17s on a long-distance bombing mission to hit the railroad marshaling yards in Debrecen, Hungary, and then continuing on to land at a makeshift Soviet base in the Ukraine.

Completing one of the first such roundtrip missions of the war, the bombers, escorted by the Mustangs, then took off from the Ukraine on D-day to hit oil depots in Romania. Near the target, dozens of German Messerschmitt Me 109s suddenly appeared. After the Mustangs had driven them off, Davis looked around and couldn't see two of his flight of four P-51s. This was not unusual. As he later noted, "The strange thing about aerial combat is that one moment the sky is filled with planes, twisting and turning, and the next moment you're by yourself." He was relieved to see his wingman nearby and when a third plane appeared in the distance he assumed that it was one of the missing Mustangs reforming. But then, as bullets began to smash into his propeller and shredded his right wing, Davis realized that it was an Me 109. His plane took more hits in its rudder and aileron and its canopy was blown off. His face and neck peppered with shrapnel, Davis was momentarily paralyzed by the freezing air—60 degrees below zero at 30,000 feet—and passed out. When he came to several seconds later, his stalled Mustang had dropped ten thousand feet. As he fought to regain control of the plane for an emergency landing, he later remembered saying to himself, "Golly, Moses, I wonder who shot me down?"

It would take some sixty-six years for the answer to arrive and tie up one of the loose ends of Davis' life.

Michael Davis

He had grown up in Zebulon, North Carolina, the son of a minister. ("Golly, Moses" was about as close to profanity as he let himself get.) After graduating from high school in 1940, he had entered Wake Forest University. He joined the Army Air Corps in June 1942 and got his wings at Napier Field, Alabama, on August 30, 1943.

As he went to war, Davis felt that he was a lucky man. "I couldn't believe I was actually flying a U.S. fighter plane in combat," he later recounted for the

North Carolina Military Historical Society's publication *Recall*. "It was something I wanted to do so bad that I couldn't believe it was becoming a fact." He named his Mustang "Bee," for "Honey Bee," his father's pet name for his mother. Not yet married or with a girlfriend of his own, he also taped his mother's picture above the plane's instrument panel.

Davis got his first kill, a Focke-Wulf 190, on June 28, 1944, in a battle over Bucharest. He scored three more victories in the skies over Hungary and Poland and became an Ace on August 22, his proudest moment in the war, as he later told writer James Oleson: "My flight of four P-51 Mustangs had finished up our assigned escort mission with plenty of fuel in our tanks so we decided to protect some crippled bombers on their return trip home. We heard a call for help behind us and saw swarms of German fighters attacking the straggling bombers. . . . In the melee that followed, I shot down two of the fighters and the three others in my flight shot down three more. We lost no more bombers on that mission."

Barrie Davis came back to the United States with six kills in November 1944 and was released from active duty a year later. Marrying and beginning a family in his hometown of Zebulon, he started a printing business and became a part-time journalist, Sunday School teacher, and renowned community leader. He left the Air Force Reserve in 1949 and joined the North Carolina National Guard, serving as a captain in the Guard's field artillery for the next twenty-eight years until he retired as a colonel.

But for all his success, there was still the nagging question of who had shot him down all those years earlier. The answer came as a result of research by military historian Jon Guttman, who discovered that Davis' antagonist was a Hungarian Ace named Ion Dobran, who had ten kills of Allied aircraft and who had survived being shot down by Davis' wingman on June 6, 1944, to become a general in the postwar period.

Davis began a sporadic correspondence with Dobran. Smelling an interesting story, *National Geographic* magazine cut through the bureaucratic red tape to fly Davis to Bucharest for a face-to-face meeting with Dobran in January 2010.

It became a diplomatic event as the Romanian government whipped up public interest for several days of touring and ceremonies featuring the two men. In their private conversations, the eighty-six-year-old Davis discovered that his wingman had come close to killing Dobran, ninety-one, when he forced his plane down, sending one slug into the back of his seat that nearly penetrated two inches of steel. Dobran told Davis that upon completing his crash landing he had immediately jumped out of the Messerschmitt and run off into the surrounding fields because he was "afraid that the Mustang would come back and shoot me."

The hands-across-the-water meeting was a significant success, involving a joint appearance before members of the Romanian air force and a helicopter trip over the Ploesti oil fields, which Allied bombers had targeted six decades earlier. Davis played his role with diplomatic aplomb, although there was one moment of slight tension with his new friend when Dobran brashly insisted that the Messerschmitt Me 109 was a far better plane than the Mustang. Davis paused for a moment and then, smiling politely, answered the Hungarian in his soft Southern drawl, "That belief cost many an Me 109 pilot his life." ★

Jefferson J. DeBlanc

COLONEL, USMCR

February 15, 1921–November 22, 2007

IN 1938, JEFFERSON "JEFF" DeBLANC was a seventeen-year-old high school student working part-time in a sugarcane factory near his home in St. Martinville, Louisiana, to earn enough money to attend Southwest Louisiana Institute. He knew what he wanted to do there: enter the government's recently established Civilian Pilot Training Program (CPTP). He had been fascinated by airplanes since he was a boy, when a U.S. Mail pilot made a forced landing near his home and allowed him to climb into the cockpit of his biplane.

The DeBlancs were one of the earliest French families to settle in Louisiana. Tall with a narrow face and an aquiline nose, Jeff displayed this heritage in his face and his courtly demeanor. He had a restless streak and, after he learned to fly in the CPTP, decided to leave Southwest Louisiana Institute his senior year, the summer of 1941, to enter the Navy Aviation Cadet Program. He transferred to the Marine Corps after getting his wings in May 1942, and was assigned to Marine Fighter Attack Squadron 112, already engaged against the Japanese at Guadalcanal. When he flew his first combat mission after arriving at Henderson Field early in November, DeBlanc had only ten hours flying the F4F Wildcat.

On November 13, his squadron intercepted twenty-five of the enemy's Mitsubishi G4M "Betty" bombers on a mission to attack U.S. shipping around Guadalcanal. Disregarding his lack of familiarity with the Wildcat, DeBlanc dove down on one of the "Bettys," aiming his fire at the plane's wing root and quickly shooting it down. He then moved in on another, disregarding the tracer bullets of the bomber's tail gunner, who slumped over as DeBlanc's machine-gun fire raked the plane from back to front and set it on fire.

By the end of the year, the Japanese had concluded that they would not be able to dislodge the Americans from Guadalcanal, but their naval and air forces kept up the fight. On January 29, 1943, DeBlanc was forced to ditch when his plane developed engine trouble during a mission. He was picked up

by a destroyer, the USS *Jenkins*. Two days later he was in the air again as part of a section of six Wildcats escorting a strike force of U.S. dive-bombers and torpedo planes on their way to hit elements of the Japanese fleet. Midway through the flight DeBlanc realized that his auxiliary fuel tank had malfunctioned and that if he continued the mission he wouldn't have enough fuel to get back to base. But he didn't want to leave the rest of the section shorthanded and decided to keep going.

As the U.S. force began to attack, DeBlanc saw Japanese F1M float planes stalking the Dauntless SBD dive-bombers. He singled out two of the enemy and opened fire, quickly destroying them. DeBlanc saw that his fuel was getting critically low. But as the American torpedo planes and dive-bombers finished their run and headed for home, he stayed with the other Wildcats to protect them against twelve Zeros diving down out of the glare of the sun.

DeBlanc rose up to engage one of the attackers and shot it down with a short burst. Then he approached a second one head-on, firing steadily until it exploded. Flying through the debris, he realized from the tracer bullets whizzing by that another Zero was on his tail. He chopped his throttle. As the Wildcat slowed, the enemy plane shot by and DeBlanc shot it down.

Before he could reorient himself, bullets shattered his cockpit, setting his instrument panel on fire, shearing off his wristwatch, and filling his back and legs with shrapnel. As his engine caught fire, he bailed out. Releasing from his chute early to avoid being targeted by enemy fighters, he hit the water hard. Buoyed by his Mae West, he surfaced and for the next several hours swam for the island, Kolumbangara, he saw in the distance.

He thought very little about having just destroyed five enemy aircraft and a great deal about what might come next. He had heard of U.S. pilots taken by natives being handed over to the Japanese for execution, but figured that if he could avoid capture his experience as a boy wandering through the Louisiana bayou might help him survive.

In pain from his wounds, DeBlanc struggled ashore and immediately headed for the jungle. He slept in a tree the first night. The next afternoon he wandered into a clearing and saw a native hut. He hid out there for three nights with coconuts his only food. On the fourth morning he awoke to see five natives with machetes standing outside the hut. ("I could see myself in the pot," DeBlanc later joked.) They put him in a bamboo cage and he feared the worst. But instead of giving him over to the Japanese, they traded him for a ten-pound sack of rice to a native working with the Australian coastwatchers, who were the American flyers' eyes and ears in the Pacific. Thirteen days after being shot down, DeBlanc was rowed out to sea in an outrigger canoe where a PBY Catalina seaplane waited to take him back to his base.

DeBlanc was rotated back to the United States and served as a flight instructor for the next several months. Then he returned to combat during the Battle of Okinawa and got his ninth and final kill, a kamikaze, on May 28, 1944.

Released from the service at the end of the war, DeBlanc was called to the White House on December 6, 1945, to receive the Medal of Honor from President Harry Truman. His citation read in part: "Remaining on the scene despite a rapidly diminishing fuel supply . . . he fought a valiant battle against terrific odds."

Late in life, DeBlanc learned the identity of the native who had "bought" him for a sack of rice and returned to the Solomons to thank the ninety-five-year-old man. As the two of them posed for a farewell photo, DeBlanc remarked, "That's full circle."

Jefferson DeBlanc retired from the Marine Corps Reserve as a colonel in 1972, earned a graduate degree, and became a teacher. ★

James E. Duffy

LIEUTENANT COMMANDER, USNR

January 23, 1920–

JIM DUFFY GREW UP READING ABOUT Charles Lindbergh and building model planes and flying them around his neighborhood. When he was a teenager an older friend took him up in a stagger-wing Beechcraft and he loved the experience so much that he vowed he would soon fly as a pilot rather than a passenger. But any idea that flying was simply fun disappeared when he volunteered for naval aviation in April 1942 and was sent to Los Alamitos in California for primary training. Soon after arriving he and other cadets were being marched to a building to get their flight gear when, in the space of a few minutes, two separate planes on training maneuvers crashed and burned in front of them.

As a boy he had lived on his grandfather's Oklahoma farm where his father sharecropped, and was carefree and easygoing, although his Irish temper and refusal to be bullied led to a succession of black eyes. His father took correspondence courses in refrigeration repair to escape the economic hardships of the Depression and when he got his certificate moved the family to Southern California, where he found work. Duffy attended schools in Monrovia and was a twenty-one-year-old attending Pasadena City College and contemplating his next move when Pearl Harbor was attacked.

He first tried to volunteer for the Army Air Corps and had gone so far as to fill out all the paperwork when the recruiter admitted that he could not promise him that he would be a flyer. Duffy said that if there were any doubts he was not interested. As he left the Army recruitment center a sergeant yelled threateningly after him that he would soon be getting a draft notice and would spend the war as a foot soldier. Duffy enlisted in the Navy the next day, after making sure that he qualified for the V-5 aviation program.

A few weeks later, after his sobering introduction to the dangers of airplanes at Los Alamitos, he was learning spins, loops, and snap rolls in an N2S Stearman biplane. Next he was sent to Corpus Christi, Texas, for formation

flying in a BT-13 Vultee monoplane trainer. Then, after more advanced training in simulated carrier landings, gunnery, and glide bombing, Duffy got his wings on July 1, 1943. He joined the newly formed squadron VF-15 in September and got his first look at the F6F Hellcat. It seemed huge to him and his first thought was, "This can't be a fighter, it has to be a bomber!" After more training VF-15 boarded the carrier USS *Hornet* on January 6, 1944, in Norfolk, Virginia, and headed for Hawaii via the Panama Canal. After arriving at Pearl Harbor, they were transferred to the USS *Essex* and headed into battle.

Duffy's first day of combat was a "breaking in" mission near Wake Island, where his flight of Hellcats ran into Japanese fighters and exchanged fire. On June 18, as the *Essex* took a major role in the Battle of the Philippine Sea, Duffy was escorting two Curtiss SB2C Helldiver dive-bombers on an attack against enemy shipping when one of the planes waggled its wings to get his attention. Its pilot then pointed to a plane below them. Assuming that it was an American, Duffy went down to investigate. "As I approached, I was surprised when I saw the red meatballs [Japanese insignia on the fuselage]. My adrenaline started to flow. I gave a short burst and it immediately started to burn. The 'Kate' [Japanese dive-bomber] nosed up, rolled over, and disappeared into the water below. I don't think it ever saw me."

His first air fight left him stunned: first, that he should actually have gotten into combat after the long months of preparation, and second, that it should have begun and ended so quickly—a mere eyeblink of time.

On the next day of the battle that soon became known as the Great Marianas Turkey Shoot, Duffy took down a Zero over Orote Field in Guam. A memorable, if somewhat surreal, moment occurred when, after a day of flying, Duffy landed on the *Essex* and then spent the next half hour or so watching the landing signal officer (LSO) "working his magic" by bringing a plane in for landing every thirty seconds or so. One final aircraft approached against the blazing sunset at a poor angle and the LSO frantically waved it off. The pilot continued in and the LSO dropped his signal paddles and ran. At the last minute the plane aborted the landing and flew over the *Essex* as all the onlookers realized that it was a Japanese fighter. As Duffy recalls, "We were barely able to close our wide-open mouths, let alone fire a gun!"

Duffy continued to fly combat missions in the Philippines for the next several months. He got his fifth kill, a Nakajima Ki 43 "Oscar" over Luzon on November 5 and became an Ace.

After the U.S. landings in Leyte Gulf were secured, the VF-15 squadron left the *Essex* and returned to the United States. It was back at Los Alamitos when the war ended.

James Duffy was released from the service on January 1, 1946. He entered the University of Southern California and, after graduating with a degree in chemical engineering, joined a company formed by his uncle, making commercial cleaning agents. He eventually became its president and CEO, serving in these capacities until his retirement in 1990. ★

Fred L. Dungan

LIEUTENANT COMMANDER, USN

July 27, 1921–

GROWING UP IN SOUTHERN CALIFORNIA, Fred Dungan's favorite holiday was July 4. After he managed to land on the USS *Hornet* on July 4, 1944, and survived life-threatening wounds he sustained while shooting down four Japanese Zeros, Dungan came to think of Independence Day as something more—a second birthday.

Like other boys of his era, Dungan fell in love with planes because of Charles Lindbergh's historic flight, and had his first ride at the age of eight in an open cockpit Fleet biplane. Dungan was attending Pasadena College in the spring of 1941 when he was accepted into the Civilian Pilot Training Program established by Congress to create a cadre of civilian pilots who could become military pilots in a national emergency.

Dungan flew a 65-horsepower Aeronca Chief with a yoke. He defrayed the plane's $6-an-hour rental cost by charging college friends to take them up for rides. He wanted to be a naval aviator and tried to enlist, but at that time there were only rumors of war and the Navy had more flyers than planes. He recalls Southern California military installations having to stage fund-raisers to buy gasoline for training exercises on the weekends: "But everything changed on December 7."

The morning after the attack he drove to the Long Beach Naval Air Installation. When he got there he saw the film star Wayne Morris, also a naval recruiter, pull up in a yellow Cadillac with a gorgeous blonde in the passenger seat. Dungan told Morris, who himself would become an Ace in the Pacific later in the war, that he was a qualified pilot and wanted to get into combat. "Follow me," Morris said, leading him into the recruitment center, where he became a naval cadet.

Cramming two years of training into five months, Dungan was sent to Project Affirm, a top secret program headquartered in Quonset Point, Rhode Island, to develop a night fighter with radar. (As part of the program, he made the first ground-controlled approach blind landing late in 1943.) In late-night

bull sessions with other pilots, Dungan laid out a futuristic vision of the role flight would play in American life once the war was over. After one of his speeches, another flyer said dismissively, "Aw, that sounds like Buck Rogers stuff." The nickname "Buck" stuck.

It was during this time that "Buck" Dungan had a chance meeting with his childhood idol Charles Lindbergh, who arrived at Quonset Point one afternoon in the cockpit of an F4U Corsair, which he was promoting as a night fighter alternative to the F6F Hellcat. Lindbergh was returning to his plane after looking around the project, and Dungan tagged along and explained why he thought the Hellcat was a better plane. Lindbergh argued with him for a moment, and then, when he saw that Dungan's mind was made up, shrugged, climbed into the Corsair, and disappeared into the clouds.

Dungan was ordered to the Pacific Fleet in January 1944, part of a five-man unit flying Hellcat night fighters, first off the USS *Yorktown* and then the USS *Hornet*. But soon he maneuvered himself into daytime missions because that was where the action was. He got his first kill near New Guinea on April 19 when he chased a Mitsubishi G4M "Betty" bomber down to two thousand feet and destroyed it. There was only one survivor from the plane's crew. He was rescued and brought to the *Yorktown*, where he insisted on seeing Dungan and congratulated him for his victory according to the samurai code.

On June 19, Dungan was taking photos of Japanese installations on Guam with another pilot. After the reconnaissance mission was over they descended through the cloud cover and saw roughly forty Japanese aircraft—an equal number of bombers and torpedo planes—in a landing pattern above an airfield. Dungan dove down and began firing. He had destroyed a bomber and strafed a torpedo plane when a formation of Zeros appeared. Dungan engaged the flight leader of the Zeros—identifiable by the markings on his fuselage—in a wild, spinning dogfight that took them out to sea. Dungan got on the Zero's tail and shredded the plane with a burst of his machine guns. The Japanese pilot opened the cockpit and saluted Dungan as his plane fell into the sea.

Two weeks later, on July 4, Dungan and his wingman, Johnny Dear, launched early for a mission aimed at the well-fortified enemy base at Chichi-Jima, north of Iwo Jima. They saw an enemy destroyer escort in open water. "Let's make a low run," Dungan radioed Dear. "Shoot at the water line." Then he called for a high run, raking the deck. "One more," he called. "This time aim for the stack." The destroyer escort began to sink.

By this time the two American planes had run into a formation of "Rufes"—Zeros with floats. When one of them passed in front of Dungan he shot it down with a short burst. When three of the enemy followed him, Dungan radioed Dear, "Hey, Johnny, I'm bringing some with me." Dear shot down two of them, and Dungan rose to take out the other one. Then he destroyed his fourth Rufe in a head-on firing match.

The dogfight had taken him over an enemy antiaircraft battery. He felt his plane taking hits and then a .30-caliber went through the buckle of his parachute harness and hit him in the neck. Bleeding badly, Dungan headed back to the *Hornet*. To keep from passing out, he shouted insults to his "guardian angel." As he managed to land on the *Hornet* he heard a crewman shout, "Get a stretcher. This man is dying."

Dungan's guardian angel saw him through after all. Within a few months he was out of the hospital. He left the Navy with a Navy Cross, a Distinguished Flying Cross, a Purple Heart, status as an Ace as a result of seven enemy kills, and a feeling that he had been born again on the Fourth of July. ★

Clyde B. East

LIEUTENANT COLONEL, USAF

July 19, 1921–July 30, 2014

EARLY ON THE MORNING OF JUNE 6, 1944, Clyde East and his wingman were in their F-6 Mustangs, reconnaissance versions of the P-51, over Laval, France, photographing German troop concentrations, when they saw two German Focke-Wulf 190 fighters about a mile behind and closing fast. Telling his wingman to take the one on the right, East turned and opened fire on the other one. "The Fw began to smoke immediately," he later said, "followed by a long tongue of fire, and started a steep descending turn to the left, probably out of control. I overran it, pulled up sharply to the left, looked back, and saw him hit the ground in a mushroom of flame and black smoke."

Then, as the clouds parted, he looked down and saw something that took his breath away—thousands of Allied ships stretching to the horizon, so close together that it seemed impossible they would not run into each other as they headed for the coast of Normandy. The invasion was beginning and East had shot down the first German plane of D-day.

It was a long way from Pittsylvania County, Virginia, where East's father worked as a sharecropper on a plantation that had been growing tobacco since before the Civil War. The sixth of nine children, East had also worked the family plot since he was a boy. As he later said of his decision to enlist in the military in June 1941, "I'd been working on a farm for a long time. I thought it was time to do something else."

Europe was at war but the United States wasn't, and East wanted action. So he hitchhiked to Canada to join the Royal Canadian Air Force, which was standing alongside Great Britain in its struggle to survive. During training he met his future wife Margaret, a native of Ontario. As he learned to fly he felt strongly that he had discovered his destiny: "I found out that this was exactly what I wanted to do."

After receiving his wings in November 1942, East was sent to England as part of the RCAF's 414 Squadron. His first assignment was patrolling the

Frank Olynyk

English Channel for German U-boats in a Spitfire. In January 1944, he transferred to the U.S. Army Air Forces as part of the 15th Tactical Reconnaissance Squadron (TRS), flying a P-51 Mustang modified with cameras to complement its .50 calibers. He named the plane "Lil Margaret" in honor of his wife-to-be.

The mission of the 15th TRS was long-range reconnaissance; air combat was secondary. After his first victory on D-day, East didn't have another kill until December 17, 1944, when he brought down a Messerschmitt Me 109 during a mission over Giessen, Germany. Then, as Patton's Third Army crossed

the Rhine to continue its thrust into Germany, East had to fight off increasing numbers of German planes to bring back the reconnaissance information that the infantry depended on. Air-to-air combat became a daily occurrence.

On March 24, 1945, he was returning from a mission over Germany when he ran into six Me 109s and shot down two of them. Over the next month and a half, he brought down nine more enemy planes—Messerschmitt and Focke-Wulf fighters, Junkers transports, Heinkel bombers, and even a torpedo-carrying biplane.

A good part of his success came from the dispassionate way he approached air combat. On one occasion he was halfway through a recon mission when he spotted an Me 109 below. He dove down immediately. As he wrote of the Messerschmitt pilot in a letter home, "He never knew what hit him. I made one pass firing about seventy-five rounds and must have killed the pilot, for the plane went straight in and burst into flame on striking the ground." After watching the Me 109 crash, East went on to complete his mission.

As scheduling officer for the squadron, he always put himself in for the longest and most dangerous missions, often going deep into the eastern part of Germany. Part of his success came from never underestimating the enemy. Even as the Luftwaffe suffered huge losses of planes and shortages of fuel and even ammunition, he continued to have deep respect for the German pilots.

By the time he returned to the United States in June 1945, East had thirteen kills, one of the highest numbers recorded by U.S. reconnaissance pilots in the European theater.

After the war, East transferred to the U.S. Air Force. He flew 130 missions during the Korean War and later served for a time as an adviser to the Italian air force. He commanded a squadron of RF-101 Voodoos in Vietnam in 1964, but one of his proudest moments came during the Missile Crisis of 1962 when he flew several of the reconnaissance missions over Cuba that established beyond a doubt the presence of Soviet missiles on the island.

Clyde East retired as a lieutenant colonel in 1965 and later worked as a military analyst for the RAND Corporation. ★

Billy G. Edens

COLONEL, USAF

January 21, 1923–

EARLY ON IN HIS LONG LIFE BILLY EDENS stopped counting the number of times someone told him that Hollywood ought to make a movie of his World War II experiences. But in truth, it was a story that had it all: becoming an Ace in a single month's nonstop aerial combat after D-day; getting shot down four times, once being given up for dead by his rescuers; being captured by the Germans, escaping from a German prison, then being taken prisoner by the Russians and escaping from a Russian prison; making the long walk from Moscow to freedom in the west.

The story began in a place called Tyronza, a town in northeastern Arkansas where Edens grew up. The town had a population of only a few hundred, most of them poor, but as the birthplace of the Southern Tenant Farmers' Rights movement, formed in the mid-1930s when Edens was a boy, Tyronza was an exciting and sometimes dangerous place to live.

After graduating from high school in 1942, Edens joined the Army Air Corps. Initially he trained in the gliders that would ultimately land U.S. forces behind enemy lines on D-day, but he wanted to be a fighter pilot and in May 1943 was accepted as an aviation cadet. After getting his wings six months later, he was given an opportunity to choose which fighter group he wanted to go to as a replacement pilot. He had recently read an article in *Reader's Digest* about the 56th, known as "Zemke's Wolf Pack" for its commander Hubert "Hub" Zemke, and already famous for the exploits of pilots such as Frances "Gabby" Gabreski, who would become the leading American Ace in the European campaign with twenty-eight kills. Edens knew he wanted to be part of this unit.

Stationed in Boxted, England, he flew the P-47 Thunderbolt, called the "Jug" by American flyers. The heaviest of the American fighters in the war, the Thunderbolt might not have been as maneuverable as the Messerschmitt Me 109, its chief opponent, particularly at lower altitudes, but it had greater durability, and this is exactly what Edens needed. Four of the P-47s he flew

during the war were shot down; he walked away from each crash in part because of the ruggedness of the plane.

The first time he went down came on his fourth mission, when he was hit by ground fire while making low strafing runs over German positions in the islands off the Netherlands. He had to bail out in

the North Sea. "It was dark and cold when I hit the water," he later remembered. "My parachute was dragging me under. I finally opened my Mae West and that popped me up. But I drank a lot of sea water."

Edens spent six hours in the freezing water until a seaplane landed to rescue him. Thinking he was dead, his rescuers used a grappling hook to pull him to the plane; it ripped into the flesh of Edens' back. They tossed him in the hold of the plane and headed to a mortuary on the English coast. Then one of the crewmen saw Eden's head move and yelled, "The bloody bloke's alive!" They worked feverishly to revive him. Miraculously, Edens was in the air again in another P-47 a few days later.

On D-day his squadron's mission was to hit targets of opportunity—enemy convoys, tanks, troop concentrations—twenty miles into France in an effort to prevent German reinforcements from reaching the Normandy beach. Two days after the Allied landing, on June 8, 1944, Edens was flying wingman to his flight leader when they saw two German Messerschmitts below. As they dived down to engage, a dozen more enemy fighters suddenly emerged from the cloud cover. In the chaos of the next few minutes, Edens shot down two Me 109s. Then he saw a Focke-Wulf 190 on the tail of his flight leader. As his friend yelled for help, Edens, who was by now out of ammunition, flew his P-47 into the rear of the German plane, bailing out at the moment of collision as the two planes exploded. He landed inside enemy territory and, after hiding in the woods overnight, was led to the American beachhead by a French boy and from there flown back to England in a light plane.

On July 5, Edens downed another Fw 190, and became an Ace two days later on the way back from a mission escorting U.S. bombers in which he shot down three Ju 52 bombers. On September 10, he was flying his final mission before being sent home, when he was hit by enemy antiaircraft fire after a strafing run. Too low to bail out, he crash landed his Thunderbolt and was immediately dragged out of the wreckage by several German soldiers who, as

he later said ruefully, "beat the hell out of me." After being held for several days in what he described as a "cattle pen," he was sent by train with other captured pilots to Stalag Luft I, a prison camp in northern Germany. After months of near starvation— Edens' weight fell from 160 pounds to less than 100—he and the other POWs heard artillery fire in the east and knew that the Russians were closing in. On April 30, the German guards left in the middle of the night and the next morning the Russians liberated the camp.

Most U.S. POWs waited to be repatriated. Wanting to control their own fate, Edens and a few others left the camp, and were eventually detained by the Red Army, marched east, and, once they reached Poland, sent to a large prison near Moscow in reeking cattle cars. After several weeks there, Edens and another captive fighter Ace named Michael Quirk, along with a bomber pilot named John Biggs, managed to escape and spent the next month and a half walking toward Germany. Ragged and emaciated, hiding from Russian soldiers and helped by Russian peasants, they finally managed to reach Berlin, where they turned themselves over to U.S. occupation forces, who threw them in jail until their identity could be confirmed.

At the war's end, Billy Edens returned to the United States, married his childhood sweetheart, and decided to make the Air Force his career. He flew 156 combat missions in F-84s in Korea, was shot down once again, and barely evaded capture by North Korean forces. He did two tours flying F-100s in Vietnam and retired as a colonel in 1974.

Whenever people called him a hero, Edens had a ready reply: "I'm no hero. I'm a fighter and survivor. And if I hadn't been a fighter, I wouldn't have been a survivor." ★

Robert P. Fash

LIEUTENANT, USNR

September 16, 1920–June 14, 2015

ROBERT FASH ALWAYS REMEMBERED THE DAY he got what he regarded as his first kill, although he didn't get credit for it—a Japanese "Betty" bomber he spotted on April 21, 1944, while engaged in a U.S. raid over Japanese positions in New Guinea. Fash had stalked the bomber cautiously, worried about the plane's tail gunner. But when there was no response as he closed to within one hundred meters he opened fire. As Fash said later on of the tail gunner, "The guy must have been reading the *Tokyo Times*. I came up behind him and shot him up." Another Hellcat pilot got credit for shooting the bomber down, but the thrill of victory for Fash was sweet nonetheless.

Growing up in East St. Louis, Illinois, Fash idolized his older brother Herbert, an outstanding athlete who seemed to be good at everything. Robert was a good baseball player himself and was starting catcher on the Illinois Wesleyan University team when war broke out. Fash followed his brother into the Navy, enlisting as an aviation cadet in June 1942. After flight training in Pensacola, he was assigned to squadron VF-50, the "Devil Cats." Snapshots of the young ensign taken at the time show him with a minimalist smile and a squint of good-natured skepticism. He somewhat resembled the film star Wayne Morris, also a naval aviator and Ace, with whom Fash would serve later in the Pacific.

VF-50 was assigned to the USS *Bataan* shortly after its shakedown cruise in early 1944. Because of the event it commemorated—the resistance, surrender, and subsequent forced "death march" of the U.S. force on the Philippine peninsula early in 1942—the commissioning of the light carrier was an emotional moment. The admiral presiding over the ceremony had stated defiantly: "Our country has always been a generous country. We give freely and I pray that we may continue to give freely, especially when it comes time to give the Japanese hell." The aviators and sailors on board the ship shared this emotion as the *Bataan* steamed into the middle of things in the Pacific.

Tom Dubanowich

On April 29 Fash was involved in what he always regarded as his proudest moment, a moment measured by American lives saved rather than enemy planes downed. His squadron was flying cover for U.S. dive-bombers attacking the heavily fortified Japanese base on Truk Lagoon. During the mission several American pilots were shot down in the coastal waters. An American OS2U Kingfisher float plane landed to rescue them. But soon there were so many flyers clinging to its pontoons that it couldn't take off again. As Japanese batteries on the island took aim at the Kingfisher, it taxied circles in the water to keep from being hit. Fash and other Hellcat pilots saw what was happening and attacked the enemy guns while the USS *Tang*, a submarine on rescue patrol, hurried to the scene to pick up all the downed airmen. For the rest of his life, Fash kept a framed newspaper clipping describing the action, with a photo showing all the Americans who had been rescued because of his and other flyers' efforts, on the wall of his den.

On June 24, Fash's squadron carried out a bombing raid against an enemy airfield on Iwo Jima. His hometown newspaper set the scene in a front-page story: "The weather was bad near the target and the squadron was forced to circle the storm and come in low. Japanese fighters were waiting in the cloud cover with a greatly superior force and swooped down." In the fight that followed, Fash shot down two Zeros. Later in the day, in another combat sweep, he got his third confirmed kill: a Japanese "Judy" dive-bomber.

In August Fash was transferred to the USS *Essex* and assigned to VF-15, known as "the Fabled Fifteen." For the next three months, he flew alongside and became a friend of the squadron's commander, David McCampbell, the leading Navy Ace

of the war with thirty-four kills, nine of them in one engagement.

On October 12, Fash shot down two more enemy fighters, making him an Ace. On October 24 he got a twin-engine Ki-48 light bomber—a "Lily" in the Allied reporting code—his final kill. The next day, when his squadron attacked the northern force of the Japanese fleet in one of the decisive moments in the climactic Battle of Leyte Gulf, one of Fash's bombs scored a hit on the Japanese carrier *Zuikaku*, helping to sink it. For his role in this action Fash was awarded the Navy Cross.

In late November Fash returned home and spent the rest of the war preparing for the invasion of the Japanese homeland, which became unnecessary when atom bombs were dropped on Hiroshima and Nagasaki. He had survived the war, but his beloved elder brother did not. On January 21, 1945, Lt. Herbert Fash, a landing signal officer on board the USS *Hancock*, was killed along with fifty other sailors when a U.S. dive-bomber returned to the ship with an unexploded bomb that detonated in a blinding flash when the plane touched down.

After the war Robert Fash began a small company called Executive Air Transport and later worked as chief pilot for the Site Oil Company. ★

Edward L. Feightner

REAR ADMIRAL, USN

October 14, 1919–

EDWARD FEIGHTNER GOT THE NICKNAME that would stay with him the rest of his life in Hawaii in the summer of 1942. After getting his wings that March, he had been ordered to report to the USS *Yorktown*. But the carrier was sunk in the Battle of Midway while Feightner was on his way to Pearl Harbor. While awaiting a new carrier posting, he was temporarily assigned to a shore unit under the command of the charismatic Edward "Butch" O'Hare, who had become the Navy's first Ace and first Medal of Honor recipient of World War II six months earlier when he single-handedly fought off a group of Japanese bombers about to attack his carrier, the USS *Lexington*.

Feightner's time on the island of Maui with O'Hare was a memorable interlude—lessons in fighter tactics and indolent days of sun and surf. (O'Hare was a dedicated skin diver whom Feightner would always remember coming to the surface of the ocean with a fish he had just speared and "laying on his back like [an] otter and eating it raw.") Over time, the other men in the unit tanned to a golden brown. But the fair-skinned Feightner turned lobster-red in the sun and one day O'Hare referred to him as "Whitey." It was like a rebaptism. The name stuck.

Feightner had grown up in the small town of Elida, Ohio. Despite his small size—five foot one, just over one hundred pounds—he had been a good enough baseball player in high school to be scouted by the St. Louis Browns. Valedictorian of his high school class of 1937, he received a scholarship to tiny Findlay College. He was in the office of the school's president one afternoon in his freshman year when a local daredevil pilot named Mike Murphy, who also had an appointment, appeared. As they were walking out he said to Feightner, "Hey, kid, you want to go flying?" Feightner said he did and Murphy not only took him up in a Ford Trimotor but when they reached cruising altitude gave him the controls. By the time he landed, Feightner was addicted to flight.

Tom Dubanowich

When he graduated from Findlay in 1941, Feightner tried to enlist in the Army Air Corps, but there was a backlog of several months in processing new pilots. He then talked to a Navy recruiter who told him, "We'll take you today." He enlisted on June 16, 1941.

When he completed flight training at the naval air station in Corpus Christi, Texas, Feightner was initially assigned to dive-bombers. He immediately checked out a SNJ trainer and flew to Washington, D.C., where his passionate appeal convinced Navy officials that he should be allowed to fly fighters.

Feightner always believed that his detour to Butch O'Hare's unit was a key moment in his career. O'Hare was a resourceful tactician who schooled the

pilots under his command in how to fight the more maneuverable Japanese Zeros. (He was a partisan of close combat: "Fly right into their tail before opening fire" was one of his maxims.) When Feightner was assigned to the USS *Enterprise* as a member of VF-10 in October 1942, he believed that he was a keener instrument of war than he would have been without the interlude in Hawaii.

VF-10 was called "The Grim Reapers" and used as its symbol the image of a skeletal representation of Death swooping down with flight goggles and wings and carrying a scythe. The unit was commanded by an officer named James Flately (known as "Reaper Leader"), who had just taken part in the Battle of the Coral Sea and who made a point of defending the F4F Wildcat against critics who felt that it was inferior to the Japanese Zero: "Let us not be too critical of our equipment. It shoots the enemy down in flames and brings most of us home."

On October 26, the *Enterprise* took part in the Battle of the Santa Cruz Islands. Feightner's first sight of the Japanese Zero in action made him aware that he was facing a formidable enemy. "They took out seven of our planes the first pass," he remembered. "They were really good." He shot down a Japanese dive-bomber attacking the carrier, but another got through and scored a direct hit. When he landed, Feightner later told his biographer Peter Mersky, he went to the hangar deck and found himself "wading around in water and fuel and dead bodies."

In November, the *Enterprise* headed to the Solomons to battle the Japanese fleet threatening to retake Henderson Field on Guadalcanal. After strafing enemy vessels carrying troops for the invasion, Feightner and other members of VF-10 remained at Henderson for several days, flying missions in support of U.S. Marines there.

On January 30, 1943, Feightner was part of a flight of Wildcats that intercepted a force of twelve Mitsubishi G4M "Betty" bombers headed for the *Enterprise*. The U.S. planes knocked down six of the attackers and the rest, blocked from the carrier, headed for the nearby cruiser USS *Chicago*, sinking it. Feightner shot down three of the enemy, leading his flight commander James Flately to remark when he returned to the *Enterprise*, "You're a fighting fool, aren't you?"

On March 30, 1944, Feightner became an Ace when he shot down a Zero, and on April 29, he got another one. In both of these engagements he used a lesson he had learned from Butch O'Hare: "Never

follow a Zero into a loop because they turn tighter and even though they start out ahead of you, they'll soon be on your tail." Instead, he simply turned hard right and opened fire on the Japanese fighters as they completed their loop. He thought of this life-saving advice again, as well as the pleasant interlude on Maui, when word came a few months later that O'Hare had been shot down in a dangerous night mission against Japanese torpedo bombers.

Now flying a new F6F Hellcat off the USS *Bunker Hill*, Feightner took part in the Battle of the Philippine Sea, which U.S. flyers called the Great Marianas Turkey Shoot because of the disproportionate numbers of Japanese planes they took down. On November 10, he was ready to take off for a strafing run of the islands off the coast of Japan when his plane experienced engine problems. He hopped into another one, which still had a bomb from a previous mission there had not been time to unload. While on the mission, Feightner saw a small Japanese warship steaming out of the harbor. He made a bombing run against it and sank it with a direct hit on its stern.

Soon after, the *Bunker Hill* headed back to the United States for an overhaul. With nine kills to his credit, Feightner was reassigned to duty as a flight instructor for the duration of the war. He stayed in the Navy and had an interesting postwar career that included work as a test pilot, flying with the Blue Angels (in one public performance he had to make an emergency landing at Chicago's O'Hare Airport, recently renamed for his old friend), and eventually as commander of the USS *Chikaskia* and the USS *Okinawa*.

Edward Feightner retired from the Navy as a rear admiral in 1974. ★

Arthur C. Fiedler

COLONEL, USAF

August 1, 1923–May 11, 2016

ARTHUR FIEDLER'S SUMMARY MOMENT as a fighter pilot in World War II came during a dogfight over Ploesti, Romania, on June 28, 1944, when he destroyed a German Messerschmitt Me 109 with his .45 pistol—without firing a shot.

His squadron of P-51s was flying at 25,000 feet when a flock of Me 109s appeared. The flight leader immediately ordered an attack: "Drop tanks and balls to the wall!" Fiedler's left auxiliary fuel tank wouldn't drop. He made every maneuver he could think of to get rid of it, but he didn't lose the tank until he thought to test-fire his guns and the concussion knocked it off. By that time, he was all alone. Heading toward where he thought the rest of his flight would be, he went through heavy cloud cover and then, when he broke into the clear, saw two Me 109s. One of them spotted Fiedler, who maneuvered the P-51 into a dive, pulled out at 13,000 feet, and opened fire, sending the German down in flames.

"I'd been given a 'probable' four days earlier," he later recalled, "and I thought, 'By God, I'm not getting another one.' So I followed him down to get pictures." The Me 109 crashed. Fiedler was pulling up when the other Messerschmitt appeared. He put several shots into the German plane's fuselage but then his guns jammed as a result of the heavy g forces. "We were about forty feet from each other, so close it was like flying in formation. He's looking at me and I'm looking at him. I'm not able to fire and not sure what to do. I figure whether I climb or dive he's probably coming after me with his 20-mm cannon. I finally decided I'm going to take out my .45 pistol and start shooting at him. As I pulled out the gun, he was looking at me. He suddenly jettisoned his canopy and just bailed out. I knew they probably wouldn't believe it back at the base, so I turned on the cameras to have proof. For a while the other guys called me Svengali because I had 'hypnotized' this German pilot."

Fiedler had wanted to fly since he was seven years old and became friends with a boy on his block in Oak Park, Illinois, whose father was a military pilot

stationed out of town. When the father came home for weekend visits he circled over the neighborhood several times before landing at a nearby field. Fiedler and all the other kids would come out to watch, dancing and yelling as the plane maneuvered above them. "My God, he's like a bird!" Fiedler remembers marveling.

He was eighteen when he joined the Army Air Corps in April 1942, a lean and lanky young man with a sharp sense of irony. Because of a shortage of instructors and planes, he wasn't called to flight school until October. After getting his wings and training in P-47 Thunderbolts, he was sent to an Army Air Corps facility in Dover, Delaware, in March 1943 as an instructor. His commanding officer told him that he would be there for the duration of the war and probably never see air combat, so Fiedler and his fiancée immediately got married. Three weeks later the Dover base was closed. Fiedler was assigned to the 325th Flight Group and sent to Lesina, Italy.

His first mission was on June 13, 1944, flying in a P-51 named "Helen," after his wife. He had never flown in a formation of more than eight planes. But on this mission, escorting bombers to Munich, there were over fifty Mustangs that were likely, according to the preflight briefing the pilots received, to run into as many as four hundred German fighters. Fiedler always remembered the sound of his heart thumping with excitement as his plane got closer to Germany.

He had excellent 20/10 vision, and on the flight path along the coast near Trieste he saw black specks in the distance and excitedly called out, "Bogeys, two o'clock high!" After a short pause the gruff voice of his flight leader came over the radio, "Naw, that's just flak." As Fiedler later recalled, "I'd never seen flak before. I was so embarrassed that I could have crawled down the tube of my oxygen mask."

Soon after, another pilot pointed out the vapor trails of a pair of Me 109s. When the flight leader ignored them, Fiedler asked himself, "Are we at war, or not?" Almost immediately the question was answered as a 109 came roaring down the left side of the formation chased by a pair of P-51s from another squadron. As he watched fire from their machine guns rip chunks out of the approaching German plane, Fiedler understood that the game he was in was played for keeps.

Flying for a time as wingman to the famed Ace "Herky" Green, Fiedler's first two kills came on June 28, 1944, one of them the Me 109 downed with his .45. About two weeks later, on July 9, 1944, he got another Me 109 over Ploesti, and then on July 26 he shot down an Fw 190 and an Me 109 over Vienna, when his squadron took on sixty-four German fighters attacking a group of B-17s. He had become an Ace in a concentrated month of combat at the age of twenty.

On September 12, Fiedler got his seventh kill and had his closest call. He was climbing up after a strafing run at enemy positions in eastern Hungary when he saw a large plane above him. He rose to intercept it, but was cautious because U.S. intelligence had recently informed pilots that the Russian army was closing on Budapest and had planes in the air. Drawing closer to the plane than he normally would have, Fiedler saw that it had an odd camouflage—wavy blue lines—and no insignia. He was within thirty feet of the tail and identified it as a German He 111 bomber just as the plane's dorsal machine gun opened up, shredding his left wing and missing his engine by six inches.

Fiedler was able to pour enough fire into the He 111 to destroy its cockpit and knock off its left engine, sending the large plane down. But his own hydraulics were shot out on his left side. His air speed and rate of climb falling, he managed to get above the overcast and head for home. The P-51's brakes were gone when he landed. He saw vehicles at the end of the runway and realized he would hit them if he didn't do something. Although going fifty miles an hour, he did a skidding ground loop that brought the plane to a stop.

A colonel rushed out in a jeep and yelled up at Fiedler as he opened his canopy, "What the hell do you think you're doing?"

Fiedler replied, "Well, sir, I got shot up by a German bomber."

"Did you get him?"

"Yes, sir."

"Good boy," the colonel said, getting into a staff car with a smile and driving off. Arthur Fiedler came home in April 1945 with eight kills, entered the University of Illinois, and graduated with a degree in mechanical engineering in 1950. He was called back to service soon after and decided to make the Air Force his career. He worked in the Air Force's Dyna-Soar space launch vehicle program and flew in Vietnam, retiring in 1975 as a colonel. ★

Richard H. Fleischer

CAPTAIN, USAAF

September 6, 1919–

RICHARD FLEISCHER SIGNED UP FOR the U.S. Army Air Forces in September 1941, just before his twenty-second birthday. He had completed two years at Northeastern University, not far from where he had grown up in Boston, but worried that he would soon be drafted. Knowing that he would be a commissioned officer making seventy-five dollars a month made the service even more attractive to him.

The only problem, as he later said with the quirky sense of humor he carried with him throughout his life, was that until then he had never been in a plane. When he finally got into training after Pearl Harbor, his instructor took him up. "He said, 'I'll be teaching you to do all this,'" Fleischer later recalled, "and then went into loops and rolls that scared the daylights out of me. When we finally landed I thought to myself, 'Let me out of here!'"

Fleischer overcame his fears and got his wings at Foster Air Force Base in Texas in October 1942. After this, he was assigned to the 348th Fighter Group, the first group in the Fifth Air Force to fly the P-47. Fleischer had over two hundred hours' flying time in the Thunderbolt over the next few months, mostly in the New England region, and later on attributed his survival to this intensive training. (This conclusion was supported by the fate of Fleischer's brother, also a pilot, who had only fifty hours in the P-47 when he arrived in Europe near the end of the war and was shot down after a few missions and taken prisoner.)

In May 1943, he boarded a troop ship in New Jersey and sailed for Australia. Once there his squadron waited a couple of weeks for its planes to arrive. When they did, the group went on to New Guinea, where Fleischer would spend the rest of his service.

The memory of his first contact with enemy aircraft in the late summer of 1943 never left him: "We were escorting C-47s dropping food to infantry positions and suddenly we were jumped. I saw golf-ball-sized tracers whizzing

Photo by Amber Barker/Looking Glass Photography. Background painting by Roy Grinnell.

by and I'm thinking, 'It's true. War is hell.' I put my P-47 into a dive to get away. The Thunderbolt was a *war plane*, heavy and tough and it could dive. I got away and was still terrified when I landed."

Back at the base, Fleischer talked to a doctor. "Doc, my mouth was so dry I couldn't swallow," he said. The doctor shrugged and said, "That's just fear. You'll get over it." He did.

He didn't get his first kill until two days after Christmas. The rest of the squadron was on a mission. Fleischer and a few other pilots had the day off. But four of them were scrambled when word came that the Americans' primitive radar showed twelve enemy planes heading toward the island of New Britain. Fleischer looked through the broken clouds and saw that they were dive-bombers beginning an attack on U.S. PT boats. What the radar had not shown was several Zeros flying cover for them at 20,000 feet above.

Wary of the rear-seat gunner in the Japanese dive-bombers, Fleischer dove down and came up from below. "I got one with hits right on the engine. Then I did a wingover and got behind a second one and took him down too." Fleischer expected the Zeros to enter the action, but they never did, perhaps fearing that there were more U.S. planes on the way. He was elated at his victory and did a victory roll on the way back to base, yelling, "Rickenbacker and Fleischer! No, make that Fleischer and Rickenbacker!"

Noting that some of the pilots in his squadron were overly aggressive, "firing at anything that moved," Fleischer forced himself to be careful when he attacked, making sure it was an enemy plane, not a friendly, before opening fire. He shot down a Zero on February 3, 1944, and a little more than a month later got two more. "I was making a head-on pass at the first one when I saw the pilot open the cockpit and jump to his death. The second kill came when the plane I was chasing snapped left into a half roll and hit the water."

By June, when he scored his sixth and final victory, Fleischer was approaching two hundred missions. "It was not like in Europe where you went home after a certain number," he said later on. "MacArthur felt he wasn't getting enough pilots and didn't want to let go of the ones he had."

The stress of constant combat was mitigated somewhat by ten-day leaves every four months to Sydney. The squadron maintained an apartment there. The men bought a 1938 Chevrolet for their common use, always scrounging for gas and trying to adjust to the right-hand steering. "It was beach time, horse races, and night spots," Fleischer recalled. "And of course we had our share of the ladies."

In October 1944, his skin yellow from the Atabrine he took to control the malaria he had contracted, Richard Fleischer was finally sent home. He had considered making the Army Air Corps his career, but, as he says, "My wife took one look at me and said, 'No more flying. Period. You've used up all your guardian angels.'" ★

Joseph J. Foss

CAPTAIN, USMCR

BRIGADIER GENERAL, ANG

April 17, 1915–January 1, 2003

JOE FOSS—KNOWN AS "SMOKEY JOE" in his World War II flying days because of the cigar he kept clenched in his teeth—always remembered the day his father declared a day off from work on the family farm in Sioux Falls, South Dakota, and took him to the Black Hills airport so the two of them could take a ride in a Ford Trimotor. It was 1931 and the Foss family, like the country as a whole, had fallen into the trough of the Great Depression. The cost of the ride—$1.50 each—made it seem like a forbidden luxury to the sixteen-year-old.

Not long after, Foss' father was killed in an automobile accident and he dedicated himself to helping his mother keep the farm from failing. But the thrill of that Trimotor flight never left him. While finishing high school he watched a team of Marine Corps aviators perform aerobatics in open cockpit biplanes and decided that he wanted to be a Marine pilot himself. He got a part-time job in a gas station, while attending the University of South Dakota, to pay for private flying lessons, and also participated in the newly enacted Civilian Pilot Training Program while earning his degree. He had over one hundred hours' flying time when he graduated. Soon after, he hitched a ride to Minnesota to enter the Marine Corps and the U.S. Navy cadet program.

A curly-haired six-footer who looked a little like John Wayne (who in fact became his friend later on), Foss got his wings in March 1941. The war in Europe still seemed far away. He spent the next few months as a flight instructor at NAS Pensacola. After the Pearl Harbor attack, Foss assumed that he would go into battle as a fighter pilot but his commanding officer told him that at twenty-six he was too old and was being sent to photo reconnaissance school instead. Foss was dissatisfied with this duty and let his superior officers know it. Finally he got himself assigned to Marine Fighter Squadron 121 ("The Green Knights"). When the unit shipped out for Guadalcanal in late September 1942, Foss, now a captain, was its executive officer.

When VMF-121 arrived, Guadalcanal's Henderson Field was a runway pocked with bomb craters from constant attacks by Japanese bombers and always under threat by Japanese troops, who occupied part of the island. Marion Carl, who would become the Marine Corps' first Ace, described the humid, malarial environment as "the only place in the world where you could be up to your knees in mud and still get dust in your eyes." Along with some stray Navy and Army Air Forces flyers, the

Marine pilots formed what became known as the Cactus Air Force ("Cactus" was the Allied code name for Guadalcanal), scrambling several times a day to intercept the enemy and keep the island from being overrun.

Flying an F4F Wildcat, Foss went on his first combat mission on October 13. A Japanese Zero attacked him from above but overshot him in his dive, and Foss blasted him out of the sky. But during the furious encounter with other enemy planes that followed his Wildcat was badly shot up and Foss had to land at Henderson with a dead engine and no flaps. The next day he went up again in another plane and destroyed another Zero. Then two more Zeros and a Mitsubishi G4M "Betty" bomber four days later.

Leading a section of eight Wildcats that would become known as "Foss' Flying Circus" because of their aggressive combat maneuvers, Foss lived with the other pilots of the Cactus Air Force in six-man tents, ate reconstituted eggs, and bathed in the Lunga River. When he wasn't flying, he and some of his men carried rifles into the jungle around Henderson Field and engaged in shoot-outs with Japanese soldiers, until the commanding officer of VMF-121 put his foot down and ordered them to stop.

On November 7, Foss shot down a Zero and two Mitsubishi F1M float biplanes. But as the second was going down, its tail gunner shredded Foss' Wildcat and he was forced to ditch in the water off Malaita Island. Initially pinned underwater, Foss finally managed to wriggle free from the wreckage and was propelled to the surface by his inflated Mae West. He bobbed in the water for hours until he was finally fished out by rescuers working with the island's Catholic mission, whose outrigger almost ran over him in the darkness. The next day he was picked up by a Navy Catalina flying boat and a day later he was back in action.

When Foss contracted malaria and was evacuated from Guadalcanal on November 19, he had shot down twenty-three enemy planes in a month of intense combat. He returned to action in early in 1943, and on January 15 shot down three more Zeros. Ten days later, as a huge force of Japanese bombers approached to hit Henderson Field with a knockout blow, Foss led a flight of four Wildcats and four Army P-38s to intercept them, forcing the enemy planes to turn back without dropping a single bomb.

This mission would be singled out in the citation that accompanied the Medal of Honor awarded to Foss by President Franklin D. Roosevelt on May 18, 1943. With his aides nervously waiting outside the door of the Oval Office, FDR spent over an hour with Foss, quizzing him closely about his view of the war. Foss later realized that the president's questions came because two of the Roosevelt sons were serving in the Pacific. A photographer snapped his picture as he left the White House wearing the medal. It appeared on the cover of *Life* magazine on June 7, making Foss a national hero.

After participating in war bond drives, Foss returned to the Pacific as commanding officer of Marine Fighting Squadron 115, but was forced out of action for good by a recurrence of malaria. After the war he came home to South Dakota and opened a flying school. He helped form the South Dakota Air National Guard, eventually rising to the rank of brigadier general, and served as director of operations for the Central Air Defense Command during the Korean War.

Campaigning up and down the state in his own plane, Foss was elected governor of South Dakota in 1954 and served two terms. Later on, he became the first commissioner of the newly formed American Football League and a host of ABC TV's *American Sportsman.* ★

Cecil G. Foster

LIEUTENANT COLONEL, USAF

August 30, 1925–July 5, 2016

THE STEELY SENSE OF WILL AND DETERMINATION his fellow pilots saw in Cecil Foster during air combat in Korea were formed in a difficult childhood. His early life became a litany of tragedy beginning in 1930, when he was five years old and growing up happily in a rambling farmhouse with five brothers and sisters in Midland County, Michigan. His mother came down with a virulent case of polio one afternoon and died suddenly. His father, who had worked as a laborer in the local oil fields, lost his job and parceled the children out to various members of the extended family. Soon after, Foster, now living with grandparents, contracted scarlet fever and almost died himself. Not long after he recovered, his grandfather suffered a severe stroke and his grandmother was forced to sell the family's cow, farm machinery, and other possessions as the Depression closed in around them. They ate all their chickens and eventually lost the farm.

Refusing to allow himself to be dragged down in the undertow of these setbacks, Foster forged a future for himself. He did well in the one-room school he attended as a boy and was always on the lookout for part-time jobs in high school. When he graduated in 1943, he enlisted in the Army Air Forces. He was initially sent to radar observation bombardier training, but he wanted to fly fighter planes and maneuvered his way into flight training at Williams Field, Arizona. World War II ended before he could get into combat, but he decided to stay in the service to see where it would take him.

He was stationed in Alaska in 1949, recently married and starting a family, when word came from Washington that there would be a reduction in force as a result of the postwar drawdown. He was released from the Air Force and returned to the lower forty-eight, where he worked without much enthusiasm as a laborer in natural gas storage facilities and as a life insurance agent. When the Korean War broke out he heard that the Air Force was in effect hiring again and reenlisted. After training in F-86 Sabre jet fighters at Nellis Air

Athena Lonsdale/Athena Photography

Force base, he was sent to Suwon, Korea, in May 1952 as part of the 51st Fighter Interceptor Wing.

On September 7, Foster, who by then had some thirty combat missions as a wingman, was enjoying a day off. He had walked over to the operations building to watch the planes taking off and landing when he heard the phone ring. The operations officer who took the call said that some Sabres had been attacked by a superior force of MiG-15s and were in trouble. Insisting on leading a flight to support them, Foster ran to the barracks to change into his flight suit then hurriedly took off.

As Foster later recounted in his book *MiG Alley to Mu Ghia Pass*, two of the four F-86s in his flight were forced to return to base because of mechanical problems. He and the other one continued toward the Yalu River, where he saw a flight of eight MiGs and "bounced" them from above. As the two Americans attacked, they saw another group of eight MiGs joining the fight, and then eight more.

For the next forty-five minutes the two Americans fought twenty-four enemy planes. When one of them rolled out to shoot, the other would cut in to cover him. Foster wasn't sure whether he was the hunter or the prey.

Another lone MiG joined the fight. Foster pulled up in a sharp right turn to engage and poured several bursts into the plane, causing it to begin a slow descent into the sea. It was his first kill. After confirming it, he and the other American headed for home.

Three weeks later Foster, in a Sabre he had named "Three Kings and a Queen" for his wife and three sons, was leading a flight back toward the Yalu when he saw a pair of MiGs. Foster was wary because he knew the Communists sometimes used isolated planes flying at lower altitude as "live bait" while several more were five thousand feet or so higher and a mile behind, ready to pounce when Americans attacked. When the MiGs turned toward him, Foster did a split-S maneuver. He fired a one-second burst at the leader that missed him but stitched a row of hits on the fuselage of the enemy wingman's plane, which began to smoke and fell into a near-vertical dive. Although he was still at 35,000 feet the pilot of the MiG bailed out. As his parachute opened, he waved his hands wildly and Foster knew he was dying from lack of oxygen.

Because the ground war was a depressing twilight stalemate, the victories of the U.S. fighter pilots made them heroes to the press and the public. Foster made up his mind not to succumb to the "MiG madness" that made some of his comrades reckless in their drive to rack up kills. Another reason for being judicious was his family. In late November he got leave to meet his wife in Japan and found that she was going to have another baby. He told her that when he got back to Korea he would have to change the name of his plane to "Four Kings and a Queen."

Back in combat he witnessed a bizarre drama while on a mission above the Yalu when he spotted a single MiG on the horizon and went after it. But just then a second MiG appeared and began firing on the first one. As Foster came closer he saw that the plane being fired upon was sleeker-looking with a slightly different wing configuration. He never figured out why the second enemy plane was firing on it, but later realized that the first plane was the USSR's new MiG-17. This was the first glimpse any pilot in his squadron had gotten of this new plane.

By late January the weather was freezing cold and Foster and the other Americans were wearing the bulky survival gear called "poopy suits" in case they had to eject. He had seven kills on the afternoon of January 24, when he went out again as leader of a flight of four Sabres. When they ran into eight MiGs, Foster isolated one of them, he later wrote, the way a cowboy might cut a steer out of a herd, and shot it down, then brought down another one soon after. When he got back to base his commanding officer told him, "Nine is enough. You should call it a war." Foster went home to meet the son he had not yet seen.

Foster later flew 165 combat missions in Vietnam, where he served as commanding officer of the 390th Tactical Fighter Squadron. On one of these missions he was hit by enemy ground fire and forced to bail out. His parachute caught in a tree leaving him dangling seventy-five feet above the ground. A "Jolly Green Giant" U.S. helicopter got to him just before the Viet Cong did.

Cecil Foster retired from the Air Force as a colonel in 1976. ★

Frank L. Gailer Jr.

BRIGADIER GENERAL, USAF

November 13, 1923–

AS A BOY, FRANK L. GAILER JR. READ BOOKS about World War I Aces, watched movies like *Dawn Patrol*, and fantasized about someday flying fighter planes himself. Aircraft carriers were becoming national news in the 1930s when he was growing up in Great Neck, Long Island, and he initially thought about becoming a Navy pilot. But his mother sent him to Staunton Military Academy in Virginia, which made him an Army man, and after attending Hofstra College for a year he volunteered for the Army Air Forces in 1942.

After graduating from flight school in 1943, Gailer was assigned to the Columbia Army Base in South Carolina to train as a B-25 bomber pilot. Columbia was where Jimmy Doolittle's men had prepared for their historic attack on Tokyo a year and a half earlier. Like most Americans, Gailer had been electrified by the Doolittle raid, but he still wanted to fly fighters. Thinking the ruse probably wouldn't work, he told his commanding officer at Columbia that he felt his size—five foot six and 120 pounds—might make it difficult for him to control a B-25. To his surprise, the officer agreed and transferred him to fighter training.

In July 1944, Gailer was sent to England as a P-51 Mustang pilot, joining Chuck Yeager, Bud Anderson, and other future Aces in the 357th Fighter Group. It was later said that William Joyce, nicknamed "Lord Haw-Haw," the British traitor who made wartime propaganda broadcasts for the Nazis from Germany in upper-class English, referred to the group derisively as "the Yoxford Boys," for the small village near the RAF base where they were stationed. The name stuck and became part of their legend.

The Yoxford Boys' mission—escorting Allied bombers deep into enemy-held territory and back again—put them into combat against the best pilots in Germany's Luftwaffe. They made the 357th into one of the premier fighter groups of the war, having one of the highest number of air combat victories and producing more Aces—forty-two—than any other unit.

On September 13, Gailer was flying as wing-man for Chuck Yeager in a mission over the Dutch city of Arnhem when they engaged a group of Messerschmitt Me 109s. Yeager destroyed one of them and got a half credit for the kill of another. Over the next week, Gailer shared in the downing of two Focke-Wulf 190 fighters. He shot down another Fw 190 on his own on October 7 and an Me 109 five days later.

Gailer was on his forty-fifth mission on November 27, 1944, when he saw two Fw 190s and dove down to line up behind them. "I fired on the wingman," he later recalled, "but my bullets hit the leader. I saw his wing come off and hit the wingman's plane, taking it down too. It was two for one. I remember saying to myself, 'I'll be darned.'"

Moments after he had officially become an Ace, Gailer saw what he thought were two more enemy fighters coming in his direction and headed right for them. They looked like Me 109s and he had his finger on the trigger, but at the last minute he realized that they were Mustangs with solid blue noses from the 352nd Fighter Group. But they didn't identify him as a friendly and began shooting. Gailer's engine was shattered and his cockpit exploded. He was struck in the shoulder and bailed out.

When he hit the ground, he was captured by a local farmer who told him that he was in Kassel, the geographical center of Germany, which meant that he would have a long walk in all directions if he tried to escape.

He was taken to Stalag Luft I, one of the largest of the German prison camps for captured Allied pilots, where he was interned with, among others, "Gabby" Gabreski, the leading U.S. Ace in the European theater with twenty-eight kills. Treatment at Stalag Luft I was not brutal as in other German camps, but food was scarce—watery soup and potato peelings—and Gailer weighed 112 pounds when the prison was liberated by Russian troops on April 30, 1945.

Initially, the Soviets insisted that the Americans would be taken to Odessa and repatriated from there. But the U.S. government had suspicions that if they were taken to Russia they might never be seen again. Its response to Soviet officials was uncompromising: these men flew into Germany and they will fly out of Germany. It launched Operation Revival, in which several dozen B-17s made round-the-clock flights to fly the Americans to Camp Lucky Strike, near Le Havre, France. After lifting off, the American pilots made a point of flying the B-17s over the ruins of Berlin, so that the former POWs could see how Allied bombing had punished the Hitler regime.

After the war, Gailer served in a succession of posts in the Canal Zone, Uruguay, as the jet adviser to a fighter wing, and as a teacher at the National War College. He spent five and a half years at the Aberdeen Proving Grounds in Maryland, taking part in chemical and biological warfare programs. In the fall of 1968 he arrived in Vietnam as head of the 35th Tactical Fighter Wing at Phan Rang Airbase, and flew 235 close air support combat missions in the F-100 Super Sabre. Later he commanded the 48th Tactical Fighter Wing in England and served as the vice commander of the 3rd Air Force.

Frank Gailer retired in 1972 as a brigadier general and spent the next forty years in the securities business in San Antonio, Texas. ⭐

Robert E. Galer

BRIGADIER GENERAL, USMC
October 24, 1913–June 27, 2005

ROBERT GALER HAD JUST FINISHED BREAKFAST and was looking out his kitchen window at the pure Hawaiian sky on the morning of December 7, 1941, when the Japanese attack on Pearl Harbor began. The Marine Air Corps Station at Ewa, where he was based, was one of the first U.S. installations hit. As the attack progressed, with Japanese warplanes passing over him a few hundred feet above the ground, Galer jumped in his car and sped to the hangars, hoping to get up in the air to fight back. But when he arrived, all the U.S. planes there were ablaze and the only thing he and a handful of other pilots could do was grab rifles, take cover in the shell of an unfinished swimming pool, and fire up impotently at the enemy aircraft roaring by.

Unlike the hundreds of thousands of young men who would show up at Army and Navy induction centers on December 8 as a result of the attack, Galer was already a seasoned pilot. He had been in Marine Corps aviation since enlisting in 1935 after graduating with a degree in engineering from the University of Washington, where he was an all-American basketball player. He had practiced carrier landings in the late 1930s in the Grumman F3F, the last fighter biplane delivered to the Navy, and had in fact been forced to ditch one off the coast of San Diego—the first of five planes he would lose. For months before Pearl Harbor his unit, Marine Fighter Squadron 211, had drilled in their new F4F Wildcats with a growing sense of inevitability that there would be conflict with Japan.

Twelve pilots from his unit, Marine Fighter Squadron 211, had shipped out from Hawaii for Wake Island a few weeks before the December 7 attack as part of an effort to establish a defensive position there. Because a detour in his training happened to have qualified him as a landing signal officer capable of bringing aircraft in for landings on carriers—an expertise temporarily in short supply in the Pacific Fleet—Galer was not part of this group. This probably saved him from being killed or captured in the opening days of the

war, since the Japanese hit Wake Island hard the day after Pearl Harbor. Three weeks later, when the remaining U.S. forces were forced to surrender, VMF 211 had lost all its planes, and those of its pilots who were not dead were prisoners of war.

In May 1942, Galer was given command of the newly formed Marine Fighter Squadron 224. The unit was sent to Guadalcanal's Henderson Field in August, becoming part of the ragtag "Cactus Air Force" (named for the Allied code word for the island) charged with defending the precarious U.S. presence there. With Marine ground forces trying to hold back Japanese troops occupying part of Guadalcanal, Galer and the other Marine aviators went up several times a day to intercept Japanese bombers and their fighter escort, who were trying desperately to dislodge the Marines from the airfield. The only advantage they had were the coastwatchers, who would report by radio when Japanese aircraft took off for their attacks on Henderson. When the information arrived—"thirty bombers, twenty fighters en route"—Galer would scramble his planes so they would be waiting for the Japanese when they arrived.

Lucky to be able to put up seven or eight planes to do battle with five times that many of the enemy, the Cactus Air Force also had to deal with the fact that its Wildcats were simply not as fast or as agile as the Japanese Zeros. Instead of dogfighting, Galer conceived of the strategy of flying high, close to 30,000 feet, and then diving down on the enemy planes to neutralize their advantages of greater maneuverability. He learned that if his planes could fight through the fighter escort and destroy the lead Japanese bomber in the formation, the others would often drop their bombs in panic and turn around.

In intense action from September 2 to October 14, Galer brought down thirteen enemy planes. He was shot down three times—once managing to crash land on an island, and the other two times pancaking into the sea. On one of these occasions he managed to swim a mile and a half to shore where coastwatchers picked him up and canoed him to a Marine outpost. He got back to Henderson Field just in time to see preparations being made for his memorial service.

At the end of 1942, Galer was pulled out of combat and returned to the United States. On March 23, 1943, he traveled to Washington, D.C., to meet with President Roosevelt and receive the Medal of Honor. His citation read in part, "Leading his squadron repeatedly in daring and aggressive raids against Japanese aerial forces, vastly superior in numbers, Maj. Galer availed himself of every favorable attack opportunity . . . though suffering the extreme physical strain attendant upon protracted fighter operations at an altitude above 25,000 feet."

Galer returned to the Pacific. Kept out of combat because he was a Medal of Honor recipient, he served as an operations officer training other Marine pilots to support the U.S. ground troops invading Iwo Jima and Okinawa.

After the war he served on the staff of the commander of the Air Force, Pacific Fleet. He was a colonel when the Korean conflict broke out and in 1952 became commanding officer of Marine Aircraft Group 12. Once again the command chain tried to prohibit him from flying in combat because of his status as a recipient of the Medal of Honor, but Galer overcame them and flew dozens of bombing and ground support missions in an F4U Corsair. On August 5, he was shot down while leading a mission over North Korea. He tried to bail out but his legs were tangled in the cockpit. Thanks to his athleticism, he finally managed to get out of the plane when he was 150 feet above the ground, just enough time for his chute to open. A Marine helicopter made a daring flight to rescue him under heavy enemy sniper fire.

"Before World War II, I lost an airplane while carrier qualifying off San Diego," Galer later noted wryly. "At Guadalcanal I got shot down three times. In Korea I got shot down about one hundred miles behind enemy lines. My smart aleck son, who is an Air Force pilot, says, 'That's five airplanes you lost. You're an enemy Ace!'"

Robert Galer retired from the Marine Corps as a brigadier general in 1957. ★

Clayton K. Gross

CAPTAIN, USAAF

November 30, 1920–January 10, 2016

KELLY GROSS WAS ALMOST SEVEN YEARS OLD in 1927 when his father got tickets for the two of them to take a fifteen-minute flight in a Ford Trimotor. His first flight was an exciting moment for the boy, but something happened shortly after the Trimotor took off from the Spokane airport that transformed it into a magical one. As the Trimotor was cruising over the Spokane airport, Gross looked out the window and saw what he later termed "the famous silver form" of *The Spirit of St. Louis* as Charles Lindbergh, on the national tour that followed his transatlantic crossing, came in for a landing.

By 1940 Gross was attending Gonzaga University as a pre-med student and—in part because of that memorable experience years earlier—participating in the national Civilian Pilot Training Program. Because of the hours he logged in the CPTP, he was a licensed pilot when he entered the Army Air Corps right after Pearl Harbor.

Sent to Randolph Field for training, Gross was one of only two men in his class of 129 chosen to fly fighters. He was assigned to the 355th Fighter Squadron, flying P-39 Airacobras, and sent to San Francisco to protect against a possible Japanese invasion of the West Coast.

In late November 1943 the 355th boarded HMS *Athlone Castle* and sailed for England. They were welcomed to Greenham Common Air Base by a general who told them, "We expect great things from you against the enemy. Not all of you will survive." They were given the latest model of the P-51 Mustang and two weeks later were in the air, supporting B-17 bombers in raids against Germany.

His squadron had frequent contact with German fighters, but Gross didn't score any victories his first few weeks. He was on an escort mission over Mannheim when he thought his luck had finally changed. He had scored multiple hits on a Messerschmitt Me 109 and was following it into what he hoped would be a death spiral when he saw tracers all around him and felt

a concussion in the back of his neck. He thought he had been wounded, a belief that seemed to be confirmed when he rubbed the base of his skull and his glove turned red. But the "blood" turned out to be hydraulic fluid and the throbbing pain in Gross' neck was caused by a shell that had rammed into the four-inch-thick steel bar behind his headrest and knocked it forward. He was still trying to understand what had happened to him when two U.S. P-47s whizzed by, one of the pilots smacking his forehead with his palm as he looked out of the cockpit in an apology for the friendly fire.

Gross finally got his first two kills on May 11, 1944, while leading a flight of P-51s escorting U.S. bombers to Germany. He saw roughly thirty German fighters approaching at about his altitude and another group of about the same size overhead. He rose to engage the second formation and found himself no more than fifty yards behind the trailing Messerschmitt. He opened fire and the German plane exploded. By this time a melee had broken out, with U.S. and German planes wheeling around each other as they desperately angled for advantage. He saw an Me 109 below him, dove down to five thousand feet, and settled on its tail. He had fired no more than one hundred rounds when the canopy of the German flew off. Gross pulled alongside it so that the German pilot could see the name painted on his fuselage—"Live Bait"—as he bailed out.

On the evening of June 5, Gross' squadron was informed that the D-day invasion would begin the following morning, and that the squadron's first mission would be escorting transport planes that were towing gliders filled with U.S. infantry to the Cherbourg area. Over the next three weeks Gross flew multiple missions a day, most of them dangerous, low-level strafing runs on retreating German troops, in which enemy antiaircraft fire brought down several members of his squadron.

On June 28, he finished his two-hundredth combat mission, which meant he would be brought back to the United States for a thirty-day leave. When he returned to duty, the squadron's mission was now supporting Patton's Third Army as it ground its way toward Germany.

In early November, Gross was no more than ten feet above the ground in a strafing run on a German convoy when dozens of enemy soldiers opened up with rifle fire. As he tried to climb out of danger, his plane failed to respond. He saw that his engine coolant was gone and he had no choice but to bail out. Hitting the ground, he ran for a stand of trees to hide, but was spotted by what he thought were two German soldiers. When they approached, he stepped out with his hands up. The soldiers turned out to be a pair of American GIs. Gross realized what they saw when they looked at him: a blonde, blue-eyed, Nordic-looking man who, in the manner of many U.S. fighter pilots, had not bothered to put on a formal uniform before scrambling for his plane.

When he tried to assure them he was American, one of them asked in a New York accent, "Where are you from?"

Gross answered, "Spokane, Washington."

The GI eyed him suspiciously, "What's the capital of Washington, then?"

Gross replied, "Olympia."

The GI looked at his buddy, "Is that right?"

The other soldier, also speaking Brooklynese, said, "How the hell should I know?"

They accepted Gross as a comrade.

By the spring of 1944, he had five kills and was an Ace. On April 14, he was on patrol over the German heartland when he saw one of the Germans' new Messerschmitt 262 jets that had just taken off below him. "I happened to be at 12,000 feet and he was at two thousand and he didn't see me coming," Gross later recalled. His initial burst set the jet on fire and it began sliding down tail first as the pilot bailed out.

Fifty years later, in 1995, Gross, who had a successful career as a dentist, was in Germany as the head of an American delegation to a convention of air Aces. He met a former German combat pilot named Kurt Lobgesong. As the two men compared combat notes they realized that Lobgesong had been the pilot of the Me 262 jet Gross had shot down a half century earlier.

"You saved my life," Lobgesong told him.

"How did I do that?" Gross asked.

The German told him that he had been wounded by fire from Gross' plane and was unable to fly while almost all the other members of his unit were getting killed during the final weeks of the war.

"You saved my life," Lobgesong repeated, saying, "Thank you," as he emotionally wrapped Gross in a bear hug.

"Any time," Gross said, hugging him back. ★

Willis E. Hardy

COMMANDER, USN

March 3, 1920–

GROWING UP ON HIS FAMILY'S FARM in a remote, sparsely populated area near Corning, California, Bill Hardy was anxious to see the world and also wanted a decent job when he graduated from high school. His mother gave him permission to sign up for the Navy at age seventeen, during his senior year in high school. But in 1938 the Depression was still smothering the economy and other young men had the same idea. Hardy had to wait a year for an opening.

Once he had enlisted, he graduated first in his class at machinist's school, and was allowed to choose a specialty. He decided to become an aviation machinist's mate because, as he later said, "it beat chipping paint or being a cook." He then became an expert draftsman and was soon instructing new aviation machinist's mates in electrical instruments and engine overhaul. After the attack on Pearl Harbor, Hardy asked for combat duty. He was sent to Naval Air Station Sand Point in Washington to supervise repairs on the PBY flying boats stationed in the Aleutian Islands, and found himself also manning machine guns on the hangar roof at night in anticipation of another Japanese surprise attack. As a plane captain, the naval equivalent of crew chief, he spent a lot of time on board the PBYs making sure they were airworthy after repair. Some of the officers Hardy worked with saw in him the makings of a good Navy pilot and recommended him for flight school. His commanding officer pulled strings so that he could take exams in lieu of the two years of college courses normally required for aviation cadets. He passed with high marks and was fast-tracked into training, receiving his wings on December 15, 1943.

A "mustang," the term used for officers who had risen through the ranks, Hardy was assigned to Squadron VF-17, known as the "Jolly Rogers" (the name was a pun on the Corsairs the unit had flown in the Solomon Islands), which was reforming as a squadron of F6F Hellcats on the carrier USS *Hornet*. The plane they flew had changed but the Jolly Rogers' aggressive élan had

not. The squadron wives stitched skulls and cross-bones on the pilots' flying helmets as they got ready for action early in 1945, the beginning of the end-game of the war. When the carrier's crew members who serviced the fighters found out that Hardy had once been an enlisted man like them, they did every-thing they could to make him look good.

During the April 1945 invasion of Okinawa, Hardy's squadron usually flew two missions a day in support of the embattled Marines trying to take the island. He remembers once dropping napalm in the entry of an enemy tunnel and seeing smoke puff up out of the ground up to a half a mile from where his bomb hit, fire having traveled rapidly through the complex underground network linking the ene-my's caves and bunkers.

The *Hornet*'s Hellcats were also trying to defend against the swarms of kamikazes Japan had launched against the U.S. task force. On the afternoon of April 6, Hardy and his wingman were assigned to try to protect U.S. picket destroyers, which were the task force's first line of defense against these suicide attacks. ("The pickets were just getting crucified," he later said of the destroyers.) Two of the Zeros that had escorted the kamikazes to their targets were head-ing back to their base when Hardy spotted them. He told his wingman to go after one of them while he went after the other. He gave it a short burst that went right into the cockpit. He saw the plane's landing gear fall and knew that the hydraulics had been hit. He pulled off to watch as the Zero slowly descended and splashed into the water below along with the second one that his wingman got.

Then he saw four enemy "Val" torpedo bombers, of the kind that had led the attack on Pearl Harbor, flying in a formation toward the U.S. Task Group. He and his wingman dove down and opened fire, each destroying two of the "Vals," which hit the water still in formation.

By this time the sun was setting and Hardy was low on fuel. He knew he should head back to the carrier, but a desperate call for help came over the radio from the commander of a picket destroyer below that was on fire, dead in the water, and about to be attacked by Japanese dive-bombers.

Vectored in by the destroyer's radar, Hardy went after one of them. Flying low to escape detection, he rose to take a shot and hit the plane's tail gunner, who slumped in the cockpit as the plane was engulfed in flames. The pilot stepped one foot onto the wing to bail out but deployed his parachute too soon and it caught fire. He tried to reel it in as he stepped back into the cockpit, and his plane smacked down into the Pacific.

"His buddy is still orbiting around," the skipper of the destroyer radioed Hardy, who immediately went after the second dive-bomber. With only one gun now operating, his first burst punctured the enemy plane's fuel tank. His second set it on fire. Seeing that his own fuel gauge was pointing toward empty, Hardy watched the dive-bomber crash and then quickly headed back to the *Hornet*.

By now it was dark; he had fifty gallons of fuel left and quite a distance to cover, and he had to maintain radio silence. He was "flying on vapors" when, by a stroke of good fortune, he saw phosphorescent wakes he knew belonged to the U.S. Task Group. He dropped down to one thousand feet and saw the *Hornet*'s blinking masthead lights. He dropped flaps and landing gear and landed. After his Hellcat skidded to a stop on the deck he thought to himself that finding his carrier and making the landing in the dark was a bigger achievement than the air combat he had waged that day.

Bill Hardy remained in the Jolly Rogers after the war ended, now flying Corsairs after the Hellcat had been retired and later the newer Bearcat. He was on the shakedown cruise of the USS *Valley Forge*. During the Korean War he was in Florida at the naval air station at Boca Chica, training night fighters and often "flying bogey" in the war games used to acquaint novice pilots with combat. He later served as executive officer for the Screaming Eagles, one of the first squadrons armed with Sidewinder missiles to serve on board a U.S. aircraft carrier, before retiring as a commander in 1959.

Throughout all these postings, there were many evenings in the bar with other officers, occasionally high-ranking ones. The Navy Cross Bill Hardy wore often started conversations that ended with the story of how he shot down five enemy aircraft in one early evening in the Pacific in 1945. As Hardy remembers these evenings, "There were several times when a four-star would sit there and listen to my story, then shake his head and say, 'I'd rather be an Ace than an admiral.'" ★

Charles D. Hauver

MAJOR, USAF

February 23, 1923–

CHARLES HAUVER ARRIVED IN ENGLAND shortly after D-day as part of the 354th Fighter Squadron. He had what in retrospect he would acknowledge was an inflated ambition for a young, untested pilot: he was determined to be an Ace. "I didn't want to shoot down any enemy planes if I couldn't shoot down five," he later recalled of his state of mind. "If not five, I didn't want any at all."

The ambition was doubly odd given the fact that unlike many other boys of his era, Hauver had never been particularly interested in flight while growing up. His imagination was never seized by Lindbergh or Rickenbacker and the other Aces of World War I. Unacquainted with his biological father, Hauver lived with his mother and her relatives while growing up in Catskill and then in Poughkeepsie, New York. He worked at odd jobs after school, turning over one dollar of the three he made every week to the family.

After graduating from high school in 1941 he took a succession of temporary jobs, "just killing time" because the international situation was so unsettled. One of these jobs was working at a drugstore near Vassar, the posh all-female college in Poughkeepsie. The young women who came into the store didn't pay much attention to Hauver at the time, although it would be a different matter when he returned for a visit a couple of years later wearing his second lieutenant's uniform.

Hauver hung out at the Poughkeepsie Elks Lodge in the months after high school along with a handful of other young men waiting for the war, which now seemed inevitable. They all fell under the influence of a member of the lodge who was informally recruiting for the Army Air Forces, and in the spring of 1942 they traveled together to New York City to enlist. "They told us to go home and wait for them to contact us," Hauver recalls. "So that's what I did. I waited and I waited and I waited. For over six months. People were treating me like a draft dodger. Finally, I said to myself, 'The hell with them. I don't care if they ever call. I'm moving on.' The very next day they called."

Alex McKnight/AM Photo Inc.

In January 1943, he traveled to San Antonio for flight school, a four-day trip in the dead of winter in a train without any heat. When he arrived, he was struck by how unfriendly the environment seemed—"dust in your eyes and mud all over your feet." The two significant things that happened to him over the next few months after pilot training were learning to fly the P-51 Mustang and getting married to a young woman he had met, in a service conducted by an Army chaplain.

He arrived in England in the late spring of 1944 and was first assigned to a training unit headed by P-51 pilots who had completed their tour, and then, in July, to the 354th Fighter Squadron stationed at Steeple Morden, the RAF base near Cambridge.

For several weeks Hauver's squadron flew escort missions for the B-17s headed for Germany and saw few enemy fighters. (On one occasion a Messerschmitt Me 109 got on the tail of his plane—named "Princess Pat" after his wife—and Hauver looked around after some evasive maneuvers and didn't see the plane. "What happened?" he asked over the radio. Another pilot laconically replied, "I got tired of watching you try to get away from him so I shot him down.") It seemed like his dream of becoming an Ace would never come true.

Then, on November 26, his squadron was attacked by two waves of seventy-five German fighters. In the brief action, which had some of the qualities of time lapse, he shot down two Focke-Wulf

190s. A month later, on December 25, he got two more kills—an Fw 190 and an Me 109 near the German town of Trier, with the Moselle River visible below. Hauver had trained himself to think of what he was doing as destroying machines, not men. But on the way home from this mission he realized that it was Christmas and felt sad for the parents of the two pilots who would never celebrate another holiday with their sons.

Hauver had been in combat for only a few months but he had completed the number of combat hours that made up a tour and knew that he would soon be sent home. On December 31, he volunteered for a last escort mission into Germany. He had completed it and was on his way back to the base when he saw a lone Fw 190 below him. Incredulous at this stroke of luck, he put his Mustang into a steep dive and shot it down, fulfilling his ambition of becoming an Ace at his last moment.

"I was seriously elated," Hauver recalls. "Back at the base I celebrated in style, coming down to a few feet above the deck and buzzing the operations shack so hard that I almost blew it off the field."

Hauver was back home early in 1945 and spent the rest of the war as a flight instructor. He mustered out in the fall and tried to find work. But the economy was slow and he had a new baby so he reenlisted. When the Korean War broke out he returned to combat, again flying the P-51. But while he hoped for more air-to-air combat, a new generation of jet fighters was now filling the skies and the Mustang was relegated principally to close air support for infantry units. He retired from the Air Force as a major in 1963.

Reminiscing about his experiences, Charles Hauver says, "I really wanted to become an Ace. I didn't think much about it over the years that followed. But now that I look back I feel pretty proud. I think it was an achievement worth wishing for." ★

Frank D. Hurlbut

LIEUTENANT COLONEL, USAF

July 20, 1922–November 11, 2013

FRANK HURLBUT WAS NINETEEN when he joined the 145th Field Artillery of the Utah National Guard early in 1940. He had always wanted to fly but never had a chance until his unit was federalized after the United States declared war on Japan. In the Army now, he requested a transfer to the Army Air Forces and somewhat to his surprise was accepted as an aviation student. Most of the other cadets in his class at Luke Field graduated as second lieutenants. Hurlbut, along with others who didn't have two years of college, was designated a "staff sergeant pilot."

After training for a year in Florida in P-39 Airacobras, Hurlbut and the other staff sergeant pilots shipped out for England on board the *Queen Mary* in December 1942. When they got there they were stepped up to "flight officers" and shipped to North Africa. They were eager to get into combat and there was a dearth of pilots; they were sent to Oran, on the Mediterranean coast of Algeria. But because they had yet to be commissioned, no one seemed to know what to do with them. The group was billeted in second-class quarters and given outmoded P-40s to fly. As Hurlbut later said, "We wandered around like lost souls, not getting any assignments. We named ourselves the 'Sixty-seven Sad Sacks' and had a sorrowful-looking cartoon logo made for our flying jackets."

Finally, in early 1943, Hurlbut was made a second lieutenant, assigned to the 96th Fighter Squadron, shipped to an abandoned airstrip in Casablanca that was being refurbished into a fighter base, and given a P-38 to fly. He was ecstatic. "What an airplane," he later said to an interviewer. "It could take rough handling and outmaneuver almost anything. And there were two engines to bring you home."

The Germans were also impressed by the P-38. After their pilots first flew against it late in 1942, the Luftwaffe high command christened it *der gabelschwanzer Teufel*—"the forked-tail devil."

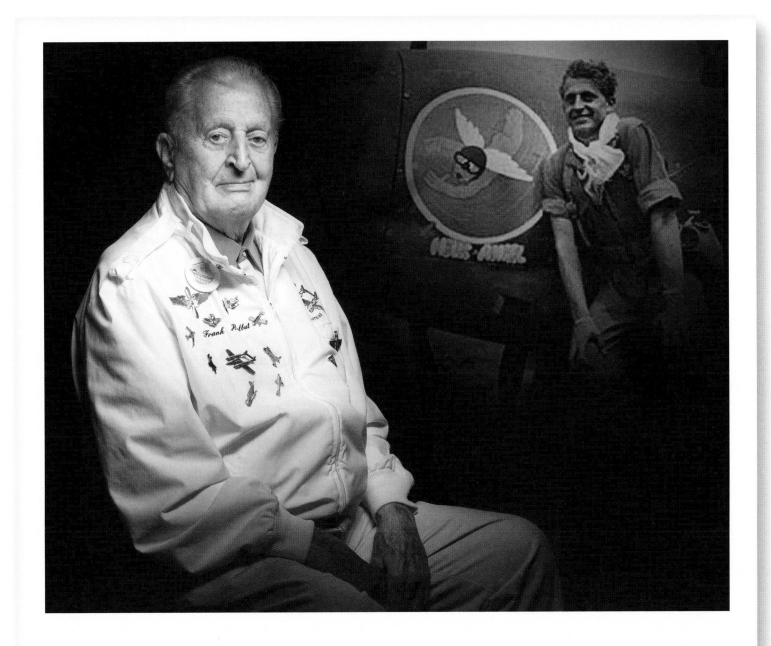

Just twenty years old when he entered combat, Hurlbut's photos show him with a crest of honey-colored hair and a sardonic, Robert Mitchum–like smile on his face. He named his P-38 "Hell's Angel."

His squadron's first missions were long-range sorties escorting U.S. B-25s into enemy-controlled areas of Sicily, Sardinia, and mainland Italy itself. On the return flights they strafed antiaircraft emplacements and truck convoys. At this relatively early stage of the war it was not unusual for the under-supplied and under-manned Americans to put up twenty P-38s against as many as one hundred enemy fighters.

Hurlbut always vividly remembered his first kill. He and the other pilots were told in an intelligence briefing that German general Erwin Rommel was trying to evacuate key personnel from his Afrika Korps. So the U.S. pilots began air sweeps over the Mediterranean, looking for enemy air transports. Late in the afternoon of April 1, they ran into a formation of large trimotor Junkers Ju 52 transports carrying German officers. The Ju 52 was a lumbering airplane in comparison to the nimble P-38, but it bristled with armament, with machine guns sticking out of every porthole and a large 20-mm cannon mounted on top of the fuselage.

Hurlbut followed his flight leader into the German formation and made a pass at one of the Ju 52s, setting it on fire. But his plane was struck several times, including a hit by a cannon shell that blew a large hole in his fuselage and passed right under his left elbow. With one of his engines spouting smoke, Hurlbut dove down to the ocean to limit his exposure and limped home a few feet off the water.

The odds always seemed stacked against the squadron. Hurlbut always remembered one briefing in which the intelligence said casually, "Today you are lucky. Yesterday there were close to eight hundred enemy fighters out there. Today on this mission in the area of Rome not more than 450 will be flying."

Over the next two months, Hurlbut brought down a Focke-Wulf 190, a Messerschmitt Me 109, and an Italian Reggiane 2001. He was credited with three more damaged that were probably kills, but gun cameras had not yet been installed in the P-38s and confirmation of victories was based on what the pilots saw in the heat of the chaotic, swirling air battles.

On July 10, Hurlbut's squadron took off from a base in Tripoli to cover the Allied invasion of Sicily. They were near Palermo when a group of Fw 190s rose like angry bees to attack them. A Lufbery Circle developed—several American and German planes simultaneously swinging around in tight left turns, each climbing and descending in an effort to get inside his opponent to gain a clear shot. Hurlbut later recalled: "I was very close to the Fw 190 and hit him with three quick bursts. He went over on one wing into a spin and crashed." He got two more kills that day, making him an Ace.

Hurlbut's toughest battle came on September 2, 1943. Twenty-four P-38s were flying cover for seventy-two B-25 bombers when they were attacked near the Italian island of Ischia by thirty enemy fighters at 16,000 feet. The fight dropped to six thousand feet as other U.S. and German planes joined the melee. Hurlbut later told interviewer Mary Lou

Neale: "An even larger fight started in at 2,000 feet, continuing down to the deck. It went on nonstop. No sooner did we think the fight was over than an additional 30 enemy aircraft dropped their belly fuel tanks and bored into the fray. At least 60 Me 109s, many Fw 190s and Italian Re 2001s were attacking us continually. Rocket projectiles were fired, bombs dropped, and you could see the puff and flash of cannons being fired every 100 yards or so. The enemy was composed of some of the finest fighter pilots Hermann Göring had to throw at us."

The P-38s fought their way down to the water so that they at least couldn't be attacked from below. Hurlbut looked around and saw aircraft crashing into the water one after the other. Suddenly four Fw 190s and four Me 109s came at him from above and at his sides and tried to separate him from the other P-38s. He could see the water below churning from their machine-gun fire that missed him. He was saved by another American pilot who shot down an enemy plane closing in on his tail.

Then a single Me 109 at his level banked around to the left, cutting directly in front of him. Hurlbut started firing, and the German pilot peeled over and crashed into the sea. His ammunition and fuel exhausted, Hurlbut headed back to the base. It was a grim homecoming because ten American pilots had been lost in the engagement.

After fifty missions Frank Hurlbut was rotated home. He was credited with nine kills, four damaged, and a probable, although he believed that his totals in all three of these categories was higher. Confident, in the manner of most fighter pilots, that the bullet with his name on it had not been made, he tried to volunteer for another fifty missions, but he had contracted a stubborn case of malaria and had to spend the rest of the war stateside as a flight instructor. He always savored the irony: after surviving the cream of the enemy's fighter pilots, he was "shot down by a mosquito." ★

Some of the material in this profile is drawn from Mary Lou Neale's interview with Frank Hurlbut in the January 2001 issue of Aviation History.

Arthur F. Jeffrey

COLONEL, USAF

November 17, 1919–April 18, 2015

WHAT SOME OF THE OTHER MEN who flew with him later called Arthur Jeffrey's "true grit" showed up first when he was just fifteen. It was 1934 and the Depression was ravaging his family, so Jeffrey took a job working nights at a lead and zinc mine near his hometown of Cardin, Oklahoma. Called "Schoolboy" by the other miners, he went directly to class when his shift ended for the next three years. He was selected salutatorian when his high school class graduated in 1938.

Work was scarce and Jeffrey joined the Army in the summer of 1939 at the age of nineteen. After two years as an enlisted man he entered aviation training, getting his wings in April 1942 after completing training in P-38s at Kelly Field, Texas. For the next two years he served as a flight instructor. Recognized as a leader by his superiors, he sometimes surprised them with an offbeat sense of humor. While teaching at the Santa Ana Army Air Base in California, the recently married Jeffrey repeatedly buzzed the apartment he shared with his wife, flying upside down and so low that she could see the pipe in his mouth. These antics stopped only when neighbors complained to the War Department.

In the spring of 1944, he was assigned to the 434th Fighter Squadron and sent to England. Eleven days after his arrival he began flying combat missions in a P-38 he christened "Boomerang." On July 5, he was strafing a German airfield near Cognac, France, when he saw a Focke-Wulf Fw 200 reconnaissance/transport aircraft below him. As Jeffrey recalled, "He was staying on the deck close to the aerodrome from where they were firing quite a lot of flak at us. I began firing in ten-second bursts at 250 yards, closing to fifty yards. The right engine caught fire and parts of it flew off." He watched the aircraft crash-land and go up in flames, but was surprised to see one crew member manage to crawl out of the wreckage and run away.

A few weeks later, on July 29, Jeffrey made combat history. He was escorting U.S. B-17s back to England after a mission over Germany when he saw that one of bombers—"terribly shot up," as he later described it, with huge holes in its wings and tail and only two engines running—had gotten separated from the rest, was beginning to lose altitude and veering off course so seriously that he calculated it would miss the British Isles altogether. He couldn't raise the B-17 on the radio, and thinking that it might have an inexperienced crew, dropped down to try to correct its flight path with hand signals. Despite the P-38's distinctive look and U.S. markings, one of the bomber's side gunners opened

fire. "At least they're alert," Jeffrey ruefully thought to himself as he moved out of range.

At this point he saw an unfamiliar looking plane with German markings suddenly take up an attack position behind the wounded B-17. It had a stubby profile and no propellers; its wheels had been jettisoned on takeoff and it was left with skids to land on. Jeffrey realized that it was a rocket-powered Messerschmitt 163 Komet, one of the experimental aircraft (it was capable of easily reaching six hundred miles an hour) the Luftwaffe introduced in the latter stages of the war.

Closing fast, the Komet made a gunnery pass at the American bomber, and Jeffrey went after it. The

Me 163 was fast, but as it tried to evade the P-38 Jeffrey was able to get close enough to open fire. The enemy plane went down in a steep vertical dive and Jeffrey followed it at over five hundred miles an hour, blacking out from the high-g pullout and recovering just in time to see the rocket plane crash. It was the first Me 163 ever shot down by an American pilot.

On August 15, Jeffrey scored a victory over a Messerschmitt Me 109 in a fight over Steenwijk, Holland. A week later he shot down a Ju 52 trimotor over the Ardennes Forest in France. Soon after this, his squadron switched from P-38s to P-51s. Because the Mustang was somewhat smaller, Jeffrey named his "Boomerang Jr."

On October 7, he was escorting a group of B-17s on a bombing run over Leipzig when he spotted what he later called a "gaggle" of Me 109s. He picked one of them and got on its tail. He opened fire as the German pilot desperately tried to evade him. He saw many strikes along the Messerschmitt's fuselage; part of the wing flew off and the plane eased over onto its back and fell to the earth. Jeffrey was an Ace.

On December 5, Jeffrey was flight leader for a section of nine Mustangs, again flying escort for American bombers, when fifty-five Focke-Wulf 190 fighters suddenly appeared. Jeffrey led the American planes into a swirling dogfight in which he shot down three of the enemy despite two of his plane's machine guns failing to operate. He was awarded a Silver Star for this action. On a December 23 mission he again shot down three more enemy planes, this time Me 109s.

By February 14, 1945, Arthur Jeffrey, now a lieutenant colonel, had shot down six more German aircraft, for a total of fourteen, and ended his tour as commanding officer of the 434th Fighter Squadron.

After the war he transferred to the Regular Army and then to the newly created Air Force, serving until his retirement as a colonel in September 1968. He rarely spoke of his wartime experiences. His son didn't find out about his father's Silver Star until he read about it on the Internet following Arthur Jeffrey's death on April 18, 2015. ★

Lynn F. Jones

CAPTAIN, USAAF

August 16, 1920–

WHEN LYNN JONES ARRIVED IN CHINA and stepped out of his P-40 Warhawk, after flying from a temporary base in India over the Hump, as Allied pilots called the east end of the Himalayas, the first U.S. flyer he saw said to him, "Hey Jones, you got any gold or something like a Parker 51 pen we can sell on the black market?" Jones immediately realized that he was in an exotic place unlike anywhere he had been before. As he later said when telling the story, "You can imagine, I was just an old country boy from Texas."

The place in Texas he was from—the town of Mercedes—was one of the oldest towns in the Rio Grande Valley, close to the area where Mexican banditos had crossed over the river into the United States in the early 1900s to terrorize local ranchers. Jones' father died of tuberculosis not long after Lynn, the youngest of six children, was born in 1920. The family survived because of the determination of his hard-working mother and the charity of uncles and aunts who lived nearby. Even so, it was, as he remembers, "touch and go" until his eldest sister graduated from high school and was able to get a job and contribute her paycheck to the family. Every day Jones himself came home after school to take care of the family's two precious cows, chickens, and other farm animals. It wasn't until he was in the tenth grade that he finally had his afternoons to himself and was able to play on the high school football team.

After graduating from high school in 1937, Jones got a job at a local printing plant working forty-four hours a week for a salary of six dollars (he was elated when he got a raise to eight dollars after a few months), which he turned over to his mother. In 1938 he was able to enter the University of Texas because an older brother, who had recently graduated with an engineering degree and was working in the oil fields of Venezuela, agreed to loan him thirty dollars a month. This, combined with the fifteen Jones himself earned working part-time, got him through.

Gabe Hernandez

In late 1940, after two and a half years of study, Jones, who had always loved airplanes, decided to enlist as a cadet in the Army Air Corps. A year later, after training in Hemet, San Jose, and Sacramento, California, he was about to get his wings when he heard that the government was asking for volunteer pilots to work for Pan American Airways in Accra, Ghana, flying supplies and munitions to the British in Egypt to help in their fight against the Germans. The $150 per month bonus being offered made Jones, who was at that point finishing advanced fighter training in Sacramento, step forward. But the day after the Japanese attack on Pearl Harbor, his commanding officer told him and the other volunteers, "You boys aren't going to Africa with Pan Am; you're staying in the U.S. Army Air Corps."

In April 1942, Jones was sent to Panama, where U.S. strategists feared Japan would strike next in an effort to close the canal. But these fears receded after the Battle of Midway in June, when the Japanese fleet lost four aircraft carriers. In August, when volunteers were needed to fly in China, Jones again stepped forward.

The 23rd Fighter Group, successor to the famed Flying Tigers of the American Volunteer Group, had been activated in China on July 4, 1942, the first fighter group activated on the field of battle in World War II. Jones was assigned to the group in early October as part of the 74th Fighter Squadron stationed at Kunming. Soon after he arrived, the other pilots nicknamed him (for reasons he never really understood) "Hoss."

For several months the 74th focused on air-to-ground attacks on Japanese infantry columns in northern Burma. Then in May 1943, the squadron was relocated to Guilin, where it began to see more air combat while escorting B-24s and B-25s to their targets. There was an unexpected element of risk in these missions, which came from the B-24's gunners themselves. "They shot at anything that came close," Jones later said. "Sometimes it seemed like they couldn't tell the difference between a long-nosed P-40 and a short-nosed Zero. We protected them but learned to keep our distance."

On June 9, Jones got his first kill when he brought down a Nakajima Ki-27 "Nate." Then on July 26, he shot down a Zero and had two more probables in an engagement over Hangchow. He had four kills on December 12 when he became an Ace in what turned out to be his most memorable dogfight. As he recalled it, Japanese bombers had appeared suddenly and caught the American base by surprise: "I was taxiing out for takeoff when the bombs began to hit. I just gave it the go. There weren't craters on the airstrip yet so I got up. Immediately there was a Zero on my tail. I had no space to dive. I was low enough to knock off chimneys. He made three passes at me. He must have been a recent recruit because he didn't hit me. I headed off to the west to get altitude and get into the fight. I came back and shot down a crippled Zero northeast of Hengyang."

Shortly after this kill, Jones learned that he had exceeded the required one hundred missions to earn a trip home. ("I was ready for a little vacation," he said later on.) He arrived in Santa Monica for reassignment and from there was sent to Baton Rouge, where he married a girl he had known in Texas. He was sent to Abilene Army Air Field, where he ultimately became director of flying training, a job he held until the end of the war.

Lynn Jones wanted to make a career in the military. But his wife, now expecting their first child, wasn't keen on the prospect of a life spent moving from one air base to another. So Jones left the Army Air Forces in September 1945 and became a successful farmer—growing vegetables and citrus in Texas and on a farm he bought in Mexico. ★

Philip L. Kirkwood

COMMANDER, USNR

April 15, 1921–August 5, 2015

WHEN PHILIP KIRKWOOD RETURNED to his home town of Wildwood, New Jersey, in May 1945, after his second tour of duty in the Pacific, there was an unexpected bonus waiting for him. While he was away in combat, a Wildwood businessman had pledged a one hundred dollar bounty for every enemy plane shot down by a local boy. He probably didn't expect one of them to get eleven kills, as Kirkwood had, but true to his word he wrote him a check for $1,100—more than half Kirkwood's annual salary as a Navy lieutenant. As it was, the businessman got off easy. One of Kirkwood's "probables" was changed to his twelfth kill not long after the check was written.

When Kirkwood was growing up, memories of the losses of World War I were still vivid. Wildwood marked Memorial Day by a ceremony in which the town gathered to watch a pilot take off from the beach and fly out over the water, where he dropped red tissue-paper poppies symbolizing sacrifice. Kirkwood later told military historian Jon Guttman in a profile for the *American Fighter Aces and Family Bulletin* that he first became "hooked on" aviation when he was the Boy Scout chosen one Memorial Day to accompany the flight and toss out the paper poppies.

After graduating from high school in 1939 he enrolled at Duke University. He wanted to learn to fly in the Civilian Pilot Training Program, but Duke didn't have one so he entered the CPTP at the University of North Carolina, Duke's great athletic nemesis.

Kirkwood was in his third year at Duke when Pearl Harbor was attacked. Now a licensed private pilot, he tried to enlist in naval aviation. But as he told Guttman, he was initially turned down by the examining dentist because of an underbite. Kirkwood, who would go into dentistry himself after the war was over, went to a different recruitment center, passed the dental exam with flying colors, and was accepted as a cadet.

Alex McKnight/AM Photo Inc.

Because the Navy's facilities at Pensacola were overbooked, he was sent to Corpus Christi, Texas, for his initial training. After going on to qualify for carrier landings at the Great Lakes on the USS *Wolverine*, a paddlewheel tour boat that had been refitted with a flight deck, Kirkwood was assigned to VF-10, the Navy squadron known as the "Grim Reapers," which had already made a name for itself on board the USS *Enterprise* during the Battle of Guadalcanal. After the *Enterprise* underwent repairs in Hawaii for the damage it had sustained in two years of sea war and sailed again early in 1944, Kirkwood was ready for his first action.

It came as the carrier, part of Task Force 58, headed toward Truk Atoll where Japan had its main base in the South Pacific, a stronghold so formidable that it was known as "the Japanese Gibraltar." The U.S. attacks on February 17–18 took a huge toll, leading to the destruction of over 275 enemy warplanes, most of them on the ground, and more than thirty destroyers, light cruisers, and other ships, transforming Truk almost overnight into a naval graveyard.

During that battle Kirkwood was credited with one Zero downed and another probable. He later told Jon Guttman that he remembered less about the air action itself than he did about the antiaircraft fire, which remained intense even as the Navy Hellcats were overwhelming Japanese fighters.

On June 19, the Hellcats of the *Enterprise* played a key role in the Great Marianas Turkey Shoot, as the Battle of the Philippine Sea was nicknamed after U.S. aircraft massacred a large number of carrier-based Japanese fighter planes with relatively few losses of their own. Part of the Japanese battle plan was to launch planes from afar, strike the ships of Task Force 58, and then land in Guam for refueling, which would allow them to return to their carriers. Kirkwood was part of a flight waiting for them in the skies over Guam. He destroyed three enemy dive-bombers that day in the space of ten minutes. And the following day he was part of the lengthy attack against the *Hiyo* that sank the enemy carrier.

After this battle the *Enterprise* headed back to Pearl Harbor for another brief refit and the pilots of VF-10 were sent to a base in the Atlantic City area, a bonus for Kirkwood because it put him close to his home in Wildwood. There they were introduced to a new fighter—the F4U Corsair. Kirkwood was impressed with the plane's killing power but aware that it was more demanding than the reliable Hellcat. After mastering the lethal but temperamental fighter, he was on board a new carrier, the *Intrepid*, for his second tour at the beginning of 1945.

Kirkwood was already an Ace with five (later raised to six) victories in mid-April when the *Intrepid* was off the shore of Okinawa supporting the Marine invasion there. In desperation, the Japanese had unleashed their "divine wind"—attacks by waves of kamikazes aimed at the U.S. ships. On April 16, Kirkwood led a flight of Corsairs to protect a pair of U.S. destroyers trying to fight off a suicide attack. He spotted several "Val" dive-bombers, along with a large number of "Nate" fighters, and went after them. As he said later on, "I didn't have enough time to analyze what was going on. Each time I'd have a second or two to blow 'em up, then gain altitude and attack again. In twenty minutes it was all over. . . . It was no big deal."

But shooting down six enemy planes and protecting the U.S. destroyers below was impressive enough to his superiors that Kirkwood received the Navy Cross for plunging "through withering antiaircraft fire to strike smashing blows against the enemy planes . . . [and] blasting them from the sky."

Back at the *Intrepid*, Kirkwood was lined up for lunch with other pilots when a kamikaze evaded the ship's guns and struck the carrier near the stern, blowing a large hole through the flight deck. Eight men were killed and twenty-one wounded. Other U.S. ships faced far greater loss of life from suicide attacks, but Kirkwood told author James Oleson that when the "All Clear" sounded and he and the other pilots raced out of the wardroom to see the death and destruction, "it was a scene you never forgot."

The *Intrepid* headed back to San Francisco for repairs, arriving in late May, which meant that the war was over for Philip Kirkwood.

Released from the Navy, he went back to Duke and earned a degree, returning to the Navy in a noncombat role during the Korean War. He graduated from the University of Pennsylvania dental school after being released from active duty in 1955. He remained in the Naval Reserve until 1986, retiring as a commander, and practiced dentistry for thirty-four years in St. Petersburg, Florida. Invited to reminisce by a television reporter during ceremonies for the Congressional Gold Medal, which was awarded to U.S. fighter Aces on May 20, 2015, Kirkwood said succinctly, "I was a good pilot. I must have been because I survived and a lot of people didn't." ★

Dean S. Laird

COMMANDER, USN

February 7, 1921–

IN 1970, DEAN LAIRD SPENT TWO MONTHS attacking Pearl Harbor. But the gun ports of the reconstructed Japanese dive-bomber he flew shot bursts of strobe lights rather than .50-caliber bullets, and his bombing runs damaged no ships. He was portraying the leader of a Japanese squadron in the movie *Tora! Tora! Tora!* The money was good, but Laird was aware of the irony: he was flying under the flag of an air force he had hunted mercilessly as a carrier-based Hellcat pilot twenty-five years earlier.

Growing up in the foothills above Sacramento, California, Laird was rangy and athletic, with a reserve that masked a wry sense of humor. A natural at baseball—he became known as "Diz" because he shared a name with that of the great pitcher Dizzy Dean—he was playing in college when the real attack on Pearl Harbor occurred. Already a licensed pilot as a result of having gone through the Civilian Pilot Training Program, Laird thought that he would follow his older brother into the Army Air Corps. But when a friend came by his house in mid-December 1941 to say that he was on his way to join the Navy, Laird, attracted by the romance of flying off an aircraft carrier, decided on the spur of the moment to go with him.

He received his wings in August 1942 and was assigned to a squadron of F4F Wildcats on board the carrier USS *Ranger*. He carried with him into battle the essential quality of all great fighter pilots: unshakable self-confidence. "It never entered my mind that I would get shot down," he later told journalists Peter Rowe and John Wilkens of the *San Diego Tribune* in an interview about his career. "I was just too good."

In mid-1943, the *Ranger*'s assignment was supporting British naval operations near the Orkney Islands. Chronically seasick, Laird volunteered for extra missions just to get above the turbulent waters of the North Atlantic. On October 4, he was flying his Wildcat through heavy weather when he saw a shadow duck into the clouds. He had learned to trust the 20/10 vision

that allowed him to spot things other pilots sometimes missed, and so he followed this specter. When the clouds broke, he saw that it was a German Ju 88 fighter-bomber. Calling out "Tally Ho!" to his section leader, he went on the attack and the two of them shot the aircraft down. Fifteen minutes later, he saw a He 115 float plane below him and swooped down on it to open fire. The Wildcat's cameras showed the float plane cartwheel when its wing hit the water, breaking the plane apart. Laird was given a quarter of the kill.

Outside of these two engagements, his assignment on board the *Ranger* offered little action and Laird decided that it was "a big waste of time."

He had always wanted to get into the more exciting air war in the Pacific and, after returning from Europe, VF-4, known as the Red Rippers, traded its Wildcats for F6F Hellcats. After training for a few months, they were assigned to the USS *Bunker Hill* in the summer of 1944. A few weeks later, the Rippers were reassigned to the USS *Essex*. Both carriers were carrying the naval battle to the Japanese.

On November 25, 1944, Laird and his comrades caught a flight of Ki-61 "Tony" fighters taking off from an airfield in the Philippines near the island of Luzon. The flight of Hellcats destroyed seven of the Ki-61s, with Laird downing one of them.

Not long after, he was part of a mission to bomb an enemy position in the Philippines. Dropping down through heavy flak, he saw his squadron commander's plane explode. Then he too was hit—the explosion severing his hydraulics and rudder cables and destroying his radio. With elevator and aileron controls still intact, Laird managed to return to the carrier, where he manually lowered his gear and made a no-flap arrested landing. As Laird jumped down from the cockpit, maintenance crew members examining the plane decided that it was beyond repair and pushed it over the side of the ship.

On January 16, 1945, Laird shot down a Japanese Zero in the China Sea. A month later, on February 16, he was part of a flight of forty U.S. fighters conducting a raid on the Hamamatsu Airfield, 150 miles from Tokyo. Laird and his wingman were escorting two F6F photo planes when he saw two Mitsubishi Ki-21 "Sally" bombers take off. "Stay up here and stand guard and I'll be right back," he radioed the wingman. Then he dove on the bombers. The first one exploded after he fired a short burst. He then made an overhead run on the second plane, setting it on fire (although he would not get credit for the kill). Back in formation, he saw flames rage inside the Ki-21's fuselage as the emergency

hatch flew off and three Japanese crewmen jumped out. None were wearing parachutes. Laird watched them fall to earth.

The next day he was part of a large formation of U.S. planes striking the Mitsubishi airplane plant near Tokyo. He opened fire on one of the Ki-61 interceptors sent up to attack the Americans. The plane caught on fire and went down. After dropping his bomb, Laird was returning to the *Essex* when he spotted a Ki-44 "Tojo" fighter below him. After he made several gunnery passes, pieces of the plane's wings and fuselage flew off, but Laird saw no fire or smoke. He followed the wounded plane for twenty miles until it finally crashed after passing over the street of a small village. "All by myself I was in the middle of Japan," he later said.

Soon after, Laird's commanding officer told him he was going home. Laird argued with him, saying he wanted to stay in the war zone. His officer shook his head and said, "You're crazy." Being sent back home to a non-combat zone was made a little easier for Laird when he was told that he would be receiving the Distinguished Flying Cross.

After the war ended, Laird held a succession of Navy jobs over the next twenty-five years. But at heart he remained a fighter pilot. He applied (and was turned down) to fly combat missions in Vietnam. Serving as the "squadron leader" of the Japanese dive-bombers in *Tora! Tora! Tora!* was as close as he ever came to combat again. He retired with the rank of commander in 1971.

Diz Laird celebrated his ninetieth birthday by going skydiving, figuring that since he had never been forced to bail out of a plane when he was a pilot, he might as well have the experience now. He plans to repeat the experience on his hundredth birthday in 2021, and has sixteen friends and family members signed up to join him. ★

Kenneth B. Lake

CAPTAIN, USN

May 14, 1924–

KENNETH LAKE JOINED THE NAVY in the fall of 1942 because he wanted to fight against America's enemies. But he had more pragmatic reasons as well: "The Navy gave you food, shelter, clothing and money besides. In every way it was an improvement over our life in the Depression."

The small town of Argyle, Illinois, where he was born was very hard hit by the economic catastrophe, and the Lake family was particularly affected. His father, a railroad man, died unexpectedly when Lake was just seven years old. He had to help his mother make ends meet and for the next few years he did yard work for neighbors and other odd jobs. As a teenager, he got up at 4 a.m. every day to do his paper route, afterward delivering milk for a local dairy before going to school. In the evenings he worked at a local restaurant in exchange for meals.

It made an impression on Lake that one of the few men in town who seemed to have reliable income was an Army sergeant. During his high school years in Belvedere, Illinois, he thought of enrolling at Texas A&M because its famous Corps of Cadets gave graduates a commission in the Army as well as a degree. But the Navy now accepted high school graduates without the two years of college it had previously required. Lake entered active duty in September 1942 as a naval cadet.

His training took him from the harsh Minneapolis winter, where the heavy cold-weather gear he had to wear made it difficult to get in and out of the N2S biplane he trained in, to the humidity and sunshine of Pensacola, Florida. He also practiced carrier landings at Lake Michigan on board the USS *Wolverine*, a one-time side-wheel passenger steamer that had been refitted with a landing deck to become a freshwater aircraft carrier for the advanced training of Navy pilots.

Early in 1944, Lake, then nineteen, and three other pilots were sent to the Long Island factory of the Grumman Aircraft Company and given four

Athena Lonsdale/Athena Photography

of the new F6F Hellcats to fly to San Diego. (Lake asked one Grumman employee how to get there and was told, "Fly to Jacksonville, Florida, and then turn right.") After delivering them, he was shipped to Pearl Harbor and then, after a few more weeks of carrier training, was assigned to VF-2 on board the recently commissioned USS *Hornet*. The *Hornet* had joined the Fast Carrier Task Force in the Marshall Islands and, after supporting the invasion of New Guinea, was ready to play a major role in the amphibious assault of the Marianas Islands. Lake recalled that the captain of the *Hornet*, after watching him make a practice landing, grumbled, "I don't want teenaged kids flying off my ship." The other pilots immediately began calling him "the Kid."

On the morning of June 19, Lake went up as part of a U.S. force scrambled when radar reported a massive wave of Japanese planes on their way to attack the task force. This was the first of four such attacks in a battle that would become known among U.S. pilots as the Great Marianas Turkey Shoot because 395 Japanese planes were shot down that day with minimal U.S. losses.

Lake saw a Zero fighter and chased it down to the top of the ocean's whitecaps. After he shot it down, he was heading back up into the action when another Zero flew in front of him. He took a 90-degree deflection shot at it, and missed. The Zero got behind him and opened fire, shattering his instruments, radio, and canopy. Lake knew he had been badly hit but he didn't know how badly until he pulled on his rudder cables and they came into the cockpit, balling up at his feet. Able to steer only by tilting his wings right and left, he headed back to where he thought the *Hornet* was.

Other Hellcats were returning to refuel and he made hand signals to them so they could radio the ship about how badly he had been hit. He managed to safely land on the pitching deck. His crew showed Lake the holes in his headrest and canopy and he understood that the bullets that made them would have shattered his skull if he hadn't been turning his head to look at the Zero attacking him. His Hellcat was so badly damaged that it was pushed overboard after its guns were removed. Lake got a new plane, went back up that afternoon, and shot down another Zero.

The nonstop action continued for the next several weeks. On June 24, Lake was a member of a flight of four Hellcats headed toward Iwo Jima to attack enemy airfields. "I was at altitude," he later recalled, "and I saw two dive-bombers take off. I flew over to them and both of the rear seat gunners bailed out before I even fired. I shot both planes down in one pass."

Then he rose to join what he described as "a big ball of a dogfight" between Hellcats and Zeros taking place above him. "It was very crowded airspace," he said later on, "and you more or less fired at anything that got in front of you." When a Zero got in front of him, Lake shot it down.

He had five kills on September 19 when he took off as part of an escort for U.S. bombers striking targets in the Philippines. When the bombers came under attack, Lake singled out one of the enemy fighters shooting at the bombers. It tried to escape into the clouds. Lake later described what happened: "I followed him and shot him when we were up into the clouds, both upside down. He blew up." One of the appreciative bomber pilots below radioed, "Hey, good show!"

Lake came home for leave at the end of September, then returned to combat on board the USS *Shangri La*. As the war came to an end, he was dropping food and medicine to prisoner-of-war camps in Japan. He was standing on the bridge of the *Shangri La* on September 5, 1945, looking through binoculars at the deck of the nearby USS *Missouri* as Japanese representatives signed the treaty of surrender.

Kenneth Lake later flew in the Korean and Vietnam wars and served as an intelligence officer in the Pentagon before his retirement as a captain in 1974. ⋆

Jack Lenox

LIEUTENANT COLONEL, USAF

February 20, 1922–

WHEN JACK LENOX WAS GROWING UP in the small town of Enid, Oklahoma, in the 1920s, the talk at the family dinner table usually centered on trains. Every morning, Jack's father walked to the railroad station, where he worked all his life, and every afternoon he walked home. Jack himself often watched the trains roll by and thought that he might work on the railroad someday, but his secret dream was to fly an airplane. "More a fantasy than a dream, really," he later said, "because I didn't see how, being in the middle of Oklahoma, I'd ever get a chance."

But when he graduated from high school in 1941, the clouds of war were gathering. He tried to get into the Navy as an aviator but the recruiter told him, "Go get a college degree and then come back and talk to us." Lenox then went to the Army Air Corps and found that he could qualify by taking a test instead of getting a degree. He enlisted in August 1941.

When he went to Kelly Field, Texas, for flight training, he was a staff sergeant among second lieutenants with college backgrounds. The aviation students all billeted and ate together but there were underlying currents of "class conflict." Another staff sergeant flying a bomber during training told his second lieutenant copilot to lower flaps and the officer replied contemptuously: "I don't take orders from a sergeant!"

After getting his wings in October 1942, Lenox became a flight officer. After several weeks in Tampa doing advanced training in P-40s, he was ordered to Dakar, Senegal, in the late summer of 1943, as a P-51 replacement pilot. But when he landed he found that there were no P-51s in the region. After what seemed to him a long wait, he was finally assigned to the 14th Fighter Group, flying a P-38. He was relieved: "The outmoded P-39s and P-40s were getting slaughtered by the Germans. Only the P-38s were holding their own."

His squadron was sent to a recently converted base in Foggia, only a few miles from the front lines of the Allied advance up the Italian peninsula. Many

Alex McKnight/AM Photo Inc.

nights Lenox and the other pilots stood outside their barracks to watch the U.S. artillery fire light up the sky. He christened his plane "Snookie," the nickname of a girl he had dated during training, and got ready to go against the Luftwaffe.

In his third combat mission on December 20, 1943, Lenox had his first encounter with German pilots, who immediately won his respect for their skill and fearlessness. His squadron was flying cover for B-17s near Athens at about 28,000 feet, five thousand feet above the bombers, when a pack of Messerschmitt Me 109s suddenly appeared. As they swarmed the B-17s, Lenox and the other P-38 pilots rolled over and dove down to engage them. He was excited and scared and noticed that his left foot was tapping the floor uncontrollably. It stopped when

he got the trailing enemy fighter in his gun sights and opened fire. As the velocity of his dive took him past the Me 109 he saw that it was smoking. He then pulled up the nose of the P-38 and aimed at the lead Messerschmitt and saw it began to smoke as well. Glad to have survived the fight and back at the U.S. base in Foggia, he was given credit for one probable and one damaged because no one had actually seen either one of the two 109s crash.

In April Lenox was sent to Egypt for a stint at a Royal Air Force gunnery school. While there, he flew the Spitfire and was amazed by the plane's maneuverability. "I learned some good things from the Brits," Lenox later recalled. "They made me a better pilot."

On May 23, two days after returning to Foggia, he was on a mission over a German airfield near Ferrara when an Me 109 came toward him with its guns blinking. Lenox opened fire and the Messerschmitt went into a steep climb, the pilot bailing out just before it stalled. The next day Lenox was cruising over Lower Austria when he saw an Me 210, a twin-engine German fighter-bomber that somewhat resembled the P-38. He moved in behind it and shot it down with a single long burst.

Lenox became an Ace on June 14 in what he always thought of as his "near miss" dogfight, because he very well could have been shot down. He was part of a flight of fifteen P-38s returning from having accompanied U.S. bombers targeting an industrial installation in central Hungary. They were lingering in the area to look for targets of opportunity below when they were jumped by fifty Me 109s. In the next fifteen minutes of chaos, Lenox shot down three of the enemy. But in the tight circles of combat, the Germans were gradually getting the best of the Americans, shooting down five P-38s and forcing all the others on the defensive. Lenox had exhausted all his ammunition and was flying for his life. Suddenly, the Messerschmitts broke off and left. "We never knew why," he said later on. "They

probably got a command to return to their base. It was a good thing for us because if they had stayed they would have shot every one of us down."

By early August Lenox had fifty missions and was eligible to rotate home. He flew an extra mission so he could say that he had gone above and beyond. He was waiting for orders to go home when his commander approached him with a deal. He needed four hours in the air to get his monthly flight pay, so why not fly down to Tunis and pick up some liquor for the squadron? Lenox agreed and the ground crew cut little doors into two belly tanks, which they stuffed with straw and attached to his plane.

He was headed back to Foggia several hours later with the whiskey safely stored in the belly tanks when he flew over Capri. He had a good friend stationed there and got it into his head that he should buzz the island. As he went into a steep dive, the belly tanks flew off. He returned to base sheepish and empty-handed. The event was never forgotten. At squadron reunions in the years after the war was long over, his entrance would always be greeted with catcalls: "Here's Jack Lenox. Maybe we'll finally find out what ever happened to our booze." ★

George G. Loving

LIEUTENANT GENERAL, USAF

August 7, 1923–

THE NAZI ADVANCE IN EUROPE SEEMED FAR AWAY from his home in Lynchburg, Virginia, but listening to radio reports with his family at the kitchen table every night, seventeen-year-old George Loving's imagination was galvanized during the Battle of Britain in the summer of 1940. He rooted for the outnumbered English flyers in their Spitfires as they defeated the mighty Luftwaffe. When Winston Churchill famously said of these pilots, "Never in the field of human conflict was so much owed by so many to so few," Loving thought to himself that he, too, would like to be a flyer someday.

That day came sooner than he expected. In January 1942, with the United States itself now at war and his first semester at Lynchburg College over, Loving hitchhiked to Roanoke to enlist in the Army Air Corps. After basic training at Maxwell Field in Alabama, site of Orville and Wilbur Wright's old flying academy, he went to Carlstrom Field in Florida for flight school. When he first arrived he heard the daunting statistics: 40 percent of the cadets would quit, get killed in accidents, or be dropped before they got their wings. Loving managed to survive and went on to fighter training in P-51s at Harding Field in Baton Rouge, Louisiana.

Loving's unit boarded the Canadian ship *Empress of Scotland* (known as *Empress of Japan* until Pearl Harbor) in July 1943 at Newport News, Virginia, and headed to Casablanca. After arriving, he and his fellow pilots were loaded onto railcars and sent to Berteaux Airfield at the northern tip of Algeria, and from there to Naples to join the 31st Fighter Group. In his book *Woodbine Red Leader*, Loving later recalled being housed in sparse apartments once occupied by workers in the nearby Alfa Romeo plant, which was now in ruins as a result of U.S. bombing. He was surprised upon joining the 31st to find that he would be flying a Spitfire. He felt that the plane didn't measure up to the Mustang in terms of performance, but it had a quality all its own—"graceful, almost birdlike"—and he still honored the Spitfire for what it had done in the summer of 1940.

Chandler Crowell/Chandler Crowell Photography

After one of his first missions escorting A-36 Apache dive-bombers to hit a key German command post, Loving described the sensation of encountering flak from enemy antiaircraft guns: "I felt like a mallard on the opening day of hunting season." Back at the base, he waited every night for German air raids. Mad symphonies erupted, composed of bomb blasts, sirens, and "ack-ack," as Loving and the other pilots raced for the underground shelters hewn out of rock, where they sat huddled with frightened Neapolitan civilians.

War was minutes of excitement and hours of tedium. The 31st was primarily flying "delousing" missions, escorting B-25s on bombing runs into Italy and eastern Europe. On Christmas morning 1943, stewards at the mess hall told Loving and the other pilots that they would each receive one egg cooked to order, the first they had had in months. That night they had turkey and were entertained by a troupe headlined by Humphrey Bogart and Betty Grable.

Loving could feel the war slowly turning to the Allies' advantage, but he worried about his role. Flying wingman in what he regarded as largely defensive missions, he later said, "I began to wonder if I'd ever have a decent opportunity for a victory." However, his spirits improved in March 1944 when, soon after he witnessed an eruption of Mount Vesuvius, the 31st got brand new silver Mustangs with red-striped tails and wingtips.

On April 18, Loving went up with fifty other P-51s on a mission along the Gulf of Venice, providing cover for P-38s hitting a Luftwaffe airfield at Udine. He heard chatter on the radio as German fighters approached, then saw two Messerschmitt Me 109s and went after them. One got away as Loving dove on the other, shredding the cockpit with a burst from his .50-caliber guns. He saw the plane enter a death spiral down to the ground.

In June, the 31st began attacks into Germany. Loving got a Focke-Wulf Fw 190 on June 13 and two weeks later brought down an Me 210.

By July Loving was eligible to come home, but volunteered to stay in combat. He was chosen to participate in Operation Frantic III, a mission in which U.S. heavy bombers flew from bases in the Soviet Union against targets not easily reached from England or Italy. Mustangs flying from a secret base in Piryatin escorted them. Loving's strongest memories were of eating heavy Russian black bread he was sure had sawdust filler in it, and of the distant camaraderie of the suspicious Soviets.

On July 30, Loving, back in Italy, brought down an Me 109 after a brief air battle and then got another one about to fire on one of his fellow Mustang pilots. He was now an Ace.

After several missions in support of the Allied amphibious landing in Marseilles in August, Loving was told by his commanding officer that he was being sent back to the United States. He finished the war as a flight instructor and after the Japanese surrender was sent to Japan as part of the occupation force. In the Korean War, he flew 113 combat missions as a fighter-bomber squadron commander, and after a four-year stint as a test pilot at the Air Proving Ground Command, he attended the Air War College, which he later commanded. Loving later served as commander of the Sixth Allied Air Force with headquarters in Turkey. He was then assigned as commander of the U.S. forces in Japan and concurrently as commander of the Fifth Air Force. He retired in 1979 as a lieutenant general. ★

James F. Low

MAJOR, USAF

September 10, 1925–

JAMES LOW GREW UP IN SAUSALITO, the sleepy community across the bay from San Francisco that became a major shipbuilding center with the outbreak of World War II. He entered the Navy in 1943, soon after graduating from high school. After serving for three years as a radar technician, Low left the Navy in May 1946. Unsure of where he was headed, he went to the University of California, Berkeley in September on the GI Bill and drifted from one major to another, supporting himself by selling encyclopedias. Low decided to become an aviation cadet in the Air Force in the summer of 1950 because he had always wanted to fly. By the time he earned his wings a little more than a year later, he knew he had found his calling.

Low was assigned to the 4th Fighter Wing, 335th Fighter Interceptor Squadron (FIS) in Korea. The pilots who flew in Korea there were a mixture of old hands such as Francis "Gabby" Gabreski, who had 28 kills during World War II (and would get another 6.5 in Korea), and younger flyers anxious to make their mark. (It was also a proving ground for future astronauts John Glenn, Buzz Aldrin, and Wally Schirra.) Low soon carved out his own legend with his aggressive—some of his fellow pilots would have said reckless—approach to combat. Acclaimed writer James Salter, who was also in the 335th FIS and in fact shot down a MiG-15 himself, used Low as the model for Ed Pell, the cocky, somewhat hotheaded figure in *The Hunters*, his classic novel of airmen in the Korean War published in 1956. Low didn't agree with or appreciate the way Salter depicted him and never understood his animus.

Nicknamed "Dad" by his classmates in flight school because he was the oldest member of the group, Low was twenty-six when he arrived in Korea. He got his first kill on his first combat mission—below Pyongyang, capital of North Korea, on May 8, 1952, when a MiG passed below him and he took it down. Little more than a month later, he shot down his fifth MiG-15 and became the only second lieutenant jet Ace. It was on Father's Day and he

Alex McKnight/AM Photo Inc.

thought of the victory as an homage to his own father. His wing commander saw Low as someone who got results and was an unstoppable "MiG killer."

After his sixth victory on July 4, Low was brought back to the United States to do public relations with the manufacturers of the Sabre jet's radar gun sight, which he (unlike Gabreski and many of the World War II pilots in Korea who still relied on "instinct") had mastered. By the end of the year he was back in combat and scored three more victories, for a total of nine MiGs downed before he came home for good.

He received a Silver Star for one of these kills, on December 2, when he was part of a fighter sweep deep into North Korea. Low saw a group of MiGs attacking American bombers. The citation for the medal tells what he did next and gives a sense of

his style as a pilot: "He immediately launched a vertical diving attack, breaking away from his flight. Although outnumbered two-to-one, Lieutenant Low attacked the enemy aircraft with such ferocity that they were forced to break off their action against the friendly aircraft and take the defensive. By superb airmanship, he . . . closed [on] the leading MiG-15 and commenced firing. Relentlessly pursuing his objective in spite of the imminent threat from the other MiG, he followed the enemy through violent evasive maneuvers and scored numerous hits in the engine section of the craft. The MiG-15 began to smoke profusely and went into a steep dive, with Lieutenant Low still in pursuit. At 2,000 feet, the enemy pilot ejected and the MiG crashed and exploded on a hillside."

On January 5, 1953, Low was the subject of a *Time* magazine story titled "Dad's Last MiG" that described his final kill, which occurred when his wingman went freelancing after a MiG and then radioed Low, "I'm out of ammo. Can you take care of it?" Just then, the MiG pulled up into the sun and Low followed and took it down with a volley of .50-caliber shells into the cockpit. The *Time* writer, who actually never interviewed Low, quoted him as saying, "I sure would have liked to have knocked down just one more. Nine is such an uneven number."

Low remained in the Air Force after the Korean War ended. In 1967, he was flying combat missions in an F-4 Phantom jet over North Vietnam when he was shot down by an air-to-air missile and captured. He was taken to the "Hanoi Hilton" and held there for a year before being released in 1968.

James Low retired from the Air Force as a major in 1973. ★

James F. Luma

FLYING OFFICER, RCAF
FIRST LIEUTENANT, USAAF

August 27, 1922–

JAMES LUMA WAS AN AMERICAN PILOT who flew for a Canadian squadron in World War II in a plane built of wood. Growing up in Helena, Montana, Luma was fascinated by airplanes—building models, reading about flying, and nurturing a dream of becoming a pilot himself. It wasn't until the end of his freshman year at Carroll College that he decided not to wait any longer to make this dream come true. He thought first of joining the U.S. military, but with war still safely isolated in Europe, the Army Air Corps was highly selective about recruits. One of the criteria that the nineteen-year-old Luma could not meet was the requirement that a cadet be at least twenty years old.

He had a stroke of good fortune when he was hitchhiking back to Montana after visiting his parents, who then lived in Seattle, to be given a ride by an American who worked as a flight instructor in Canada. This man told Luma that the Royal Canadian Air Force accepted U.S. citizens older than eighteen with their parents' approval. Luma recalls practically yelling, "Stop the car!" He hitchhiked back to Seattle, got his parents' permission, and pawned his watch for ten dollars to pay for the bus ride to British Columbia.

Luma joined the Royal Canadian Air Force (RCAF) in Vancouver in July 1941 and received his wings the following May. He was sent to England in May 1943 and began training in Night Intruders. He transferred to the U.S. Army Air Forces in June because he wanted to qualify for the ten-thousand-dollar life insurance policy offered by the U.S. War Department, and was then re-posted to the RCAF's 418, the Night Intruders—wearing an American uniform but serving in a Canadian squadron.

The 418th flew the de Havilland Mark VI Mosquito, a twin-engine fighter-bomber that British flight engineers had designed in the mid-1930s to be made of wood—a core of balsa with thin laminations of hardwood—because of anticipated wartime shortages of aluminum and other metals. It made a dramatic mark on the air war in Europe, but failed when the British sent it to

Burma, because of the tropical insects that feasted on the glue holding its wood laminates together.

Built for a two-man crew—a pilot and a navigator—the Mosquito was the fastest plane in the European theater until the introduction of the P-51 Mustang with the Rolls-Royce Merlin engine. It was also one of the deadliest, with four .30-caliber machine guns in the nose and four 20-mm cannon in the lower fuselage. It was the premier Allied Night Intruder, stalking the bombers the Luftwaffe sent on night raids and the German night fighters that protected them. Photographs taken at the time show the youthful Luma in his fleece flight jacket, pensively smoking a pipe beside his plane "Moonbeam

McSwine," named eccentrically by the Canadians after a character from the "Li'l Abner" comic strip.

The Germans feared the Mosquito and experimented with a variety of countermeasures to stop it—sending up decoy planes bristling with gunners and armament to lure it into a confrontation; setting up counterfeit airfields with replica aircraft lit by phony landing lights to lure the Night Intruders into a trap of antiaircraft batteries. But the Mosquito continued to take a toll on German aircraft.

Targets were selected by British intelligence, often using information relayed by French Resistance agents. Missions were confirmed at the last minute. Luma spent twenty-seven fruitless nights in the ready room before he was finally scrambled. He went on seventeen Night Intruder missions before making contact with the enemy. The first German plane he saw was his first kill.

It came on January 21, 1944, when Luma and his navigator were flying over the German base at Wunstorf looking for targets of opportunity. Normally Luftwaffe pilots, knowing that Mosquitos might be lurking in the darkness, were careful about any light that might give them away. But Luma and his navigator spotted the faint glimmers of light on the nose and tail of a plane just taking off. (The pilot was careless, Luma would later theorize, because he was an Ace who had taken down seven British bombers that night and was anxious to get back into the air after refueling to shoot down more.) Luma let the twin-engine Messerschmitt Me 410 heavy fighter pass below him and gain altitude. As he approached it, he had a moment of "buck fever" because it was his first combat, and overshot it. Lowering his landing gear to cut his air speed, he circled around, lined up behind the 410, fired a short burst, and pushed his stick forward to escape the debris from the fireball.

Three weeks later on February 13, Luma caught up with a lone He 177 bomber "down moon" in a bright night sky. ("We didn't like a full moon," he later remarked, "and always tried to apply for leave when it appeared.") For some reason the bomber's tail gunner didn't see them and Luma shot the 177 down after following it for several miles.

On March 6, on a mission near Spain's border with France, he got his third kill—an unsuspecting Fw 190 fighter. During this engagement, the Mosquito's starboard engine went out and Luma had to fly six hundred miles back to his base in England on one engine. As he skimmed the choppy waters of the Channel at five hundred feet, he was tracked by British radar and an air-sea rescue plane waited with its engine idling in case he had to ditch.

On March 21, Luma led a rare daytime mission—called a "daylight ranger" by the Night Intruder pilots—along with another plane to strafe an enemy airfield on the French-German border. Relying on the Mosquito's speed to get in and out, they made two swift passes, destroying several German planes on the ground, and then pulled up and headed for home. While still over French territory, he saw a Ju 34 single-engine transport and shot it down. Then, twelve minutes later, he opened fire on a Ju 52 trimotor transport, destroying both its engines and sending it down.

After these last kills, which made him an Ace, Luma was transferred to photo reconnaissance, flying weather missions over Berlin with the U.S. 802nd Reconnaissance Group, where he served until the end of the war in Europe.

After the war James Luma followed his nose for adventure in his work as a commercial pilot. He flew transports for Korean National Airways during the war in Korea; for Air Ventures in Katanga during the civil war in Congo; for Vietnamese Air Transport during the war in Vietnam; and for Trans Mediterranean Airways in Lebanon. He was flying 707s for Air Berlin when he hit the mandatory retirement age of sixty in 1982. ★

Winton W. Marshall

LIEUTENANT GENERAL, USAF

July 6, 1919–September 19, 2015

IN THE HAIR-RAISING CHAOS OF DOGFIGHTS IN KOREA, when he was dodging fire from MiG-15s attacking him in the same instant that he was flying through the debris of enemy planes that he had just destroyed, Winton Marshall sometimes flashed back to his first days as a military pilot, when he was depressed not to have experienced combat.

He had volunteered for the Army Air Forces in the spring of 1942, a thin twenty-two-year-old (so thin that his friends started calling him "Bones") from Detroit who was hoping to get revenge on the Japanese for Pearl Harbor. After getting his wings, he was assigned to Las Vegas Army Air Field, later Nellis Air Force Base, and became chief of the P-39 training section there. He was hoping to see action in Europe, but early in 1945 he was sent to Panama as a pilot with the 28th Fighter Squadron and spent the remainder of the war there guarding the Canal Zone. One of the few spoils of war was meeting his future wife Millie, who had herself flown in Europe as a member of the original Women Air Force Service Pilots (WASP).

Thinking his time had passed, Marshall served in the late 1940s as a test pilot for the F-84 Thunderjet, which first entered service in 1947 but was plagued by design problems and didn't become fully operational until 1949. Then, in May 1951, Marshall finally got a chance for aerial combat when he went to Korea as commander of the 335th Fighter Squadron, flying the F-86 Sabre jet.

It was a critical moment in the war. Until the introduction of the F-86, the U.S. air forces there had been hard-pressed to deal with the superior MiG-15, the Soviet Union's top-line fighter. But the Sabre more than leveled the aerial playing field, becoming the dominant aircraft of the war. In response to its formidability, in fact, the USSR, theoretically not involved in the Korean "conflict," sent some of its best pilots to fight in the air war, which had become focused in the area known as "MiG Alley" on the border between North Korea and China.

Marco Garcia/Marco Garcia Photography

The arrival of these elite Soviet flyers was accompanied by a change in tactics. In the early days of air combat in Korea, the MiG pilots, using their planes' superior climbing ability, had usually attacked the U.S. fighters from below. But by the time Marshall arrived, the enemy had changed to a "coordinated high side attack," with Communist commanders now putting planes above as well as below the American Sabre jets, so that a pair of F-86s now typically faced four MiG-15s coming at them from different altitudes. As Marshall later told aviation historian Larry Davis: "While you were turning into the two planes making the high-angle attack, two more were looking up your tailpipe."

Flying an F-86 named "Mr. Bones V," Marshall already had one kill when he was part of a large U.S. force that went up against an even larger enemy formation on September 2, 1951. Marshall didn't know it at the time, but according to aviation writer Diego Zampini, who studied records of the engagement released after the fall of the USSR, the pilot he shot down in the melee that followed was an experienced Russian lieutenant named S. T. Kolpikov.

On November 28, Marshall had an even more memorable engagement, one of which he later said, "Never did I have to fight so hard to survive." Having just rolled out from the attacks of two MiGs, Marshall later told Larry Davis that he watched as his "cockpit was surrounded by a hail of bright tracers from the cannons of the MiG on my tail. They looked the size of oranges as they went by my canopy." Marshall jerked the stick so hard that his plane seemed to stop in the air. As the MiG behind him thundered by he shot it down with a single burst.

But the action, which would last twenty minutes, was far from over as yet another MiG closed in on Marshall from behind. Again he slammed his stick back. But the enemy pilot did the same, sticking with him. Marshall engaged in what he thought was a neat evasive maneuver—a snap roll that ended in an inverted spin with zero air speed. But when he looked out of his canopy, there was the MiG, still right with him. Both planes ended in a flat spin with little air speed. Marshall jerked the stick and pulled the rudders and went into a more controlled spin. So did the other pilot. He recovered from the spin and the other pilot did too, except that this time the MiG was directly in front of him. Marshall opened fire and the MiG exploded.

Zampini records that the pilot of the MiG was G. T. Shatalov, another elite Soviet pilot who was himself an Ace, with five U.S. planes to his credit in Korea. Marshall didn't yet know his identity, but said of his antagonist, "I half regretted the loss of such a great pilot even though he was on the other side. . . . I would have loved to have sat down for a beer or vodka at the officers' club with that guy, trading fighter pilot stories together."

On November 30, Marshall was engaging a group of Tu-2 propeller-driven bombers when another La-11 took a long shot at "Mr. Bones V" and riddled its fuselage and canopy with cannon shells. Marshall fell out of the air and barely managed to regain control of his plane to keep from hitting the Yellow Sea. He landed safely, and doctors treated his shrapnel wounds. The opposing pilot was so certain he had gotten Marshall that he claimed him as a kill.

Marshall was an Ace with 6.5 kills when he left combat and returned to the United States in January 1952. Later on, as commander of the 15th Fighter Interceptor Squadron at Davis-Monthan Air Force Base, he was beginning a flight when he saw a B-47 bomber catch fire at the end of the runway. He quickly taxied his F-86 to the burning bomber and blew out the fire with the exhaust from his jet. He later deadpanned that he had been acting as "a fire Marshall."

Winton Marshall remained in the Air Force for the next quarter century, having a variety of commands including vice commander in chief of the U.S. Pacific Air Forces. He retired as a lieutenant general in 1977. ★

W. Robert Maxwell

COMMANDER, USNR

July 1, 1919– March 30, 2016

ROBERT MAXWELL SHOT DOWN seven Japanese planes and had three probables in heavy combat in the Pacific during the second half of 1944. But however dramatic these experiences were, they were always overshadowed by what had happened to Maxwell a year earlier, on May 2, 1943, during one of his first missions when the F6F Hellcat he was then flying collided with another U.S. plane and crashed into the sea. Thus began a saga of survival in which Maxwell discovered within himself a strength and resourcefulness he didn't know he possessed.

He grew up a carefree youngster in Wausau, Wisconsin, spending many free hours at the local airport doing odd jobs for pilots in the hope that they would make his day by taking him up for a short ride. He was in his third year at the University of Wisconsin in the spring of 1941 when he volunteered for naval aviation. A desire to avoid the recently instituted draft had something to do with his decision, but less than the sight of naval recruiting officers driving around the Madison campus in snazzy convertibles with good-looking coeds sitting beside them.

Maxwell was going through flight training in Pensacola when Pearl Harbor was attacked. After getting his wings in May 1942, he was assigned to VF-11 at Naval Air Station San Diego. A friend from Wausau also in VF-11 was killed in a training accident. Accompanying the body home for burial, Maxwell later told journalist Peg Eastman, made him realize that war was a game played for keeps.

By April 1943, VF-11 was conducting land-based operations on Guadalcanal. On May 2, what turned out to be a sixteen-day ordeal for Maxwell began as a routine mission escorting a strike force of dive-bombers attacking a Japanese position near the island of New Georgia. Maxwell and the other Hellcats were weaving protectively over the dive-bombers when his flight leader suddenly dropped down and to the left. As his wingman, Maxwell started to

John Slemp/Aerographs Aviation Photography

go down and look for him but his Wildcat collided with the flight leader's aircraft. As Maxwell bailed out, he watched his plane break in half and plummet into the sea.

Slipping his life raft off his leg while still under water, Maxwell inflated it and climbed in. He opened the first aid kit and applied sulfa powder to gashes on his chin and leg. He inventoried his emergency rations: a six-square chocolate bar and a canteen of water. He ate one of the squares, sipped some water, and began paddling toward what he thought was the nearest land—Tetepari, an uninhabited island in the New Georgia chain.

Over the next four days he parceled out the chocolate squares and water and fought the heavy squalls that drove him further out to sea, until the wind changed and he at last saw land. Then his raft was picked up by a huge wave and slammed down onto the beach.

Later describing his saga to military historian Eric Hammel, Maxwell told how he concentrated on details as a way of dispelling panic as he carefully preserved the raft and his remaining equipment. Subsisting on coconuts and a couple of small crabs he trapped, he spent the next eight days making his way through the jungles, swamps, and coral shoreline of Tetepari, headed in the direction of Rendova, an island he knew to be inhabited. His trek would later be used by the Navy as a textbook case of survival strategies in lessons for other airmen.

On May 13, Maxwell made new oars to replace those he had lost, constructed oarlocks out of rope he found, and re-inflated the raft he had kept with him. Then he crossed the three-mile channel to Rendova. As he emerged from the rough surf, some islanders passing by in a canoe yelled at him and then came ashore to pick him up. They took him to a village on the east coast of Rendova. Given food and water, he showed the natives where he lived in the United States on a worn map one of them produced. The next day the chief of the village made contact with an Australian coastwatcher in New Georgia, who sent back a basket with ten packs of cigarettes and assurances that he would get word to American authorities that Maxwell was alive.

Finally, on May 18, a PBY flying boat was sent for him from Guadalcanal. Maxwell was sent to New Zealand for two months of hospitalization. He returned to the United States for leave, then was reassigned to VF-51 in March 1944 aboard the USS *San Jacinto*, the same carrier on which future President George H. W. Bush was then serving as a TBM Avenger pilot.

Resuming the combat duty his personal ordeal had interrupted, Maxwell shot down a twin-engine "Betty" bomber and an "Emily" flying boat near Saipan on June 11. Four days later he shot down three Kawasaki Ki-61 "Tony" fighters in an engagement that lasted until near darkness, when he led his flight of four F6F Hellcats back to the *San Jacinto*, dodging friendly fire to bring them home in a difficult night landing.

On June 19, Maxwell became an Ace when he downed a "Judy" dive-bomber. He got his seventh and final kill, another "Tony" interceptor, on October 5.

After completing his tour, Robert Maxwell spent the rest of the war as a flight instructor. When he left active duty he got what would become a career job with the Wausau Insurance Company and entered the Naval Reserve, retiring as a commander in 1958.

Reflecting on his solitary ordeal at sea and on land in the Pacific late in life, Maxwell told author James Oleson, "Today when I see programs titled *Survivor*, I do not watch. But I sure know what that word means." ★

Frank E. McCauley

MAJOR, USAF

November 9, 1916–

AS A BOY WORKING IN ALFALFA AND CORN FIELDS on his family's farm in Hicksville, Ohio, Frank McCauley always remembered pausing whenever the local hardware store owner flew over in his plane, the only one in the community, and wondering what kept it up in the air. McCauley tried to convince his father to build a small airstrip on the farm, in hopes that it would attract the barnstormers who sometimes showed up unexpectedly in this part of northwestern Ohio like traveling magic shows. His father said that the land was for alfalfa, not airplanes, but he did lend McCauley the family car once so that he could help a flyer who damaged a wing when landing at another Hicksville farm.

After graduating from high school in 1934, McCauley attended Bowling Green State University for a time then transferred to Michigan State University. After graduating in 1940, he figured that he would soon be drafted—conscription having been reinstituted that year—so he enlisted in the infantry. After a few months handling weapons and learning to build fortifications for future ground combat, he asked to be transferred to the Army Air Corps.

He was sent to flight school at Randolph Field, Texas, and got his wings in July 1942. Then he was assigned to the 56th Fighter Group in Bridgeport, Connecticut, for advanced training. He expected to be flying P-40s, but his squadron, the 61st, was the first to receive the brand new P-47. When he first saw the plane, McCauley exclaimed, "That is *big*!" His eight-plane training flight called itself "Snow White and the Seven Dwarves." Each had the name of one of the dwarves painted on his fuselage; McCauley chose "Happy."

He was ordered to practice intercepting "bogeys" over New York City. He got excited when he saw a flight of planes with red circles on their wings and fuselages—the insignia, he had heard, of the Japanese—and rushed back to the base to make a report. "They were Canadian," he later commented. "I felt a bit silly after that."

Athena Lonsdale/Athena Photography

McCauley's squadron sailed for England on board the *Queen Elizabeth* in December 1943. There were 12,000 military personnel aboard the ship, sixteen men in each state room. After landing in Scotland, the squadron was sent to an RAF base in Northamptonshire. Not yet used to Americans, the British airmen struck McCauley as standoffish and remote. He and some of the other pilots tried to soften them up by staging get-togethers, but that generated little camaraderie. The winter was brutally cold and the Americans broke up furniture in their rooms to burn when there was not enough coal.

The 56th was commanded by the legendary Hubert "Hub" Zemke, who had been in England during the Battle of Britain and had observed the tactics of Spitfire and Messerschmitt pilots. During its first few months in England, Zemke put the 56th through extensive training. Other units grumbled about the large and heavy P-47, whose slow climbing rate and acceleration, they felt, made it inferior to the Luftwaffe fighters. But Zemke saw the Thunderbolt's strength—very fast in a dive because of its weight—and developed "dive, fire, and recover" tactics that made the P-47 into a formidable weapon despite its cumbersomeness. Frank McCauley adopted these tactics and later noted, "I always tried to attack from above and always with the sun at my back."

He would always remember the adrenaline high of getting into the cockpit of the "Rat Racer," as he re-named his Thunderbolt, feeling that "Happy" was insufficiently warlike: "I was never afraid. I was eager to get into that plane. I enjoyed every bit of it." The first time he got a German fighter in his gun sights in the late spring of 1943, in fact, he was overexcited and opened fire too soon, losing the opportunity for a kill.

His first victory came on August 17 near Lièges, Belgium, when a flight of B-17s his squadron was escorting was attacked by enemy fighters. McCauley and another P-47 dived down on a twin-engine Messerschmitt 110 fighter-bomber and opened fire at the exact same time, sharing the kill when the plane exploded in a fireball. A few minutes later McCauley got his own Focke-Wulf 190, watching the pilot bail out after he had riddled the plane's fuselage with machine-gun fire.

McCauley had three more kills over the next few weeks in escort missions over France and Germany. But the thrill of victory was always mitigated by the losses of the bombers he was escorting to their targets. "Every time we lost one, you knew that ten men went down with it. What was heartbreaking was that you weren't able to do anything about it. That was our job—to make sure it didn't happen."

His last combat mission on October 14 was particularly sweet because he was able to save some endangered bombers. It was at the end of a mission over Germany. The P-47s had gotten the B-17s to their targets in Germany and were headed back to England when McCauley spotted a group of German fighters waiting for the Thunderbolts to leave so they could pounce on the vulnerable bombers. Although low on fuel, McCauley and other Americans turned back and attacked the Messerschmitts. While driving them off, he shot down an Me 110. He was proud to become an Ace, but it was even more gratifying to have protected the B-17s. "We saved those bombers," McCauley later said. "That was the most satisfaction we could get."

Soon after this mission, his forty-sixth, McCauley was made an operations officer for the 495th Fighter Training Group, spending the rest of the war showing replacement pilots how to make the P-47 into a lethal weapon. "These pilots had never flown in heavy clouds, never done aerobatics. We had our work cut out for us to make sure they'd last for a few missions, at least."

McCauley was testing a plane over the English Channel as part of his work as a trainer on June 6, 1944, when he broke through cloud cover and saw the unforgettable sight of an armada of Allied ships on their way to the French coast, bunched so close together that it seemed possible to step from one to another. He realized that the skies over the Channel were a dangerous place to be that day and quickly headed back to England.

As the air war in Europe was coming to an end, McCauley went home in a B-24. After spending time with family and friends in Ohio, he was sent to Edwards Air Force Base in California. He met a girl at the USO canteen in Hollywood and married her. He spent seven years in the reserve, resigning his commission thirty days before his unit was called to Korea. "Whether or not I dodged a bullet," he later said, "I'll never know."

In 2010, at the age of ninety-four, Frank McCauley went skydiving because, as he said, he had never had to bail out during the war and "wanted to know how it felt." ★

Joseph D. McGraw

CAPTAIN, USN

November 17, 1923– July 24, 2015

IMMEDIATELY AFTER GRADUATING from high school, Joseph McGraw, known as "Jo-Jo," joined some friends from his hometown of Syracuse in enlisting in the Navy as an aviation cadet in September 1942. Memories of Pearl Harbor were still raw. The local newspaper dubbed them "the Syracuse Avengers."

After getting his wings in the summer of 1943, McGraw joined VC-10, a recently commissioned squadron known as "the Mallards," whose pilots completed their carrier qualification on Lake Michigan on board the *Wolverine*, a former side-wheeler excursion craft refitted with a large improvised landing deck. It would have been appropriate, given the nickname the newspaper had given to his Syracuse group, if McGraw had been assigned to the TBF Avenger dive-bombers some members of the unit flew. But he thought of himself as a born fighter pilot and maneuvered to be assigned to the FM-2 Wildcat, an improved version of the Navy's standard carrier-based fighter at the beginning of the war. The "wilder Wildcat" that McGraw would take into battle was faster and lighter than the original and better able to engage the Japanese Zero on equal terms.

In the late spring of 1944, VC-10 was assigned to the USS *Gambier Bay*, one of the CVE escort carriers, which were half the size of the "fleet" carriers, much slower, and without as much armament and firepower, but far cheaper and quicker to build. (Cynical crew members claimed that the designation CVE stood for "Combustible, Vulnerable, and Expendable.") One of the missions of the "baby flattop," as these escort carriers were called, was ferrying planes to the big carriers and participating in U.S. island-hopping attacks on Japanese strongholds in the Pacific.

The *Gambier Bay*'s first taste of combat came in June when it supported the Marine invasion of Saipan. McGraw, shown in wartime photographs as a long-faced young man with a piercing stare, high cheekbones, and an ironic

smile that tilted the edges of his mouth upward, was anxious for action. According to historian David Sears, who featured him in his book *The Last Epic Naval Battle*, when Japanese fighters failed to appear on his early missions, McGraw one day pulled out his .38 pistol, cracked open his cockpit, and fired down at what he assumed was enemy territory below, just to feel that he was in the fight.

He soon had more action than he could handle. On one mission he was about ready to land on the *Gambier Bay* when he saw a Japanese bomber readying an attack on the ship. He rolled over to open fire, but just then the bomber's wing was knocked off by U.S. antiaircraft fire, which hit McGraw as well, wounding his plane so badly that, when he did manage to land, his plane came close to skidding off the end of the carrier.

Not long after, he was on a strafing run against a Japanese airfield on Saipan when his plane shuddered after being hit by enemy guns. He looked back and saw that half of his tail had been shot away. As his Wildcat veered out of control, McGraw bailed out and spent several hours bobbing in the ocean before he was picked up by a U.S. destroyer.

On June 18, he scored his first kill, downing a Japanese "Betty" bomber over Saipan.

The *Gambier Bay* supported Marines invading Guam and Peleliu, then joined the large U.S. task force in the Leyte Gulf preparing for a showdown with the remainder of the Japanese fleet, including the *Yamato*, the largest and most heavily armed battleship in the war.

On October 24, McGraw was on patrol with another Wildcat when he saw above him two dozen of the enemy twin-engine light bombers called "Lilys," on their way to attack the U.S. fleet. Climbing up to intercept them, McGraw scored direct hits on the right engine and wing of one of them, sending it down in flames. Dodging the Japanese fighters that were trying to protect the bombers, he got on the tail of another "Lily" and found himself looking directly at the plane's rear gunner, who shot a few holes in McGraw's Wildcat before McGraw sent the bomber down into the water below.

At dawn the next morning McGraw was having a quick cup of coffee in the mess hall when word came that the Japanese fleet was moving to attack the *Gambier Bay*. He raced another pilot for the next available Wildcat and strapped himself in as enemy battleships and destroyers opened fire. A shell hit the deck of the ship as the Wildcat in line ahead of McGraw took off. He gunned his engine without waiting for a signal from the launch officer and got airborne.

As David Sears told the story, after McGraw made a strafing run over the *Yamato* a message came over his radio telling him and the other pilots that the *Gambier Bay* was going down: "Your nearest field is Tacloban at Leyte. God bless you." Afraid that he wouldn't be able to get back into the fight if he headed landward, McGraw got permission to land on another escort carrier, the *Manila Bay*, where he refueled, rearmed, and took off for another strike.

By mid-afternoon he had returned to the *Manila Bay* for more fuel and then re-launched yet again as part of a four-plane section. In the chaos of the mammoth naval and air battle, he saw eighteen Japanese "Val" bombers accompanied by a dozen Zeros headed for U.S. shipping. He dived down on one of the "Vals" and shot it down. Then he hit one of the Zeros trying to protect the bombers with a long burst and the plane exploded. Another of the enemy fighters came toward him and tried to ram his Wildcat. McGraw managed to pull up and escape the collision. As he circled around to return to the action, the sky, crowded a few minutes earlier, was suddenly empty, an "eerie moment" for him.

Soon after this mission, Joseph McGraw was sent home to spend the rest of the war as an instructor. After entering college and majoring in aeronautical engineering, he was recalled to duty in Korea, where he flew sixty missions in an F9F Panther jet off the USS *Boxer*. After retiring as a captain in 1967, he flew missions for the U.S. Forest Service at the controls of one of the "borate bombers," fighting fires every summer throughout the western states. ★

Donald M. McPherson

ENSIGN, USNR

May 25, 1922–

IT WAS MARCH 19, 1945, and Donald McPherson, flying an F6F Hellcat off the USS *Essex* in his first combat mission, was about to undergo his baptism by fire. As his squadron attacked airfields on the Japanese mainland, McPherson saw an enemy bomber struggling to take off to keep from being destroyed on the ground. He swooped down on it, but in the middle of his dive the Hellcat's engine suddenly quit. With the ground looming up, he somehow got the engine restarted and managed to pull out. He limped back to the carrier and after a hard landing discovered just how lucky he was when his crew found that a 20-mm cannon shell had smashed into his fuselage and severed the cable controlling the aircraft's tail section.

Born in 1922 as the youngest of seven children, McPherson grew up on a Nebraska farm where times were hard even before the Depression. The University of Nebraska was only thirty miles away in Lincoln and he dreamed of going there, but his parents couldn't afford the tuition, and after graduating from high school at sixteen McPherson went to work on the farm helping his family make ends meet. When he turned nineteen his father urged him to enlist in the Navy and try to become a pilot so he wouldn't be drafted into the infantry. He was accepted for flight training and got his wings in the summer of 1944.

By early 1945 McPherson was in VF-83 on board the *Essex*, enjoying the predawn missions most of all because the pilots who flew them were served steak for breakfast. On April 6 he got "lucky," as he later said. He was returning from a mission, flying low, about 1,500 feet, on the way back to the carrier when he spotted two Japanese dive-bombers skimming the water below him. "I had my trigger guard off safe and was ready to fire," he later remembered, "and all I had to do was push the nose down and put the sight on the first plane and squeeze the trigger." As McPherson's shells tore into the plane, the Japanese pilot slumped down in the cockpit and the plane crashed into the

Ariel Fried/Ariel Fried Photography

water. The second dive-bomber turned to run and McPherson chased it down and destroyed it too.

Over the next few weeks, VF-83 supported the U.S. invasion of Okinawa, bombing the caves where enemy troops lay in wait to ambush U.S. soldiers. Then, as the Japanese sent waves of kamikazes against the American fleet, McPherson and the other Navy pilots tried frantically to guard the ships. On May 4, as 250 kamikazes approached, the U.S. fly-ers tried to get as many as they could. McPherson shot down three enemy planes in quick succession, becoming an Ace. Another pilot got six. All told, his squadron shot down over one hundred Japanese aircraft in less than an hour. "But," as McPherson said sadly, "we didn't get them all." Four U.S. Navy ships were sunk in the attack and many others seriously damaged.

The loss of all those American lives haunted McPherson in the years that followed. But decades later, as journalist Steve Liewer wrote in the *Omaha World-Herald*, McPherson got some consolation from a telephone call from a former crew member of the USS *Ingraham*, a destroyer VF-83 had been trying to guard that day. After studying an archive of photos taken during the attack, the caller said, he had determined that the *Ingraham*, already badly damaged, would certainly have been taken down by

another kamikaze headed straight for it if McPherson hadn't suddenly appeared and destroyed the Japanese plane before it could hit the ship.

McPherson was on the deck of the *Essex* when the first atomic bomb was dropped on Hiroshima, and he saw the mushroom cloud boil up on the horizon. Later on, his squadron dropped packs containing comic cards and candies over POW camps where American prisoners were waiting to be repatriated. He was in the air over the USS *Missouri* when the Japanese formally surrendered.

Donald McPherson came back home to the farm, married and started a family, and became involved in his community's life as a Boy Scout leader and Little League coach. He was employed as a rural letter carrier and continued to farm until he was almost ninety years old. ★

Henry Meigs II

FIRST LIEUTENANT, USAAFR
COLONEL, ANG (KANG)

June 12, 1921–November 28, 2014

HENRY MEIGS II HAD ONE OF THE MOST ILLUSTRIOUS genealogies of World War II American fighter Aces. The first Meigs (Vincent) arrived in Connecticut in 1636 and established the family that would play an important role in U.S. history. The uniquely named Return Jonathan Meigs (from a plea by his mother to his father, Jonathan, after she briefly spurned him: "Return, Jonathan") was a onetime friend of Benedict Arnold, the Revolutionary War hero-turned-traitor. Montgomery Meigs was a Civil War general and friend of Abraham Lincoln who helped found Arlington Cemetery and design the Capitol dome. The first Henry Meigs was a congressman from New York and later president of the city's board of aldermen.

Henry II grew up in New York City, in a home on upper Fifth Avenue across from Central Park. According to his wife Sarah, he was "not particularly burdened by and not even very knowledgeable about this [his family's] history." He attended private schools and always recalled getting a quarter each day from his mother for bus fare and using half of it for candy. Feeling that it was inevitable that the United States would be dragged into the European war, he entered the Army Air Corps right before Pearl Harbor. He trained at Shaw Field in South Carolina and received his wings in October 1942.

Meigs was initially assigned to the 339th Fighter Squadron of the 347th Fighter Group which, beginning in February 1943, played a key role in the Allied effort to drive the Japanese out of the Solomon Islands. When the United States established a tenuous foothold on Guadalcanal, the Japanese responded with a ferocious bombing campaign, including nighttime attacks by "Betty" bombers the Marines called "Bedcheck Charlies." The Air Corps established the 6th Night Fighter Squadron (NFS) to combat these attacks.

The P-70 Nighthawk was first used for these night missions, but it was inefficient at high altitudes, and by the time Meigs transferred to the 6th NFS in the summer of 1943, it was using radar-equipped P-38s. Photos taken of him

Frank Olynyk

at the time show him standing under the wing of his plane with a Betty Grable pinup painted on its nose. He wears a thin mustache and a shoulder holster containing a .45 pistol, and has the insouciant good looks of a young Errol Flynn.

Meigs scored his first victory over Guadalcanal on the night of August 13 against a "Betty" bomber that blundered into U.S. searchlights. On September 21, with U.S. Marines watching the light show, he shot down two more "Bettys" in the space of a minute—a feat that made the newspapers in far-off England.

By the end of the year, with the Japanese assault against Guadalcanal defeated, Meigs transferred to the 12th Fighter Squadron and began flying daytime missions. In heavy action over the Duke of York

Island, New Guinea, he was given credit for three Zero "probables" on January 7 and a confirmed Zero on February 9. He bagged two more Zeros six days later.

By the late spring of 1944, Meigs was back in the United States, living outside of New York on a barracks ship. He met a recent Sarah Lawrence graduate named Sarah Willis whose father Simeon Willis had recently become governor of Kentucky, the first Republican elected in that state in decades. Meigs was a Republican too, and he and Sarah spent their first few dates complaining about FDR, who was running for an unprecedented fourth term. They were married in the Kentucky Governor's Mansion on Christmas 1944.

Sarah recalled her father taking Meigs aside soon after the wedding and telling him, "Being a hot pilot won't get you anywhere in the civilian world. You need a profession." Meigs asked the governor what he recommended and Willis answered without hesitation, "Lawyer."

Meigs took his advice and attended the University of Kentucky Law School, then embarked on a distinguished legal career that he pursued while also playing a key role in establishing the Kentucky Air National Guard. Meigs became a Franklin County judge in 1960 and issued precedent-making rulings on the separation of powers in state government and other important cases while becoming a champion of judicial reform. He sometimes gave friends little plaques he had made reading, "Flying is the second-biggest thrill in life. The first is landing." ★

Robert C. Milliken

LIEUTENANT, USAAF

June 6, 1922–

ROBERT MILLIKEN WAS A FIVE-YEAR-OLD living on his grandfather's homestead near the small town of Hanna, Wyoming, in a house without electricity or running water, when news came that Charles Lindbergh would be doing a flyover. It was 1927 and Lindy had just captivated America and the world by his transatlantic flight to Paris. He had returned to instant heroism and was now taking a victory lap across America, navigating the terrain by following railroad tracks. Milliken lived near the Union Pacific and every few miles, as Lindbergh passed a station, the railway telegraph offices gave updates on his approach. In an unforgettable moment, Milliken stood transfixed, looking up with one hand shading his eyes, as *The Spirit of St. Louis* passed overhead. Like so many American boys of his generation, he had been immediately addicted to flight by watching the Lone Eagle.

After graduating from high school, Milliken enrolled in the University of Wyoming, taking a job as night janitor in a hotel to help pay expenses. He was eating the free breakfast he got as part of his compensation on the morning of December 7, 1941, when word came of the Japanese attack on Pearl Harbor. Milliken immediately signed up for the Army Air Corps. "But they had no airfield, no planes, no instructors," he later recalled. "They told me to go home and wait to hear from them."

The wait stretched out for weeks, then months. It wasn't until late 1942 that Milliken got the call. He didn't get his wings until the late fall of 1943, when he finished his training at Williams Field, Arizona.

He shipped out for Europe on board the *Queen Mary*, on a voyage stalked by U-boats that had been given the added incentive of a cash bounty the German government had placed on the head of the ship's captain. After landing in Scotland, Milliken traveled by rail to the RAF Warmwell base in Dorset, where he joined the 474th Fighter Group as a P-38 pilot.

He had several combat missions before one he would never forget. It came on the morning of June 6, 1944, D-day, also his twenty-second birthday, when his squadron flew in support of the Allied invasion of Europe. As the sun rose and the clouds parted, he saw below the sight of a lifetime—an armada of hundreds of ships headed toward Normandy. Upon learning that two German Messerschmitts had buzzed the beaches of Normandy, his squadron hurried to engage them. But the two enemy planes didn't fire a shot and quickly headed east, away from the action. Milliken's first kill, a Focke-Wulf 190, didn't come until a month later after a brief battle over central France.

By August the 474th was at a temporary airfield at Saint-Lambert, where the Army Corps of Engineers had quickly constructed a mesh track runway. It was assigned to missions escorting bombers into Germany and also attacking the retreating German army along the front lines of the ground conflict.

On September 12, the 474th was attacking Aachen, one of the strong points of the Germans' Siegfried Line and also one of the first cities on German soil to be captured. The mission of the P-38s was to take out Aachen's powerful searchlights, thus blinding the Germans to night attacks. Milliken had just finished strafing them when he looked up and saw a large group of German fighters. "I felt like I was suspended in time for a minute," he later told journalist Christine Peterson of the *Casper Star Tribune*. "It seemed like everything stopped."

"Then a 190 attacked me head-on," he recalled. "I could see his tracers passing right over me. I raised up a bit and blew him out of the sky." Out of the corner of his eye he saw another enemy plane maneuvering to fire on one of his fellow pilots, who had bailed out of his damaged Lightning and was descending slowly toward the ground in his parachute. Milliken quickly got on the tail of the German plane and brought it down with a sustained burst, saving the American flyer's life. He saw the pilot of the Fw 190 he had just destroyed bail out himself, slamming into the tail of his plane as his parachute opened. He later learned that this was a top German Ace who would return to combat after

his injuries had healed and go on to shoot down a number of U.S. planes before the war was over.

By the end of 1944, Milliken, with four kills, had flown enough missions to go home, but volunteered for more. On December 18, he was leading a flight of four P-38s in support of U.S. troops fighting in the Battle of the Bulge when he spotted a force of Messerschmitt Me 109s attacking an outnumbered group of P-47 Thunderbolts. He opened fire on one of the enemy planes and saw the P-38's powerful cannon tear gaping holes in its fuselage, sending it into a death spiral and making Milliken an Ace.

Robert Milliken was sent home just before the war ended. He got married and began a family as well as a business—selling aircraft and giving flying lessons. ★

Sanford K. Moats

LIEUTENANT GENERAL, USAF

December 4, 1921–

"SANDY" MOATS WOULD HAVE A DAZZLING career in the Air Force during the postwar era, becoming a lieutenant general and holding a variety of high-echelon jobs, including commander of the Sixteenth Air Force and vice commander of the Tactical Air Command at Langley Air Force Base, Virginia. Yet his strongest memory would always be of serving as a P-51 pilot at the end of World War II at a temporary airfield in Belgium during the Battle of the Bulge, when he shot down four Messerschmitt Me 109s in the space of a few minutes and became an Ace.

Moats was a wry, observant twenty-one-year-old studying engineering at Kansas State University late in 1942 when he got his draft notice. Not particularly anxious to fight in the trenches, he applied for the Army Air Corps. He completed flight training and was commissioned a second lieutenant in December 1943. In 1944, his unit, the 487th Fighter Squadron of the 352nd Fighter Group (the "Blue Nosed Bastards"), crossed the Atlantic on the *Queen Mary*, landed in Scotland, and began operating out of northern England.

Moats' first mission was on June 10, 1944—four days after the D-day invasion. He was chasing one of the few German fighter planes operating over Normandy in his Mustang when he had a propeller failure and was forced to land on the dirt runway U.S. Army engineers had scratched out near the beach. Waiting for his plane to be repaired, he hitched a ride a few miles inland to see the fighting taking place among the hedgerows. He noticed bodies of many enemy soldiers laid out there, all of them with bullet holes in their foreheads. He asked a passing sergeant about it and got the enigmatic response, "They've been marked."

Back at the beach a day later, his plane was declared ready to fly. He took off and headed back to his base, but midway over the Channel oil erupted from the engine and covered his windshield. Unable to see where he was going, Moats radioed for help and two RAF Spitfires arrived, one on each of his wings, to guide him to a blind landing.

Moats got his first combat victory on July 18, a Ju 88 bomber over Rostock, northern Germany. He fired a burst into the plane's tail, taking out the gunner, and then shot out both of the engines, sending it cartwheeling down. Three days later he shared the kill of an Me 109 with George Preddy, who eventually became the leading Mustang Ace of the European theater with twenty-six kills.

Late in 1944, the 487th was sent to a small airfield in Belgium near the Ardennes Forest to support U.S. forces in the Battle of the Bulge. On Christmas Eve they landed on the steel-grilled runway that had been laid down by Army engineers. With the planes unable to fly for several days because of foul weather, Moats had time on his hands. He wanted a German helmet or some other war memento and

got some GIs to take him to the front in a jeep. With shells landing a quarter of a mile away, the vehicle flailed through the snow to the top of a hill where Moats had a surreal encounter with an infantryman standing there. "Where are the Germans?" he asked. The soldier pointed to a spot a few hundred feet away where a German officer was organizing perhaps eight hundred troops. "Why aren't you shooting at them?" Moats asked. "Why should I?" the GI answered, "They're not shooting at me." Moats smelled something sweet and asked about it. The soldier pointed at a nearby shack and said, "There's a cook over there making apple pies. Why don't you go get yourself one?" Moats got a pie and then left.

It was snowing heavily on New Year's Eve and Moats went to bed early, sleeping under several blankets on a cot in one of the tents set up in the forest for U.S. pilots. The next morning it was brutally cold but crystal clear. He went to the operations tent and joined the other flyers in toasting bread on top of a large potbellied stove. At first they were told that there would be no mission that day, but then they were ordered into their planes. Twelve Mustangs were sitting idling on the runway when the commanding officer suddenly said, "Let's go!" Some seventy Messerschmitt and Focke-Wulf fighters were heading their way in a last-ditch effort by the Luftwaffe to break U.S. air supremacy.

Just as Moats got his Mustang up, he was bracketed by tracer bullets from the guns of an attacking Me 109. The plane was going too fast and overshot him. As it did Moats fired a concentrated burst and the Messerschmitt hit the ground. He saw another Me 109 attacking a nearby marshaling yard and shot it down. Because of the large number of planes in the area, the action was fierce and concentrated, taking place at about two thousand feet right above the airfield. Moats got behind another Me 109 and opened fire. Both wings of the Messerschmitt flew off. Moats didn't know it at the time but his crew, who had worried over him for several dozen missions and shared vicariously in his victories, were cheering below as the German plane crashed. He got his fourth kill of the day a few minutes later.

Sandy Moats was in Paris when the war ended. He was surprised one day when he was informed that he had been selected to be part of a delegation of fifty servicemen who would travel back to the United States with Gen. Dwight Eisenhower. "Most were bird colonels," he later remembered, "and I was a lowly captain and the only fighter pilot among them." The entourage landed in Bermuda and was fitted out with new hand-tailored uniforms before continuing the trip to Washington for a dinner with President Truman and Gen. George Marshall, and then a ticker-tape parade down Fifth Avenue. Moats enjoyed himself, but the question of why he had been chosen for the delegation continued to nag. The answer finally dawned on him: it was because he, like Eisenhower, was from Kansas, and the general just wanted to have someone from his home state with him on this victory tour. ★

George P. Novotny

FIRST LIEUTENANT, USAAF

February 22, 1920–

SOME PILOTS IN WORLD WAR II FELT that their combat experiences, taking place high above the dramatic clash of armies, existed in a vacuum and that few Americans could know what they did or appreciate what they achieved. That was not the case for George Novotny, a P-47 Ace who flew in North Africa and Italy. Back home in Toledo, his girlfriend and future wife, Ruth Kleman, worked at an Autolite plant devoted to war production. Every time Novotny scored a kill, the plant manager would announce it over the intercom with a flourish—"Miss Kleman's boyfriend just got another victory!"—and all the other workers would set down their tools and break into enthusiastic applause.

Novotny's father was a Czech immigrant who came to America through the "golden doors" of Ellis Island at the turn of the century. The elder Novotny had a good job as a skilled carpenter working for the Toledo Shipbuilding Company and while he spoke Slovak around the house he encouraged his children (George was the fifth of eight) to make English their first language and think of themselves as American born and bred. He lost his good job during the Depression and was forced to accept relief, but he and George's mother kept their kids' focus on education and success.

George was a standout football player in high school, but he excelled at baseball, pitching three consecutive no-hitters in his senior year. After graduating in 1939, he played both sports for two and a half years at Toledo's De Sales College. He volunteered for the Army Air Forces right after the attack on Pearl Harbor and was sent to Maxwell Field in Alabama for his initial training. He requested assignment to fighters rather than bombers because, as his daughter Mary later said, "He was the sort of man who wanted to rely on his own abilities and control his own destiny."

Novotny got his wings in January 1943, and did advanced training in P-40s at Harding Field in Baton Rouge. He was assigned to the 54th Fighter

Alex McKnight/AM Photos Inc.

Group in May 1943 and took a roundabout route to North Africa, first heading to Brazil on a commercial TWA flight and from there to Casablanca, Morocco.

He took a few flights "just to get used to the terrain," as he wrote home. Then he was re-assigned to the 325th Fighter Group in Tunis. He was flying a P-40 when he got his first kill over Cagliari, Sardinia, on July 20, 1943—an Italian Macchi C.202 fighter ironically—as it later seemed—known as the Folgore, or "Thunderbolt." Then he downed a Messerschmitt Me 109 ten days later and another 109 on August 28.

Soon afterward, his squadron got P-47 Thunderbolts with the 325th's distinctive checkerboard design painted on their tails. The name Novotny gave his plane—"Ruthless Ruthie"—came from a pun: he was "Ruth-less," in the sense that he was without his fiancée, and also ruthless in his approach to combat. On November 21, Novotny flew cover with other P-47s for the transport carrying FDR to Tehran for a "Big Three" war strategy conference with Stalin and Churchill.

On January 30, 1944, after his squadron was transferred to Foggia in southern Italy, Novotny had what he later called "the biggest day in this pilot's combat career." With three other P-47s, he flew north along the coast at fifty feet above the waves to Villaorba. Novotny later recalled that "at the aerodrome there, I got behind a Ju 52 [trimotor transport] turning left. I opened fire and it hit the ground in flames. I circled and attacked another Ju 52 . . . and I saw this plane hit the ground and explode." At this point he saw an He 111 light bomber coming at him head-on. As he later said, "I fired and the plane fell to the ground in pieces."

It was the daring of the raid as much as the planes destroyed that led the members of the squadron to nickname Novotny and the three others "the Fearsome Foursome."

On March 18, Novotny shot down an Me 109 south of Fiume and on April 6, he got a highly regarded Italian Macchi C.205 Veltro "Greyhound" fighter in the same area. Soon after that he was sent home and, after marrying the namesake of his plane on July 1, 1944, he became a flight instructor, training, among others, flyers for the Free French Air Force.

The wartime career of "Ruthless Ruthie" took a somewhat bizarre turn after Novotny's return to the United States. The plane was given to a squadron of the famed Tuskegee Airmen operating in Italy. On May 29, 1944, one of the airmen, a pilot named Lloyd Hathcock, took off on what was supposed to be a flight ferrying the P-47 to a friendly airfield. But he made a navigational error and instead landed at the Rome Littorio airport, then still in German hands. Hathcock was sent to a POW camp and "Ruthless Ruthie" was seized, repainted in German markings and sent to the Zirkus Rosarius, the Luftwaffe's special unit tasked with testing captured Allied aircraft to understand their strengths and vulnerabilities.

George Novotny continued to wonder every so often about what finally happened to "Ruthless Ruthie" in the postwar years, as he attended the University of Michigan, worked for Capitol Airlines and TWA, and ended his career as assistant manager of Detroit Metro Airport. ★

Fred F. Ohr

MAJOR, USAAF

July 15, 1919–September 6, 2015

FRED OHR ALWAYS VIVIDLY REMEMBERED THE DAY in the middle of the Depression when he and his family, Korean immigrants originally named Wu, were working on their subsistence farm just outside Boise, Idaho, and he heard a sound overhead. He looked up and watched transfixed as a biplane flew by. He later admitted to his mother that he himself had the "impossible dream" of flying some day. "She told me that if the desire is great enough the dream will happen," he later recalled. He discounted her remark at the time but it was very much on his mind on the day in 1944 when he became the U.S. Army Air Forces' first Korean-American Ace.

While still in high school Ohr had repeatedly attempted to join the military, seeing it as a way to enlarge his possibilities in life. His ethnicity seemed to be a greater obstacle than the fact that he was underage. The Army rejected him without offering an explanation. When he tried the Navy a few months later, the response was more detailed, but also more disheartening. "The admiral is at sea right now," Ohr remembered the recruiter telling him, "and when he gets back to port I'll ask him if he needs another cabin boy."

When he graduated from high school in 1938 politicians were talking about reinstituting national conscription. Ohr joined the Idaho National Guard in the hope that this would protect him from the coming draft long enough to get through college. He was assigned to the 116th Cavalry Regiment and became a horse handler.

In early 1941, after Ohr had transferred to the U.S. Field Artillery and completed two years at the College of Idaho, one of his friends, about to take the Air Corps exam, begged Ohr to come with him and take it too to help steady his nerves. Ohr agreed and was shocked after completing the exam when a colonel in the recruitment center said to him, "Go home and get your personal effects in order because come September you'll be in flight training." Running out of the room for fear that the officer would change his mind, he

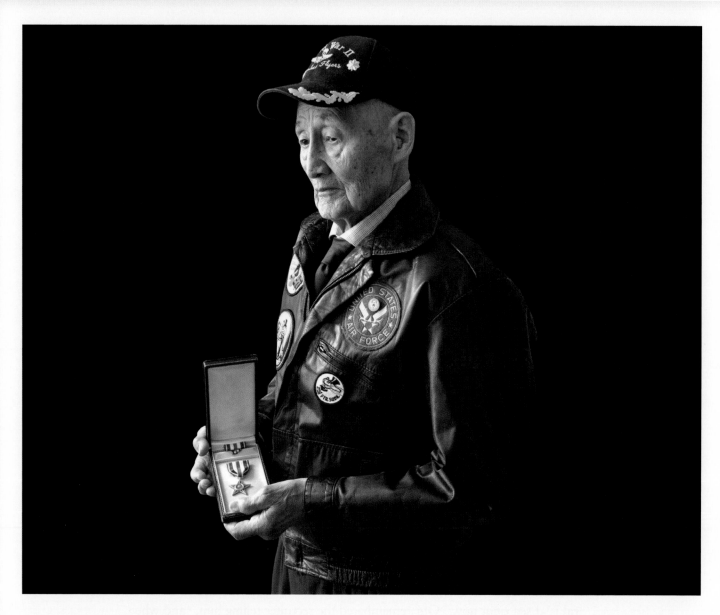

Peter Panayiotou/Panayiotou Photography

entered flight training in November 1941 and was commissioned a year later.

His training had not included fighters and when Ohr was first sent to North Africa early in 1943 he worked as a member of an air crew servicing planes. But there was a desperate shortage of pilots for the Spitfires the 2nd squadron was then flying. Ohr was told that he was being pressed into duty because of the manpower shortage and would be given three days to master a year's worth of knowledge, from battle tactics to combat formations. The

officer assigned as his instructor told him, "You have to develop a fighter pilot's mentality." Ohr looked at him and said, "What's that?" He soon came up with his own answer to the question: "If all else fails and you have nothing left, take the enemy down with you."

Ohr got his first kill flying a Spitfire on April 9, 1943—a German Ju 88 bomber he shot down over Kairouan in Tunisia. By then he was integrated into the squadron, occasionally experiencing bigotry because of his Korean ethnicity but always able to handle it deftly without playing the role of victim. He later told military historian James Oleson of an episode when his commanding officer took him aside with a grim look on his face. Ohr asked him what was wrong and the officer handed him a letter. As Ohr later recalled, "I got as far as the 'Subject'—Asian commissioned pilot Officer (yellow)—and gave the letter back and asked, 'Are they going to take my wings?'" The officer said he would "take action" if anyone tried. To dispel the gloom, Ohr replied, "Colonel, I'll tell you what. Tell them Freddy Ohr went on a *horrendous* mission and got so *scared* that he turned WHITE!" The colonel broke up in laughter and made sure that nothing ever came of the letter.

As the action got tougher, Ohr once got a laugh out of the other pilots by informing them that he had decided that from that time onward he would be a "kamikaze," going all out on every mission.

By the spring of 1944, North Africa was secured and the 2nd Squadron, now flying brand-new P-51 Mustangs, moved to Sicily and Corsica and turned its attention to Italy and eastern Europe. Ohr was always aware of how good the German pilots waiting for them were—some of them having been in air combat since the Spanish Civil War.

By July 9, Ohr, now a captain with four kills became an Ace when he downed a Messerschmitt Me 109 over Ploesti, Romania. He added a final kill on July 27.

He ended his service in November 1944 as commanding officer of the 2nd Squadron: "It was during my fourth tour when they told me I had to go home. I didn't want to. When I wasn't flying I felt I was missing something. I was addicted to the adrenaline. But they said I'd been there too long and had to go home."

Freddy (as all his friends called him) Ohr ended the war as a major. After leaving the Army Air Forces, he attended the University of California, Berkeley and Northwestern and became a successful dental surgeon. ★

Jeremiah J. O'Keefe Sr.

FIRST LIEUTENANT, USMC

July 12, 1923–

GROWING UP IN OCEAN SPRINGS, MISSISSIPPI, in the late 1920s, Jeremiah O'Keefe felt the strong pull of history. The town was the site of the first permanent French outpost in America, established in 1699. O'Keefe's grandfather had arrived there a century and a half later, fleeing the Irish potato famine, and had opened an undertaking business after the Civil War, becoming successful enough to establish the O'Keefes in a beautiful antebellum home. The family lost it at the beginning of the Depression. The day they were forced to leave Ocean Springs, Jeremiah, then nine years old, pledged to his sister that he would get the home back some day.

He was studying at the Soule Business School in New Orleans on December 7, 1941. The Japanese attack stunned him. ("I didn't even know where Pearl Harbor was," he later recalled.) He enlisted in the Navy the next day but, because of bureaucratic delays in processing so many new recruits, he was sent to a local junior college to take a Civilian Pilot Training Program course. After completing it he was called to active duty and earned his wings at the Pensacola Navy base in May 1943, at the age of nineteen, opting for Marine Corps rather than naval aviation in part because his father had been a Marine in World War I.

Initially assigned to multiengine aircraft, he and a handful of his friends who had suffered the same fate asked for help from Maj. Marion Carl, who was back in the United States after becoming the first Marine Ace in the early days of the war at Guadalcanal. As a result of the strings Carl pulled, O'Keefe was rerouted into fighter training at El Centro, California, where he joined Marine Fighter Squadron 323, known as the "Death Rattlers," and began training in the F4U Corsair.

VMF-323 shipped out for the Pacific in July 1944. After a lengthy stopover in Hawaii the squadron flew in missions over Guadalcanal, then Espiritu Santo. After U.S. forces seized Japan's Kadena air base on Okinawa early in

Andrew Achong/Andrew Achong Photography

April 1945, the Death Rattlers were stationed there to try to keep Japanese kamikazes from hitting U.S. ships. This battle was, as O'Keefe later said, "the only substantial action we were ever in."

Early on the morning of April 22, Easter Sunday, O'Keefe helped a Marine chaplain hold services and then took off in his Corsair as part of a four-plane patrol. They had been up for an hour without seeing anything when word came from the radar-equipped American picket ships below that a large number of aircraft were headed down from Japan. The Corsairs rushed to engage.

Spotting the U.S. planes, the swarm of Japanese "Vals" (the Allies' name for the Aichi D3 dive-bomber) dispersed to present more difficult targets. O'Keefe picked out one of the "bandits" and opened fire, watching it disintegrate. Then he saw six more kamikazes and went after them. As he commented later on, "It was my intention to shoot all of them down. I started with the leader. He left the formation and I decided I'd stay with him until I settled the matter."

Once he had the "Val" lined up, O'Keefe opened fire and the plane blew up. He turned to get back into the fight and saw that another enemy plane was coming right at him. He began firing but even though the "Val" was hit, its pilot kept coming, aiming for a collision. "He wanted to take me down with him," O'Keefe later recalled, "but I wasn't ready to go." His concentrated fire blew the kamikaze out of the sky.

He quickly rose to take out another "Val" whose pilot didn't see him coming. Running low on fuel and ammunition, he saw that one of the kamikazes had gotten through the American patrol and was heading toward the fleet. Pushing his Corsair to the limit, he got close enough to shoot the "Val" down with a final burst.

The executive officer of the squadron had six kills that day. The commanding officer got five and so did O'Keefe, becoming an "Ace in a day." *Time* magazine published a story about the battle under the headline, "One Deal, Three Aces."

A few days later, on April 28, O'Keefe was piloting one of twelve Corsairs participating in what he thought would be an uneventful patrol. But then he spotted five unidentified aircraft in the distance and got permission from his flight leader to investigate. Getting closer he saw that they were Ki-27 fighters U.S. intelligence referred to as "Nates." O'Keefe singled out the leader and opened fire, his shells ripping up the fuselage and cockpit. As that plane went down in flames, he rose to fire on another, sending it, too, spiraling into the ocean. These were his last kills.

Two months later Jerry O'Keefe came home to the United States. After the war he earned a degree at Loyola University, took over the family funeral business, and began an insurance company. He served one term in the Mississippi legislature and served as mayor of Biloxi for eight years. After he became a success, he made good on his promise and bought back the family home the O'Keefes had lost fifty years earlier. ★

Ralph S. Parr

COLONEL, USAF

July 1, 1924–December 7, 2012

REMINISCING ABOUT THE VARIOUS AIRCRAFT he had flown long after his days as a pilot were over, Ralph Parr once told interviewer Scott Huddleston of the San Antonio *Express-News,* "Well, I just enjoyed flying whatever plane I was sitting in." In combat, those planes included the P-38 Lightning in World War II, the F-86 Sabre jet in Korea, and the F-4 Phantom in Vietnam. In these three wars he flew a total of 641 combat missions and became a double Ace as well as one of the most decorated pilots in the U.S. military, the only person to have been awarded both the Distinguished Service Cross and the medal that replaced it, the Air Force Cross.

Parr thought of his love of flying as almost genetic and remembered the exact moment the romance began. "My father was an amazing aviator himself," he recalled. "When I turned five he asked me if I'd like to go up in a plane as a birthday present. I thought that was just the greatest thing."

"Hooked" by this experience, he was always looking skyward while growing up. His birthplace of Portsmouth, Virginia, was a Navy town because of the shipyards there, but when Parr turned eighteen in 1942 he enlisted in the Army Air Corps. Receiving his wings in February 1944, he was able to get to the Pacific for the last two months of the war, flying a P-38 with the 7th Fighter Squadron. He didn't see much combat, but he did fly over Hiroshima and Nagasaki after the atomic bomb attacks, and the sight of the smoking ruins of these cities left a deep impression.

After the war, he joined the Air Force Reserve and was able to get back on active duty before the Korean War broke out. He began his first tour shortly after North Korea invaded the South, flying the F-80, America's first generation jet fighter. After 165 missions that showed him, among other things, that the F-80 was no match for the Russian MiG-15s, he returned to the United States and honed his skills in the new F-86 Sabre, and was back in Korea for a second tour in May 1953.

Frank Olynyk

Flying an F-86 named "Vent de la Mort"—loosely, "Whisper of Death"—Parr got his first kill on June 7 in what was soon regarded in Air Force circles as one of the most harrowing dogfights of the war. The mission was simple, Parr later said: "Lure the MiGs into a fight and kill as many as possible." It was a good day for combat: the visibility twenty miles from the Yalu River was so good that "if you'd gotten higher up you could have seen Paris." When a flight of MiGs "bounced" the F-86s from nine o'clock, Parr drew a bead on one of them and got permission from his flight leader to go after it. The pilot of the MiG saw him coming and went straight down into a power dive. Parr followed, reaching a speed of over 670 miles an hour and grunting like a weightlifter to counter the g forces

as he pulled back hard on the stick to pull out at the treetops below.

"As I closed rapidly to about four thousand feet," Parr later said, "I noticed that there were two, there were four, no there were eight MiGs. Then off to my left I saw eight more." (Parr later remarked, "There were sixteen. I had them surrounded.") He set his sights on the leader of the group. The experienced pilot broke right and then left and "jinked" the plane expertly. Parr followed the MiG like a mirror image in a twisting ballet of maneuvers. At one point his Sabre was on its back, directly above the MiG and moving at exactly the same speed. "I looked down right into his canopy," Parr later said, "and I could see everything including the laces on his boots."

As the airborne pas de deux continued, with Parr matching and mirroring the other pilot's moves, it became a question of whether either of them would make a mistake. Suddenly the other pilot gave a little too much throttle and got slightly ahead of Parr who murmured to himself, "Friend, that's going to cost you." Now directly behind the MiG and so close that the F-86 was violently buffeted in its jet wash, Parr managed to get into firing position: "Then I let him have it." The MiG broke up and crashed.

But the battle wasn't over. Parr saw four of the remaining enemy planes diving on him. Three overshot him, one stayed momentarily on his tail. Parr rolled his plane so that the last MiG also overshot and then he came in behind and shot it down.

In eight minutes of intense combat that seemed to Parr like eight hours, he engaged sixteen MiGs, shot down two, and damaged a third. The engagement would become legendary among American pilots in Korea.

Over the next month and a half, with the war winding down, Parr got seven more kills over "MiG Alley." His tenth, making him a double Ace, came on July 27, just hours before the armistice, when he shot down a Russian Ilyushin IL-12 transport carrying officials to the diplomatic events in Panmunjom. The USSR, which, according to rumor, had several of its own officials on the plane, made the shoot-down into a diplomatic incident. Parr was not apologetic: "They were in the wrong place at the wrong time doing the wrong thing."

In 1967, Parr, now a colonel, returned to combat in an F-4 Phantom in Vietnam. In his first tour, he flew 226 missions with the 12th Tactical Fighter Wing (TFW). One of them occurred on March 16, 1968, over Khe Sanh, where Marines were under the guns of infiltrating North Vietnamese troops. Parr was escorting a C-130 transport attempting to resupply the Marines when it came under heavy ground fire. The Marine commander on the ground advised the transport to abort the mission, but Parr instead attacked the enemy mortar and artillery positions within two hundred meters of the American troops, making eight separate passes under heavy fire, neutralizing them and returning to base with twenty-seven hits in his Phantom. According to military historian Frank Olynyk, the Marines recommended Parr for the Medal of Honor, but the paperwork was lost, and after a long delay he instead received the Air Force Cross.

Ralph Parr came back for a second tour in Vietnam and flew another 201 missions as commanding officer of the 12th TFW. He retired from the Air Force in 1976. ★

Frederick R. Payne

BRIGADIER GENERAL, USMC

July 31, 1911–August 6, 2015

FREDERICK PAYNE, CALLED "FRITZ" by his fellow pilots, was ready for World War II long before America was, although he came to the military by a roundabout route.

Payne's father, a graduate of the Naval Academy who had participated in Commodore George Dewey's victory over the Spanish at Manila Bay and served as a naval officer in World War I, assumed that Frederick would follow in his footsteps. Frederick did attend the prestigious Culver Military Academy in Indiana and, after graduating in 1930, go on to Annapolis. But the nation was bogged down in the Depression and the role of the military seemed to be diminishing. Struck by wanderlust, Payne left the Naval Academy after two years and traveled west. After a year at San Diego State Teachers College, he transferred to the University of Arizona. By the time he earned a degree in 1935, Hitler had consolidated his dictatorship and was pouring money into his Luftwaffe. Seeing a war on the distant horizon that would likely involve his country, Payne tried to enlist as a flyer in the Navy. The Navy's cadet program was full, but his father was able to pull strings with the Marine Corps, which accepted Payne for pilot training in the summer of 1935.

He was almost twenty-four when he first soloed on July 1, 1935, at Floyd Bennett Field in New York, the setting later on for dramatic flights by aviators such as Wiley Post and Amelia Earhart. Howard Hughes took off and landed there on his record-setting circumnavigation of the globe in 1938.

After finishing advanced training at Pensacola, Payne got his wings in the fall of 1936, and began training in the F2A Buffalo, the first monoplane fighter equipped with a tailhook for carrier landings. When Pearl Harbor was attacked, he was serving with Marine Fighter Squadron 221, which left San Diego the next day, December 8, 1941, on board the USS *Saratoga*.

The *Saratoga* was diverted to reinforce the embattled Marines on Wake Island. When Wake fell, it returned to Pearl Harbor. Payne was made executive officer of a new squadron, VMF-212 (the "Hell Hounds"), which was

Marc Glassman/Marc Glassman Photography

based on a hastily constructed airstrip on the island of Efate and became the first Marine squadron to enter combat in the South Pacific.

The Battle of the Coral Sea in May 1942, and even more so the Battle of Midway a month later, slowed Japan's advance in the Pacific. The Solomon Islands, especially Guadalcanal, would serve as the first step for an American counteroffensive designed to deny Japan the bases it needed to enable its naval forces to dominate sea lanes and threaten U.S.-Australian supply lines.

On August 7, the Marines invaded Guadalcanal and occupied the airfield Japanese engineers had been building there, christening it Henderson Field in honor of Lofton Henderson, killed at the Battle of Midway, the first Marine pilot to die in the war. A month later VMF-212 arrived at Henderson, joining what became known as the "Cactus Air Force." ("Cactus" came from the Allied code word for Guadalcanal, not from the local vegetation.)

Payne and the other Marine pilots lived in primitive tents with mud floors in the middle of a marshy coconut plantation aptly nicknamed "Mosquito Grove." Tropical disease was a constant threat. So was enemy attack—by air, by sea, and on the ground. Henderson Field itself was a strip roughly cut out of the jungle, the dirt runway itself hit so frequently by Japanese artillery and naval fire that its potholes claimed as many U.S. planes as enemy action did. As Marines on the ground struggled to keep Japanese troops from retaking Henderson, the outnumbered Cactus Air Force, knowing that it had an opportunity to turn the tide of the war, slugged it out with Japanese aircraft in what at times seemed a dubious battle to protect the fragile U.S. handhold on Guadalcanal.

Several times a day, Payne and the other members of his squadron headed up in their F4F Wildcats to intercept the Japanese "Betty" bombers and their fighter escorts, which constantly attacked Henderson. On September 28, Payne had his first kill when he shared credit with another U.S. pilot for shooting down a "Betty" on a bombing run. On October 8, he got two more bombers. On October 21, he shot down a Zero and two days later downed another one, becoming an Ace.

His Wildcat often returned to base with a hemstitching of bullet holes in the wings and fuselage from clashes with enemy fighters. But Payne's only serious brush with death came not from the machine guns of Japanese Zeros, but from malaria. He had been ignoring the effects of the disease for weeks, but on one flight became desperately ill and vomited into his mask, blocking his oxygen supply and causing him to black out as the Wildcat spiraled downward. "When I came to," Payne later told journalist Denise Goolsby, "I was at about eight thousand feet and the plane was going down." He managed to get the Wildcat under control in time to level out and safely make it back to Henderson.

Payne was extracted from Guadalcanal in November 1942, and spent the next few months in combat in Kwajalein, Hollandia, Guam, and other battles. Then he was brought home to serve the rest of the war as commanding officer of Marine squadrons forming up to go into combat throughout the Pacific. After the war he served in Korea, and was a military liaison during U.S. nuclear testing in the mid-1950s. He retired from the Marine Corps as a brigadier general in 1958.

When Frederick Payne died at age one hundred and four on August 6, 2015, he was the oldest of America's surviving fighter Aces. ★

Steve N. Pisanos

PILOT OFFICER, RAF
COLONEL, USAF

November 10, 1919–June 6, 2016

AFTER MEETING STEVE PISANOS in London during World War II, newsman Walter Cronkite wrote: "His is a Horatio Alger story, set in the exciting world of flight and deadly duels above the clouds." Pisanos' story was all the more dramatic for beginning, unlike Horatio Alger's, in a foreign country under a different name with absolutely no expectation that America or heroic wartime adventures above the clouds would ever be part of it.

"Steve" was first Spyridon Pisanos, born in a suburb of Athens in 1919, one of six kids who grew up in a two-room house and shared an outdoor privy with a neighbor. A sense of the life he might make out of the life he was given came one morning when Pisanos was twelve years old and heard a buzzing sound in the sky while walking to school. He looked up and saw a biplane bearing the insignia of the Hellenic Air Force. In a flash he decided that he would someday become a pilot himself. From then on he skipped school to hang around the local aerodrome, eventually being allowed to help sweep the hangars and do odd jobs. Over the next few years, as he wrote later on in his autobiography *The Flying Greek*, he watched American movies like *Wings*, *Dawn Patrol*, and *Hell's Angels* when they were shown in Athens theaters, and decided that his impossible dream could be realized only if he managed to get to the United States.

At the age of eighteen, he signed on as a deckhand on a Greek freighter. When it docked in Baltimore he jumped ship with five dollars in his pocket and one English sentence: "Ticket for New York." He managed to get to Manhattan and found a job at a Greek bakery. Studying English in a Greek-English dictionary on the streetcar on the way to work, he haunted Floyd Bennett Airfield as he had the aerodrome in Athens. He paid five dollars out of his weekly fifteen-dollar salary for a flight lesson. The instructor who first took him up in a Piper Cub called him "Steve." Pisanos adopted it as his American name.

He received his pilot's license in 1941 as the Nazi armies were conquering Europe. He wanted to fly against the Luftwaffe. But America was still neutral and in any case as a non-citizen he wouldn't have been accepted by the Army Air Corps. He heard about an English group recruiting pilots for the RAF. He applied and was accepted, and after brief training in California traveled to Canada and then to England by ship and became part of the American Volunteer 71st RAF Eagle Squadron.

Pisanos had completed weeks of Spitfire missions over the English Channel when the United States entered the war and the Eagle Squadron became part of the Fourth Air Force. He was now flying P-47

Thunderbolts. Sometimes called the "Jug" because of its bulky body, the Thunderbolt could challenge the Messerschmitts at high altitudes. The more Pisanos flew it the better he liked it.

On May 3, 1943, Pisanos got a call from the U.S. ambassador's office in London offering him American citizenship. He was the first immigrant to be naturalized on foreign soil, one of the reasons Walter Cronkite, then a war correspondent working under Edward R. Murrow, interviewed him.

Flying escort for the "Big Friends"—B-17s hitting German positions all over the Continent—Pisanos' squadron went up almost every day. On May 21, he tangled with a Focke-Wulf 190, shooting up its cowling and sending it into a steep dive over Ghent. He was given a "probable," later raised to a kill based on the testimony of other U.S. pilots. On August 12 he brought down a Messerschmitt Me 109 over Holland.

Pisanos' squadron was assigned the upgraded P-51 Mustangs, whose greater range allowed them to escort bomber formations all the way to Berlin and back without having to break off midmission because of lack of fuel. On January 29, 1945, he brought down two Me 109s near the German city of Aachen. On March 5, he destroyed two more, becoming an Ace. But as he was returning to base after this mission, his plane was hit by flak near the French coast. His engine quit and he was forced to crash-land in farmland near Le Havre. It was at this point that what had been a combat story became a story of survival and resistance, described in detail by Pisanos in his autobiography.

Knocked unconscious in the crash, he came to fifty feet or so from the crumpled Mustang. Two German soldiers appeared in the field and began firing at him with their rifles. He sprinted toward a wooded area and managed to evade them. On the run for several days, he came to a French farmhouse and was taken in by the family living there. They managed to put him in contact with the French Resis-

tance, which shuttled him from one safe house to another over the next few weeks.

The usual escape route for downed Allied flyers was through Spain, but the Resistance deemed such a journey too difficult at this time. They arranged false identity papers for Pisanos, dressed him in peasant clothes, and assigned one of their female members to pose as his wife. She in turn got a baby from an orphanage to pose as their child, and they walked to Paris with other refugees.

By now the Allies had landed at Normandy and were moving west. Pisanos worked with the Resistance to harass the Nazis behind their lines, staging clandestine missions to blow up locomotives and derail trains, ambushing a German truck convoy, and machine-gunning German troops during the liberation of Paris.

After six months on the run, Pisanos was finally repatriated to his old unit. He expected to soon be back in combat with his friends, but his commanding officers forbade him from flying over the Continent for fear that if he was shot down again and captured, he might be tortured into revealing the Resistance networks he had worked with. He spent the rest of the war training pilots in England.

After the war, Steve Pisanos married and started a family. He flew as a commercial pilot with TWA for a couple of years, before reenlisting in the newly constituted U.S. Air Force. Before retiring as a colonel in 1974, he flight-tested new jet fighters, worked on the Air Force's guided missile program, flew in Vietnam, and served as military attaché to the Greek government when it adopted American fighter aircraft.

He always regarded as a second birthday that morning in 1940 when he impulsively jumped ship in Baltimore and first set foot in a new world. "My life is the American Dream," he says. "There is no other country in the world where someone like me could do what I've done." ⋆

Tilman E. Pool

LIEUTENANT, USN

December 24, 1923–

WITH THE DEPRESSION STILL WEIGHING heavily on Texas, Tilman Pool set aside thoughts of college and started work at a printing company two days after he graduated from high school in 1941. His father had recently suffered a stroke; Tilman felt he had to help his family. "I didn't feel sorry for myself," he later said. "Everyone around us was in the same boat, living day to day."

Pearl Harbor changed everything. Pool decided to volunteer for the service in mid-1942 because he knew that after his eighteenth birthday he would soon be drafted and because most of his friends, boys he had played basketball and baseball with while growing up in Houston, were enlisting. Carrying with him some of his home state's frontier attitudes, Pool decided that he wanted to go to war in a fighter plane, a Westerner's showdown weapon. He first tried to enlist in the Army Air Forces but was told that, because of the large numbers of volunteers, it would be at least six months before he could enter a flight class. So he went to the Navy, was accepted as a cadet, and entered V5 flight training three weeks later at Southwest Texas State Teachers College in San Marcos, Texas.

"Tilly," as the other men called him, was nineteen when he got his wings in November 1943. He flew Grumman F4F Wildcats during operational training at Sanford, Florida, then he was sent to the Great Lakes in February 1944 to qualify for carrier landings on board the USS *Wolverine*, the side-wheel steamer the Navy had refitted as a freshwater training carrier. He was then sent to Pearl Harbor flying the newer F6F Hellcat.

Two months later Pool was in the Marshall Islands as part of VF-39, a land-based squadron engaged in bombing missions against the Japanese islands. "The living conditions were terrible," he said later on. "We discovered what all land-based Navy units knew—that you suffer when you're far away from naval supply lines."

In September, he was rotated back home for a month and then reassigned to VF-17, which was sent to the USS *Hornet* in time to take part in the first carrier strikes on the Japanese mainland—Tokyo and the Yokohama Naval Base. Soon after, Pool was flying close ground support missions against the dug-in Japanese infantry as part of the U.S. invasion of Iwo Jima. He remembers flying low enough to see a Marine pilot radio director on the ground close to the targets, marking them with fluorescent cloth activated by sunlight. They were readily visible from above as Pool and the other Hellcats swooped low to hit the dug-out caves and caverns with their bombs and strafing.

On March 18, Pool was part of an eight-plane attack against Kanoya Air Base (from which more than half of all kamikaze attacks were launched). As he recovered from his strafing run a large number of Zeros dove down on him and the other Hellcats. During the swirling twenty-minute dogfight that followed, Pool shot down one enemy fighter and had another probable. Hand signaling his flight leader that he was low on fuel, he started to head back to the *Hornet*. A Zero followed and Pool quickly shot it down before running out of ammunition. Coming up alongside the Zero as it started to roll down into the water below, he saw the pilot slumped down in the cockpit.

The following day, after a mission striking enemy shipping, Pool's flight was told that U.S. radar had spotted a large number of enemy planes near Hiroshima. When he got there he began to target a Zero, but a Marine pilot got it before he could open fire. Then he looked down and saw a "Frank" (the Allied reporting term for the Nakajima Ki-84) below him being chased by four Hellcats. Like other U.S. pilots he considered this the enemy's best fighter plane and believed that the Japanese assigned their best pilots to fly it. He watched the Hellcats attempt to close on it without success and thought that it had escaped. But then the "Frank" unaccountably made a hard left turn that brought it near Pool, who dove down and opened fire. As the enemy plane burst into flames about one hundred feet above the ground, the pilot bailed out, almost immediately hitting a tree below. Pool later learned that the pilot, who survived the fall, was a sixteen-kill Ace who had shot down two Hellcats earlier that day.

On April 7, the *Hornet* was part of a U.S. force searching for the *Yamato*, Japan's premium battleship and the largest warship yet constructed. Armed with 1,000-pound bombs, Pool's squadron went up to locate the biggest naval prize of the war. Breaking down through thick cloud cover, he finally saw it, "this thing that looks to me like an island." Too low to dive bomb, he and the other Hellcats had to do a more gradual "glide bomb." As the *Yamato* engaged in violent evasive maneuvers, Pool saw his bomb hit the water right next to a Japanese cruiser and dam-age the rudder. Successive waves of U.S. carrier-based planes finished off the huge ship.

Five days later, Pool and three other Hellcats were on patrol to intercept any enemy planes headed toward Okinawa. One of the Hellcats developed engine trouble. Following protocol, another escorted it back to the *Hornet*. With his wingman, Pool headed toward an area where U.S. radar picket ships below said an air battle was going on. He looked up and saw eight planes coming down from above. At first he thought they were Navy because they were flying in the U.S. "four finger" formation, "but then I saw the red 'meat ball' on the fuselages and realized they were enemy. I turned hard right and got on the leader and kept getting rounds into him as he hit the sea." Another of the "Franks" got on Pool's tail, but his wingman shot it down. The six remaining "Franks" battled with the two Americans in a dizzying series of turns and "snap shots" until other U.S. planes appeared and the enemy withdrew.

On the way back to the *Hornet*, Pool and his wingman jumped three Zeros. One of them came close enough to hit the tail wheel of Pool's Hellcat; he shot it down. It was his sixth and final kill.

By mid-summer 1945 Tilman Pool was back home, driving through Louisiana on his way from the West Coast to reassignment at the Navy Air Base in Pensacola, when he heard over his car radio that Japan had surrendered. He left active duty in the Navy in July 1947. ⋆

Ralston M. Pound

COMMANDER, USNR

December 31, 1920–

WHEN HE WAS A TEENAGER, RALSTON POUND fell in with a crowd of boys who got a reputation as troublemakers in his hometown of Charlotte, North Carolina. Although the Pound family was hit hard by the Depression—Ralston remembers his father, owner of a small supply store, walking four miles to work and back from their home on the outskirts of town every day to save money on gas—they scraped together the money to send him away to a West Virginia military school. Rather than seeing it as exile or punishment, Pound actually enjoyed the sense of discipline the school provided and felt that it helped him get "straightened out."

By 1939, Pound was enrolled in North Carolina State College. He studied engineering, but actually studied flying more intensively as a result of having entered the school's Civilian Pilot Training Program and receiving a pilot's license. Many in the United States may have believed that the country could avoid involvement in the wars spreading through Europe and Asia, but Pound had a different view because of the steady presence of military recruiters on the college campus. He listened to presentations by recruiters for the Army Air Corps, but decided to enter naval aviation in the summer of 1941, one year away from graduation.

Pound had begun his training at the naval air station in Atlanta when Pearl Harbor was attacked. In the spring of 1942, he was sent to Opa-Locka, near Miami, for fighter training, and received his wings there on September 2, 1942. After advanced training at Cecil Field, in Jacksonville, Florida, he was sent to Naval Air Station Norfolk for carrier qualification in the F4F Wildcat.

Pound was assigned to VF-16, continuing training while the USS *Lexington* was in the final stages of construction. (It was supposed to have been the USS *Cabot* when its keel was laid in 1940, but was renamed the *Lexington* when the carrier bearing that name was sunk in the 1942 Battle of the Coral Sea.) Now flying the F6F Hellcat, Pound was on board the new ship when

David Jaffe/Lift-Off Studios

it made its shakedown cruise in the Caribbean and then headed for Pearl Harbor through the Panama Canal in June 1943.

The *Lexington* had supported the U.S. landings in the Gilbert Islands and raided Japanese shipping at Kwajalein Atoll when Pound took off on the morning of December 4, 1943. Many thoughts were swirling in his mind, chief among them "not getting shot down." His flight encountered the enemy over Truk Lagoon and he immediately shot down a Zero and then, fifteen minutes later, spotted a Mitsubishi A6M3 carrier-based fighter known by the Allies as the "Hamp." He set it on fire with a quick burst and watched it fall into the ocean.

That night, Pound was savoring his victories when a huge explosion rocked the *Lexington*. It had been hit by a Japanese torpedo and had to limp back to Pearl Harbor, where VF-16 put ashore, and the carrier continued on to the Bremerton, Washington, shipyards.

While the Lexington was being repaired, Pound volunteered to serve in a squadron on the USS *Essex*. He was annoyed because as a newcomer he was not assigned to "the good missions" where there would be a likelihood of combat. Instead he was relegated to flying "around and around in circles at 25,000 feet on patrol above the fleet."

When the *Lexington* returned to service in March 1944, Pound was back on board as part of VF-16 and once again in combat situations. On April 29, he shot down three Zeros in quick succession during further strikes on Truk and became an Ace.

In June, as the *Lexington* supported the invasion of the Marianas, Pound was at eight thousand feet, starting a strafing run on Japanese planes still on the ground, when he saw his flight leader's plane hit by an antiaircraft shell. "It just disintegrated in a ball of fire," he later said. "There was nothing left of it or him."

Pound got his last kill, a Japanese "Judy" dive-bomber, on June 19. When he did the balance sheet he was proud of his six kills, but he had also lost a roommate during the past year, and several close friends on the *Lexington*.

His tour completed, Pound returned to the United States in late July 1944 and was assigned to the naval air station in Sanford, Florida, for refresher training. Early in 1945, he was assigned to the newly constructed USS *Lake Champlain*, which, after its shakedown cruise to Guantanamo Bay in May, was preparing to head back to the Pacific when the Japanese surrendered.

Released from the Navy in September 1945, Ralston Pound returned to Charlotte to join his father's office supply business, eventually becoming its president. He joined the Naval Reserve, retiring as a commander in 1969. ★

Luther D. Prater

CAPTAIN, USN

October 9, 1921–

EARLY ON THE MORNING OF DECEMBER 7, 1941, "Del" (from his middle name Delano) Prater was in the air as a passenger in a friend's plane. It was his first flight and he was thrilled—until they landed and found out that Japan had just attacked Pearl Harbor.

He had grown up in Bonanza, Kentucky, which he later described as "a crossroads town with a grocery store and a high school, and that was about it." He graduated from that high school in 1937 and then from the University of Kentucky in 1941. He planned on going to law school, but an academic adviser urged him to wait until the turbulent situation in Europe became clearer. Instead he decided to create a holding pattern by enrolling in graduate school for a year to study public administration. After his first flight on the "day of infamy," he also decided to get a private pilot's license and was ready when a Navy recruiting team looking for aviators showed up at the university looking for recruits in the spring of 1942. He took the Navy physical and was told to finish his graduate school year and report in July.

At six foot two, Prater would have been tall for the Army Air Corps, but the Navy's Wildcat and later the Hellcat were a bit more spacious than AAC planes. He got his wings in May 1943 at Pensacola and then did advanced training at Naval Air Station Opa-Locka. After practicing carrier landings at the Great Lakes, he was ordered to San Diego and then to Los Alamitos to join VF-19 being formed there.

By August 1, 1943, VF-19 was on board the USS *Lexington*. Prater's first mission, a strafing run over Guam, was a sobering one when the squadron suffered the loss of two pilots. The melancholy turned to elation three days later when Prater shared the kill of a Zero, the first victory scored by VF-19, after climbing from a strafing run against an enemy airfield: "I looked up and there was this big object right above and there was this big red ball on its side. We all tried to maneuver to get a shot at it. Another pilot and I got the best position. We both started firing and it caught fire and the pilot just bailed out!"

Prater didn't get another victory until October 10, when he got a "Judy" dive-bomber near Okinawa. Two days later, he had his biggest day in an engagement near Formosa when he shot down a Ki-27 "Nate" fighter, a Zero, and a Ki-43 "Oscar" fighter. In the second of these three kills, the Japanese pilot came at Prater head-on. Both planes opened fire. For a moment it seemed like a game of "chicken," with neither pilot changing course. But then the Zero began smoking; it exploded very close to him and Prater felt lucky to escape its debris.

After this dogfighting melee he and his squadron leader went looking for targets to strafe. They saw a grass field with parked enemy planes and dove on it. The squadron leader either blacked out when pulling up or was hit by ground fire; his plane crashed.

Prater's three kills that day made him an Ace, but he had lost a friend.

Prater had 7.5 kills on November 5, when he got his final victory—a Zero that blundered into his path while he was leading his section on a combat air patrol. A little more than a month later he was ordered home.

In the spring of 1945, he transitioned to the Corsair and assigned to a new air group being formed, consisting of fighters and dive-bombers, for "something big." After training in Santa Rosa, California, and Hawaii, the group was waiting to be put on a carrier when the atomic bomb was dropped on Hiroshima. Prater later learned that the "something big" was to have been supporting a ground invasion of Japan.

The Navy put the Navy Cross, Silver Star, and Distinguished Flying Cross Del Prater had been awarded into the formula that allowed him to get early release in mid-September. He decided to stay in Southern California and enter the stock brokerage business. He retired from the Naval Reserve in 1969 as a captain. ★

Donald L. Quigley

LIEUTENANT COLONEL, USAAFR

December 28, 1919–

DONALD QUIGLEY WAS TWENTY YEARS OLD and operating an engraving machine in his hometown of Marion, Pennsylvania, in the summer of 1940 when the Battle of Britain was taking place. His imagination was galvanized by newsreels of pilots scrambling to their Spitfires and taking off from grassy fields to do battle with swarms of German fighters. These dramatic images made him decide to volunteer for the Army Air Corps in the spring of 1941 and become a fighter pilot himself.

Graduating from flight school a few days after Pearl Harbor, "Quig" as the other cadets called him, was assigned to the 75th Fighter Squadron. It had been formed from the remnants of the disbanded American Volunteer Group—the "Flying Tigers"—that had flown under the leadership of the legendary Claire Chennault for the Chinese government after it was attacked by the Japanese. Now in the Army Air Forces, Chennault commanded the 75th and two other squadrons filled with former Flying Tigers pilots, all of them still flying P-40 Warhawks with the iconic shark mouth painted on their noses. Quigley named his plane "Rene the Queen" in honor of his wife Irene. Donald Lopez, a future assistant director of the Smithsonian's Air and Space museum who also served in the 75th, later wrote of him: "He was about 5'8", dapper, with a trim mustache and looked the way we thought a fighter pilot should—something like David Niven in *Dawn Patrol*."

The 75th sailed for India in May 1943 and by the fall was flying missions from bases there, supporting Allied ground forces battling the Japanese in northern Burma. There was relatively little air combat. Most missions involved strafing and fragmentation-bomb attacks on enemy shipping off the Burma coast and on its inland waterways; these attacks usually ended with Japanese sailors and ships blown to bits, and the water, Quigley always remembered, red with blood.

Todd A. Yarrington/Yarrington Studio

Early in 1944 the 75th was transferred to south-eastern China and began to engage Japanese aircraft on an almost daily basis. By June, Quigley had scored two "probable" kills in combat against Ki-43 "Oscar" fighters. Now a major, he was given command of the squadron in July. His first outright victory came on July 5, when his flight of ten P-40s was escorting twelve B-25s on a bombing run over Changsha in Hunan Province. Quigley spotted six "Oscars" on the horizon and ordered his flight to go after them. He shot one down immediately.

Twelve days later he got another—a rookie pilot, he believed, because he had forgotten to drop his tanks as the engagement began. On July 28 he shot down a "Hamp," the name American intelligence had given the updated version of the Zero. On August 4 he shot down a "Val" dive-bomber, and got another the next day.

Quigley was now an Ace whose 177 missions made him eligible to come home. On August 10, he was leading a flight on a mission to attack a large concentration of enemy troops along the Xiang River near Hengyang. He was on his third strafing run when his plane shuddered from a hit by ground fire and burst into flames. He was close to the ground and briefly thought about trying to make a crash landing, but his cockpit quickly filled with smoke, blinding him. "I'm getting out of this plane," he murmured to himself and made a low-altitude bailout. The other pilots in his flight assumed that he hadn't made it, but his parachute just barely managed to open before he hit the ground.

Disoriented, Quigley cleared his head and then raced toward a dried-up rice paddy, hoping to hide in the tall weeds until nightfall. But he was soon surrounded and captured by enemy soldiers, who roughed him up with gun butts. He thought he would be shot but, as he later learned, Japanese intelligence wanted downed American flyers for interrogation.

He would be imprisoned for the next thirteen months, at first alone in a five foot by five foot cell with just enough space to lie down corner to corner, and then with eleven other U.S. fighter and bomber pilots. This group called itself "the Diddled Dozen" because it was moved from place to place, seemingly without any chance of repatriation or of being put in a regular POW facility. Housed first in an underground bunker in Shanghai, they were sent in a boxcar to Peking, then to Pusan, Korea, and then to the Japanese mainland as the war was coming to an end. During their more than a year of captivity, the Dozen were ragged, lice-infested, and always hungry. (Quigley's children remember him reproaching them when they ridiculed prisoners in war movies for using rats for food: "You have no idea what you'll eat when you're starving.")

Their last prison was at a small airfield near Sapporo, where they were housed when Hiroshima and Nagasaki were bombed. More than a month later, on September 11, they were finally informed by a Japanese officer that the war was over. Then, in an almost comic scene, they were taken to a former ice cream factory that had been started up again and given some ice cream. Soon after, some Americans arrived and took them to an airfield where a transport plane was waiting to take them to a U.S. Army base.

Donald Quigley thought about making the military a career, but decided that "old pilots like me were a dime a dozen." He retired as a lieutenant colonel, returned to his hometown of Marion, and started a successful engraving business of his own, where he worked for the next sixty years. ★

Alden P. Rigby

MAJOR, USAF

January 4, 1923–May 3, 2015

GROWING UP IN FAIRVIEW, UTAH, one of ten children in a devout Mormon family, Alden Rigby conceived of a blueprint for his life while still a teenager. He would go to college after completing high school, marry his childhood sweetheart Eleen, and eventually return to work on the family farm after completing his Mormon mission. He was an eighteen-year-old freshman at Brigham Young University on the first step toward the realization of this dream when the Japanese attacked Pearl Harbor. He accepted a different kind of mission—that of a fighter pilot flying a P-51 Mustang in the air battle over Europe.

Unlike others he served with in the war, Rigby had not been swept up in the romance of flight as a boy. When he went to Fort Douglas, Utah, to enlist early in 1943, he was given the choice between paratrooper and aviation cadet. "I'd never been in an aircraft," he recalled, "but I thought that would be the lesser of two evils."

Because of his success as a cadet, Rigby became a stateside flight instructor in P-51s for several months after getting his wings. Then, just after D-day, he shipped out for Bodney, England, as a member of the 487th Fighter Squadron of the 352nd Fighter Group, which would become known by the Luftwaffe as "the Blue Nosed Bastards of Bodney" because of the distinctive blue markings on the noses of their Mustangs.

Rigby had the names of his wife and baby daughter—"Eleen and Jerry"—painted on the fuselage of his Mustang, and a large "R" on the tail. He began combat missions across the Channel into Europe, where the Germans were now in retreat. He wrote home faithfully at least once a day, although Eleen would sometimes go more than a week without hearing from him and then get a windfall of seven or eight letters all at once. Their bond was strengthened by the distance between them and the dangers he faced. "I often told my wife that I had more to live and fight for than anyone," Rigby later said. "I knew that she was going with me on every mission."

August Miller/August Miller Photo LLC

His first kill came on November 27, 1944. His squadron's Mustangs were allowed to go after targets of opportunity while they were on their way back to base after escorting U.S. bombers to their targets in Germany. Rigby had made three strafing passes on an enemy installation, and had pulled up to four thousand feet to get ready for another run, when he saw a Messerschmitt Me 109 rising up from below. As Rigby opened fire the German pilot headed for a cloud. As Rigby later said: "This cloud was not very big [and] . . . when he came out of it, I fired a few more [rounds]. Off came the canopy and out comes the pilot." Rigby circled the parachute of the descending German for two or three thousand feet: "Either he was waving at me or shaking his fist. . . . When he lands I just waggle my wings as a salute to him and go back to England."

His day in the sun came a little more than a month later on a cloudy New Year's Day, 1945. His squadron had been ordered to Y-29, the name given to a small field near Asch, Belgium, where their mission was to support U.S. troops desperately trying to blunt the surprise German offensive in the Battle of the Bulge. The Army Corps of Engineers had cleared the area and laid down steel planking as an airstrip. There was thick forest behind and in front of the field. There were already fifty or so P-47s stationed at Y-29 when the Mustangs arrived.

The U.S. planes were socked in by thick fog and unable to fly for over a week. Finally, on the morning of January 1, Rigby and about a dozen others were in their Mustangs idling on the makeshift runway while their officers tried to convince Air Force brass that they should be allowed to take off, despite continuing bad weather, on what they thought would be a mission escorting U.S. bombers to Berlin. None of the Americans knew that the German High Command, as part of their last-ditch offensive, had withdrawn some 1,200 aircraft from the eastern front to strike Allied bases in the Netherlands, France, and Belgium, and that a large force of these planes was headed their way.

Rigby was fourth in line for takeoff when U.S. antiaircraft guns suddenly opened fire all around him. He looked up and saw fifty or sixty Focke-Wulf Fw 190s about to dive down on the base. "There we are, on the ground, and we know they're going to take us out," he later recalled. "We figured we had little or no chance to survive this attack."

Not waiting for the green go-light from the makeshift U.S. control tower, the P-51 pilots rammed their throttles forward. Hit by waves of prop wash from the planes in front of him, Rigby struggled to control his Mustang. He and the others managed to get airborne only because a group of eight P-47s had taken off moments earlier from a parallel strip and was breaking up the German formations.

Only four hundred feet above the ground, Rigby saw that an Fw 190 was on the tail of his flight leader. He shouted over the radio, "Break left!" When the Mustang veered, Rigby opened fire on the Fw 190. As he later said, "I saw that plane light up all the way from its nose to its tail. I could see the flashes of the armor-piercing bullets striking metal."

As the Focke-Wulf hit the ground, Rigby saw another below him at treetop level. As he lined up on it, he realized that his gun sight was no longer operating. Not able to aim, he sprayed the plane with a long burst and it went down. Then he looked up and saw a U.S. P-47 with a wing on fire trying to hold off a Focke-Wulf coming in for the kill. Rigby climbed steeply, came between the two planes, and knocked the Fw 190 out of the sky with another long burst.

He believed that he was out of ammunition, but the fight was still going on and he stayed in the middle of it. He saw a Focke-Wulf in a dogfight with two Mustangs and headed toward it. When the Fw 190 came by him, Rigby pressed his trigger and his last few bullets shattered the enemy's cockpit.

When the remaining German planes left the scene and the Mustangs landed, the score was twenty-four Fw 190s downed with no U.S. losses. After flying a second mission that afternoon, Rigby and the others returned to be greeted by Gen. Jimmy Doolittle who had heard about what was already being called "the Miracle of Y-29."

Because two other Mustangs had also been engaged against the last Fw 190, Rigby did not claim credit for the kill. But in 2000, after reviewing Eighth Air Force records of the battle over Y-29, the American Fighter Aces Victory Confirmation Board awarded him the victory, making him the last Ace of World War II. But for Rigby, an even better honor was the letter he received about the same time from the son of the P-47 pilot (dead now) he had saved during the fight. The son wanted Rigby to know that he and his nine brothers and sisters, and their twenty-eight children, all owed their lives to him. ⋆

R. Stephen Ritchie

BRIGADIER GENERAL, USAFR

June 25, 1942–

STEVE RITCHIE NEVER FORGOT THE FIRST TIME he was targeted by Russian surface-to-air missiles (SAMs). It was April 16, 1972, on his first mission to Hanoi. Three SAMs, accelerating to 1,600 miles per hour, came between Ritchie and his wingman at approximately one hundred feet, but failed to detonate (they were supposed to be lethal at 150 feet). Ritchie later told the story many times and always ended with: "Thank goodness for that Soviet quality control!"

Ritchie's hard-charging competitiveness was evident as a boy growing up in North Carolina. He played all sports and was a star quarterback in high school. He was not recruited for Air Force Academy football, but made the roster as a walk-on and became a starting halfback for the Falcons in 1962–63, displaying on the gridiron the "intelligent aggression" one writer would later see as the hallmark of his combat career.

Ritchie graduated first in his pilot class and was one of a handful to fly the F-104 as a second lieutenant. He volunteered for Vietnam in 1968 and flew the first F-4 Fast Forward Air Controller (FAC) mission. The Fast FAC Program was started by famed pilot George "Bud" Day in 1967, flying F-100s, and proved to be one of the most successful missions in the Southeast Asian conflict. Circling at dangerously low altitudes, FAC aircraft marked targets, called in strikes, and determined their effectiveness.

During one of his missions, Ritchie located some enemy supplies along the Ho Chi Minh Trail. When none of the aircraft he called in for strikes was able to destroy the cache of matériel, he decided to attack it himself (breaking the very rules he had written). Diving out of the sun in the hope that enemy gunners would be blinded, he was about to open fire on a strafing run when his F-4 bolted wildly as the right engine was destroyed. After he made it back to Da Nang on one engine it was discovered that a 37-mm shell had passed directly into the intake on the other engine and exited, miraculously without exploding. Ritchie never forgot his thousand-to-one survival miracle.

In 1969, Ritchie was assigned to the Air Force Fighter Weapons School at Nellis Air Force Base, where he introduced the Fast FAC mission to the school's curriculum and taught the initial cadre of instructors. A generation later, Lt. Col. Mark Welsh (a future Air Force chief of staff), Lt. Col. Terry Adams, and others implemented the Fast FAC mission using the F-16 in the first Gulf War with a program called "Killer Scout."

In 1972, Ritchie volunteered again for Vietnam. On May 10, he was number three in a flight of F-4s, led by his Air Force Academy classmate and friend, Maj. Bob Lodge, who was on his third combat tour. Having planned this special mission for weeks, Lodge proceeded inbound to Hanoi at treetop level below enemy radar, and contacted four MiG-21s. Lodge and his wingman fired their missiles head-on at approximately seven miles, getting two kills. Meanwhile, Ritchie made visual contact with the third MiG and wrenched his F-4D Phantom to gain an inside advantage. Like a quarterback leading his receiver, he fired two Sparrows. The second missile detonated under the MiG and its pilot bailed out.

But this moment of triumph turned to tragedy as Lodge became "target fixated" behind the fourth MiG and failed to heed warnings that two MiG-19s were on his tail. They shot down the big Phantom with 30-mm fire. Roger Locker, the plane's weapon systems officer, bailed out. But Lodge had told Ritchie and others that he would never eject, because of his special access to classified information, and went in with the plane.

On May 31, Ritchie was reminded of the unpredictability of the Sparrow missile. "We were in a left turn east of Hanoi when I fired four missiles at a MiG-21," he recalls. The first three malfunctioned, but luckily the last one hit the MiG hard enough to blow the canopy and entire front end off the aircraft."

On July 8 Ritchie launched on what he later called "the most exciting air-to-air mission I ever flew . . . when I drew on all my life experiences. All the training, education, teamwork, discipline, and practice came together in an instant in time."

This intense experience began when another F-4 had been hit by MiGs and its pilot, separated from his flight, radioed his position as he limped back to base. Knowing there was a "cripple" flying alone, the North Vietnamese dispatched two MiG-21s to take it out. As Ritchie sprinted to cover the wounded F-4 he was vectored to within two miles of the MiGs by DISCO (call sign of the RC-121 early warning aircraft with special radar and intelligence capabilities). Spotting the lead MiG at ten o'clock, he turned left in full afterburner to pass it head-on, then executed a six g slicing turn and a barrel roll to come up behind the second MiG. He downed it with two Sparrows, and then, flying through the debris and ignoring the battle damage it caused, he maneuvered hard to achieve a four o'clock position on the lead MiG. Knowing that he was beyond maximum angle off, inside minimum range, and pulling too many g's, he nonetheless locked on the radar from the front cockpit and fired. As the missile seemed to veer off course to the left, Ritchie was shouting: "Come right! Hard right!" As if the Sparrow had received his frantic instructions, it suddenly made a near 90-degree turn, "splashing" the MiG dead center in the fuselage.

On August 28, Ritchie's flight was headed home from a mission over Haiphong when DISCO warned of two MiG 21s "Blue Bandits" returning to Hanoi. Ritchie realized that he was on course to intercept. Soon his weapons officer saw the "Bandits" ahead at 25,000 feet and secured a radar lock. Ritchie initiated a climbing turn and fired two missiles with no luck. Now trailing the MiGs, he launched two more Sparrows. The first missed, but the second—his fourth and last—scored a direct hit.

There was a huge celebration at the Udorn Air Base Club that night for the first Air Force Ace in Vietnam. No one knew it that evening, but because of how the nature of air warfare would change in the future, Ritchie would probably be the last U.S. fighter pilot Ace.

Stephen Ritchie later transferred to the Air Force Reserve, continuing to fly jets at air shows as a part of the Air Force recruiting program. On January 29, 1999, after flying a T-38 demonstration, he was retired in his "g-suit" on the Randolph Air Force Base Flight Line by one of his former students at the Fighter Weapons School, Gen. Mike Ryan, the Air Force chief of staff. ★

LeRoy W. Robinson

COMMANDER, USNR
December 13, 1923–March 27, 2016

LEROY ROBINSON SOMETIMES JOKED that he was surprised that his parents hadn't named him "Last," because they always made a point of saying that he was the last of their eight children. The first was his brother Richard, whom LeRoy idolized while they were growing up in the small town of Prosperity, South Carolina. Richard graduated from the Naval Academy in Annapolis, became a naval officer, and was serving on board a destroyer, the USS *Downes*, when it was badly damaged during the Japanese attack on Pearl Harbor, although Richard himself survived. LeRoy volunteered for naval aviation shortly afterward because of his big brother.

Robinson received his wings at Pensacola on October 1, 1943. By a cruel twist of fate, his brother Richard decided to leave shipboard duty and become a naval pilot because LeRoy was so enamored of flight. After completing his own aviation training, Richard was assigned to pilot PBY flying boats and was killed in action in the Pacific in 1944.

LeRoy Robinson joined VF-2 on board the recently commissioned USS *Hornet* in May 1944. As part of Task Force 58, the carrier supported U.S. forces as they attacked Saipan in mid-June, trying to secure the island as a strategic point from which the new B-29 bombers could attack the Japanese mainland. And then a week later the *Hornet* became part of the pivotal Battle of the Philippine Sea.

Like the other F6F Hellcat pilots, Robinson was given a .38 six-shooter to wear in a shoulder harness. Before takeoff he inventoried the backpack containing his survival gear. It held a variety of items. He understood the food, morphine, and water. But why, he asked the more experienced pilots, was there a lasso in the backpack? The answer: to throw over the periscope of a possible rescue submarine surfacing to help a downed pilot. Robinson was skeptical until a member of his squadron, shot down over the water, used his lasso to hook on to a sub that then reeled him in.

John Slemp/Aerographs Aviation Photography

Robinson got his first kill on June 11 near Guam. He was skimming the water looking for another Hellcat pilot who had gone down when he saw another plane behind him. Because it was painted brown, Robinson's first thought was, "What's the Army doing out here in Navy territory?" Then he looked closer and saw the "red meatball" on the plane's fuselage and realized that it was a Japanese

Zero. The fighter was coming fast and passed beneath Robinson to avoid a collision. After turning, it reappeared in front of him; he fired a short burst and "splashed" the Zero.

On June 19 he was in the air taking part in the Great Marianas Turkey Shoot. Robinson shot down two more Zeros that day. But even though the battle became a great victory for American forces, his abiding memory of the aerial action was of utter chaos at close quarters. At times he saw Zeros shooting at other Zeros and Hellcats shooting at other Hellcats.

A week later, on June 19, Robinson became an Ace when he shot down two "Kate" torpedo bombers that were part of an enemy attack against Task Force 58. Before the second one went down its rear-seat gunner scored solid hits on the engine of Robinson's Hellcat and set it on fire. As he later said, "I had no intention of bailing out. I regarded my parachute not as something to use but as something to sit on because I was a little short for a pilot."

Hot oil was pouring out of the engine onto his windshield when he maneuvered for a landing on the *Hornet*. Unable to see, Robinson opened the cockpit. Then the oil sprayed on his goggles. When he lifted them to make sure he was lined up for a landing, the oil hit his face and burned his eyes. He managed to get the Hellcat down and it was so badly damaged that the crew immediately pushed it over the edge of the deck into the sea.

After the Battle of Okinawa, LeRoy Robinson returned to the United States, where he served as a flight instructor for the duration of the war. He left active duty in 1947 but stayed in the Naval Reserve, and became a pilot for Delta Airlines after earning a degree from the University of South Carolina. Called back to duty during the Korean War, he chose to fly transports rather than fighters because he felt that the "rules of engagement"—especially not being able to attack MiG bases across the Yalu River in China—put U.S. fighter pilots at too great a disadvantage. He retired from the reserve as a commander in 1965. ★

George I. Ruddell

COLONEL, USAF

January 21, 1919–February 27, 2015

A POWERFULLY BUILT MAN with a forceful personality, George Ruddell was a popular commander of the 39th Fighter Squadron in Korea, respected for driving himself as hard as he drove his men. Speaking of how demanding it was to fly with Ruddell, one of his wingmen later said: "The only setting that Lieutenant Colonel Ruddell knew on his throttle was full forward from take-off to landing."

Ruddell was a Canadian whose family left Winnipeg not long after his birth to settle in Utah and then Southern California. Having become possessed by the idea of flying as a result of books he read about Eddie Rickenbacker and the other Aces of World War I, he began showing up at the old Telegraph and Atlantic airfield in Los Angeles as a teenager, helping move planes in and out of their hangars and selling tickets for $1.50 for ten-minute rides over the Rose Bowl and the L.A. Coliseum. In return, local pilots took him up in Taylor Cubs. His mother had made him promise not to fly because one of her old boyfriends had died flying into power lines. But Ruddell couldn't help himself. By the summer of 1936, when he was just seventeen, he was soloing regularly, and got his pilot's license two years later. He enlisted in the Army Air Forces a month and a half before Pearl Harbor and received his wings in six months.

After serving a combat tour in the Aleutian Islands flying P-40s, he asked to be sent to a fighter unit in England. He arrived there in 1943 as part of the 514th Fighter Squadron. Piloting a P-47, he flew missions over France, shot down two German Messerschmitt Me 109 fighters, and shared the kill of a Focke-Wulf 190 with another U.S. pilot. His squadron supported the D-day invasion. One of Ruddell's strongest memories was of finding the German Seventh Army in retreat just south of the Loire River—fifteen miles of vehicles, tanks, and horse-drawn equipment: "All three of our squadrons flew mission after mission, utterly destroying that force."

Michael Schoenholtz/Michael Schoenholtz, LLC

After the war Ruddell, now a major, transitioned to jets and commanded two fighter squadrons. In 1952 he volunteered for Korea and took charge of the 39th Fighter Squadron of the 51st Fighter Wing in November. A week later, flying an F-86 Sabre jet with three command stripes on the nose, which he had named "MiG Mad Mavis" after his wife, Ruddell brought down his first MiG-15 in the vicinity of Igu-dong.

It wasn't until six months later, on April 11, 1953, that he got his next kill. A day later he was flying lead in a mission over the Yalu River in "MiG Alley" when his wingman spotted six MiGs. (Ruddell's vision was not as sharp as that of most of the pilots he commanded; they jokingly—and only behind his back—referred to him as "Colonel Weak Eyes.") Ruddell got on the tail of one of the enemy planes, opened fire, and saw smoke. He climbed up and came down firing to finish off the MiG. "I hit his cockpit," he later recalled. "He bailed out."

This kill gave Ruddell five and a half victories (between the two wars in which he fought) and made him an Ace. Yet he was hungry for more and over the next two months shot down five more MiGs.

As with many of his fellow pilots, combat was almost addictive for Ruddell. Known as a fair but "very tough" officer, he had rigidly enforced rules of engagement about not crossing the Yalu into China in pursuit of enemy planes. As one of his pilots later said, "He said he'd cut our heads off, decapitate us if we went north of the river." But on at least one occasion Ruddell's own desire for action got the better of his obedience to orders.

John Bolt, also an Ace with kills in World War II and Korea, was a Marine pilot serving under Ruddell as part of a Marine Corps exchange program with the Air Force. (The men in the squadron called Bolt a "wetback" because he had "swum" over this boundary.) He later told of how one evening Ruddell had invited him to have a drink in "a little cubbyhole he had in his quarters." They talked about how the Chinese and Soviet pilots were using U.S. policy directives about not crossing the Yalu to stage hit-and-run attacks, in which they would offer combat and then run back to Chinese territory when the American F-86s appeared.

As Bolt recalled, Ruddell wanted to be a good officer who enforced the rules of engagement, but he was also suffering from a bad case of "MiG fever" and anxious to go after enemy planes using Chinese territory as a sanctuary, even if it meant jeopardizing his career. While they were drinking and talking, Ruddell became so agitated that tears began running down his cheeks. "I want to go across the river," he told Bolt. "I've got to have some action."

The two men designed a plan: they would take a flight of four F-86s to MiG Alley. Ruddell would order two planes to loiter on the southern edge of the river and provide a radar profile for U.S. communication while he and Bolt would pursue any MiGs they saw that headed north of the river into what they thought was safety. Switching from combat frequency to training frequency, the two men communicated with a private code they had devised. ("Twin," Ruddell said as he crossed into Chinese airspace; "Cities," Bolt answered as he followed.)

A pair of MiGs appeared below them and they gave chase. Ruddell dove down on one of them. But he had forgotten to turn on his windscreen defroster and ice crystals prevented him from clearly seeing the enemy. Bolt had turned on his defroster; he swooped down to shred the MiG with machine-gun fire and sent it into a death spiral. Back at base, after the story of their action had been told, a sign appeared in the officer's recreation area reading "Marine Wetback Steals Colonel's MiG."

George Ruddell ended the Korean War with a total of eight kills. With the addition of his two and a half victories in World War II, he was a double Ace.

After the war, he commanded the 479th and 33rd Tactical Fighter Wings. He retired from the Air Force as a colonel in 1970. ★

Leslie C. Smith

BRIGADIER GENERAL, USAF

October 31, 1918–

A RECENT GRADUATE OF FRESNO STATE COLLEGE working in a bank in Palo Alto, California, Leslie Smith felt that the United States would almost certainly be dragged into the cauldron of war boiling over on the European continent in 1941. The draft had recently been reinstituted and while it was still technically a peacetime draft, he wasn't surprised when he received his notice that summer. He couldn't see himself as an infantryman and so, although he had never been up in an airplane, he signed up for the Army Air Forces a month before Pearl Harbor was attacked. The first thing he did after being accepted as a cadet was go to a local airfield and rent a plane—and a pilot—for an hour's flying time.

He was sent to Corsicana, Texas, for his primary training. Assuming that the entire West enjoyed a climate as mild as Northern California, he was surprised to find that this part of the Lone Star State was miserably cold in the winter. After completing advanced training at San Antonio's Kelly Field in the spring of 1942, he was posted to the 56th Fighter Group at the Army Air Forces facility in Bridgeport, Connecticut. It was here that Smith was introduced to the P-47 Thunderbolt, the plane he would soon fly against German fighters in Europe. It looked huge and formidable, almost otherworldly, to someone who until then had only flown trainers. "A monster plane," as he later put it. "My short legs made it difficult even to climb up onto the wing."

He had been training in planes with 400 horsepower. The P-47 had six times that amount at 2,400 hp. The first time he took it up the plane seemed to have a mind of its own. "I just sort of hung on," he later remembered. "I finally realized that it wasn't going to kill me and made it turn." He got lost on this maiden flight and was afraid that he wouldn't make it home until he found the Pequonnock River and used it to orient himself and find his base.

By January 1943 Smith knew he was about to ship out, but had no idea of where he would be heading. Because of German submarines stalking

Eric Muetterties/Studio 52-Eric Muetterties Photography

American troop carriers off the eastern seaboard, such information was tightly embargoed. In the dead of winter he and the other men in his unit were ostentatiously issued desert uniforms to deceive enemy spies. Once they were packed onto the *Queen Elizabeth* with 12,000 other servicemen, they threw them overboard. The passage was exceptionally rough. Smith noticed that members of bomber squadrons were constantly seasick while he and the other P-47 pilots, accustomed to stomach-churning aerial maneuvers, looked forward to their meals.

They landed at Scotland and went by train to Kings Cliffe in England, an RAF base. There they waited for their P-47s. When the Thunderbolts arrived, red recognition bands were painted around their cowlings and rudders to distinguish them from the German Focke-Wulf 190, the only other radial engine fighter in the European theater.

In April, after weeks of training and reorganization, the 56th flew its first operational mission. Smith says that he and most of the other pilots out for the first time were all secretly sure they would get shot down, but they saw no enemy aircraft on the bomber escort mission.

When German fighters did appear, they sometimes seemed to be uninterested in combat and would simply fly through the bomber formation to disrupt it and keep on going. Smith was credited with an Fw 190 damaged in July, but for several months after that had little opportunity to engage the enemy.

But early in 1944, Smith's squadron started to encounter "huge flocks" of enemy planes. He recalls close to 150 Focke-Wulfs and Messerschmitts attacking the bombers the Thunderbolts were escorting on January 21, 1944. Another U.S. squadron was on the other side of the bombers when the enemy struck. "We had to get up and over the bombers," Smith says. "Then I'm staring down at what looks like a whirlpool" with U.S. and German planes twisting and twirling down into it in tight circles. He saw a P-47 following down two 190s with a third 190 on his tail. He dove down into the melee and was credited with another Focke-Wulf damaged.

On February 22 Smith ran into a pair of 190s. The first one began to smoke when he poured fire into it and immediately went down. The second headed toward ground level to escape, but the P-47, although not particularly maneuverable, was able to use its weight to gain speed in a dive, and Smith quickly caught up with the second 190 and shot it down.

Over the next four months he got two more Fws and two Messerschmitt Me 109s. In one of these kills the German plane was heading down fast and Smith decided to follow it to document its crash with his camera. Afterwards he had the sickening feeling that by pressing his attack he had prevented the pilot from getting out of the plane: "We weren't killing a pilot but destroying an airplane. The Japanese shot pilots bailing out and the Germans did when they became desperate at the end of the war.

We never did." He was relieved when the film he had taken showed that the German pilot had managed to bail out before the plane crashed.

In his months of combat, Smith observed his fellow pilots closely. "The people who got the most kills were very aggressive," he later said, implying that they were not only aggressive but sometimes reckless, dangerously so. "I just wanted to get in there, do some damage, and then come back. There were pilots who didn't want to engage at all. They flew their missions without ever coming close to shooting down an enemy plane. We wanted them just to go home and become instructors or something like that."

After completing seventy-five missions, Smith was eligible to return home. But because of its losses, the 56th was short on experienced pilots who had exhibited leadership qualities. The group commander asked him to stay for another twenty-five missions as a squadron leader. Smith agreed. When he reached one hundred missions the group commander asked him to stay until he shot down another enemy plane. It took him thirty-eight more missions to get his seventh and final kill—the day after Christmas, 1944.

After the war Leslie Smith came home hoping to continue flying as a commercial pilot, but the airlines only wanted bomber pilots because of their experience with multi-engine planes. The bank he had once worked for rehired him. He occasionally checked out a Piper Cub at a local airport, but he missed flying fast airplanes so he joined the newly formed California Air National Guard in 1947 as a lieutenant colonel. He became commanding officer of its 144th Fighter Group and eventually retired as a brigadier general. ★

Donald J. Strait

MAJOR GENERAL, USAF
April 28, 1918–March 30, 2015

LIKE MANY BOYS WHO GREW UP in the "Age of Lindbergh," Donald Strait regarded flight as the great adventure. He always remembered with pleasure getting up early on Saturday mornings, fixing his own lunch, and then riding his bike eight miles to the local airport (a significant effort for a seven-year-old), spending the entire day there watching the planes land, talking to mechanics and crew, and, if he was lucky, a pilot or two.

Graduating from high school in Verona, New Jersey, in 1936, without much interest in college, Strait took a clerk's job at Prudential Insurance, a way of supporting himself while he pursued his ambition of playing professional baseball. He pitched for a local semi-pro team and was good enough to attract interest from the New York Giants. But when he was about to sign a contract with the team, he injured his arm in a weekend game and his dream of a baseball career was over.

He felt himself at a dead end until he read, in an article in a local paper, that the 119th Air Observation Squadron of New Jersey's National Guard was looking for eight new recruits. When he showed up for an interview he saw over one hundred other young men there for the same reason. He was one of the eight chosen ones.

Strait was first trained as an aircraft armorer, then as a rear-seat gunner in the O-46 observation planes the squadron flew. The unit was coming home on a Sunday from a December weekend exercise when people stopped their vehicles as they passed through Baltimore to tell them that the Japanese had bombed Pearl Harbor.

Strait signed up as a cadet in the Army Air Forces and received his wings in January 1943. His first assignment, flying P-47 Thunderbolts in the winter at Westover Field, Massachusetts, involved weather that made anything he later experienced, including flying combat missions from English bases, seem smooth by comparison. "The snow on the runways was just like glass," he

Jimmy Williams/Jimmy Williams Productions

later remembered in an oral history done for the Air National Guard. "We had terrible accidents, guys taking off, losing control, going through snow banks, across fields, hitting barns and such."

Before sailing for England in the summer of 1943 as part of the 356th Fighter Group, Strait and the other pilots in his squadron packed the cockpits of their P-47s with candy, liquor, records, and other personal items. When they picked the planes up at the U.S. Air Depot in Burtonwood two weeks later, these stockpiles were all gone.

Strait's first combat missions in October 1943 were largely unopposed sweeps over northern France and Holland. When he came home from one of them he asked his crew what he should name his plane. After a day or so he got his response from the crew chief: "Jersey Jerk." Somewhat offended, Strait asked why. The chief replied, "Sir, let me tell you why we want to name it that. Any guy who would take off in a single-engine airplane, cross the North Sea in wintertime, and take a chance of getting his ass shot off by the Luftwaffe has to be a jerk." Strait thought a moment then said, "Name it."

He scored his first combat victory on February 6, 1944. His flight spotted a couple of Focke-Wulf Fw 190s below and Strait immediately dived on one of them, his guns scoring hits as he chased it down and watched the pilot bail out. He had two more kills by mid-May and could have rotated home, but he decided to remain in combat when he was offered command of the 361st Fighter Squadron.

Strait was cocky and aggressive—"hard charging," in the phrase often used to describe him by his superiors. "I wanted to excel," he himself said. "I wanted nobody to beat me." He made captain in 1944, less than a year after beginning combat; he made major a year after that.

Soon after he took command of the 361st in November, twenty new P-51 Mustangs were ferried into Strait's air base one morning and his squadron's twenty P-47s were taken away that same afternoon. At that point he had three kills in the Thunderbolt. But the P-51 was a keener weapon. In the next three months he would quickly down ten more German fighters. "If I'd had the Mustang at the beginning," he later said, "I would have had forty victories."

Strait was never disturbed by bad odds. On November 26, as journalist Stephen Sherman later wrote, his squadron of Mustangs was flying escort for B-17s bombing the heavily defended Ruhr area when one of the pilots called out that forty "bandits" were approaching from the south. As the Mustangs dropped their tanks to attack, Strait saw over one hundred more German fighters also heading for the American bombers from another direction. Yelling over the radio, "We've got the whole damn Luftwaffe," he engaged immediately, knocked one Messerschmitt down, and then spotted another and exploded it with concentrated fire, stopping his attack only when low fuel levels forced his planes to head for home.

By late February 1945, Strait had 13.5 kills. When the war ended in May, he was ordered back to the United States. He requested reassignment to the Pacific front, but was told that he had done enough.

Strait rejoined the New Jersey Air National Guard after the war and eventually became its commanding officer. He was recalled to active duty during the Korean War, the Cuban Missile Crisis, and the war in Vietnam. He retired from the Air Force as a major general in 1978.

As Blair Haworth, editor of his oral history, later noted, Donald Strait's first duty was in an aircraft with fixed landing gear that had just recently got an enclosed cockpit, and his last was in a supersonic fighter heavier than the bombers he had escorted over Germany thirty years earlier. In this sense, Strait's career summarized the emergence of the United States as the world's premier air power. ★

James E. Swett

COLONEL, USMCR

June 15, 1920–January 18, 2009

MARINE PILOT JAMES SWETT ALWAYS REMEMBERED the sensation of taxiing his F4F Wildcat for takeoff from Guadalcanal's Henderson Field on the morning of April 7, 1943. It was the twenty-two-year-old's first combat mission and he was jittery with excitement. As he later said, "God knows how I would have felt if I'd known what was in store for me." What was in store were seven enemy kills, then getting shot down himself and almost drowning—all in an intense fifteen minutes of action over Tulagi Island.

Swett had entered naval aviation in August 1941 as an experienced flyer. When he enrolled at Northern California's College of San Mateo in 1939, he decided to get a pilot's license. Even after completing his training in early 1942, and taking a commission in the Marines, he still had over four hundred more hours in the air in private planes than in military aircraft.

Swett was assigned to Marine Fighter Squadron (VMF) 221 and sent to Guadalcanal in late March 1943. Six months earlier the Marine ground force on the island had been fighting for its survival in an effort to control the vital airfield, Henderson Field, which was a key to U.S. efforts to go on the offensive in the Pacific. By the time Swett arrived, the Marines had won the Battle of Guadalcanal, the first major U.S. victory against Japan. Enemy troops that had occupied part of the island had withdrawn and Henderson was more or less secure. But the U.S. hold was still tenuous, threatened by continuing attacks from a large concentration of Japanese ships and aircraft in the area.

On April 7, Swett's flight of four F4F Wildcats was scrambled when up to 150 Japanese aircraft—a U.S. pilot in the area radioed back, "There's millions of them!"—were reported heading toward nearby Tulagi Island to attack U.S. ships in its harbor. They quickly got airborne and intercepted a large force of Japanese Aichi D3A "Val" dive-bombers, escorted by Zero fighters flying high cover. The Wildcats went after the "Vals" before the Zeros could engage.

Swett got on the tail of three of the dive-bombers and quickly shot down two of them. As he was lining up on the third, his Wildcat suddenly shuddered and he saw that one wing had been shredded by friendly fire from U.S. antiaircraft installations below. He continued his attack on the third "Val" and brought it down.

He looked around and saw a formation of another six dive-bombers and, although his plane was now moving sluggishly because of the damaged wing, he went after them. In a few minutes of frenzied action, he shot down four more "Vals." He was going after a fifth when he ran out of ammunition. At that moment his cockpit was shot up by the dive-bomber's tail gunner, peppering his back and arms with shrapnel. His Wildcat on fire and too low for him to bail out, Swett decided to ditch the plane.

He hit the water hard and began to sink immediately. Swett was twenty-five feet down before he managed to wriggle out of the cockpit, his Mae West propelling him to the surface. In addition to his shrapnel wounds, he had broken his nose, which was bleeding so heavily he worried that sharks would be attracted. He managed to inflate his one-man raft and got into it. Three hours later he was approached by a U.S. picket ship. One of its sailors yelled to Swett, "You an American?" He yelled back, "Hell, yes!" and was taken on board and given two shots—one of Scotch and another of morphine.

After a short rest in an Australian hospital, Swett returned to combat at a new base in the Russell Islands, this time flying an F4U Corsair. On June 30, he shot down two Japanese "Betty" bombers over Rendova. Ten days later, he got another "Betty" and a Zero that was attacking his wingman. He didn't see another Zero on his tail, which opened fire on Swett's plane and brought it down. This time he was rescued by local natives in an outrigger and taken to Australian coastwatchers, who arranged for a PBY seaplane to come and get him.

In early October, Swett learned that he was to receive the Medal of Honor. He refused to return to the United States for the ceremony and the medal was presented to him on October 9 by Gen. Ralph Mitchell, commander of Marine Aviation in the Pacific. Swett was back in combat on October 18, shooting down a Zero over Kahili Air Field. When he brought down two more enemy dive-bombers attacking a U.S. task force on November 2, his total enemy kills were 14.5.

In December 1943, Swett came home for a thirty-day leave, getting married and traveling to Washington to receive congratulations from President Roosevelt.

Swett returned to the Pacific and flew off the USS *Bunker Hill* in support of the American landings at Iwo Jima and Okinawa. On May 11, 1945, defending the ship against Japanese kamikazes, Swett scored his final kill, "tearing up" a Yokosuka D4Y dive-bomber with the Corsair's four 20-mm cannon. But two kamikazes managed to hit the *Bunker Hill* that day, setting off explosions that killed four hundred U.S. sailors. Swett and other flyers were forced to land their orphan Corsairs on the USS *Enterprise* and then watch as their planes were immediately pushed over into the ocean because there was no room for them

After this engagement, Swett returned to the El Toro Marine base in California, joining a squadron that was planning for the invasion of Japan until the bombing of Hiroshima and Nagasaki forced a Japanese surrender.

After the war, James Swett commanded a Marine squadron. He was held back when it was sent to Korea because of his status as a Medal of Honor recipient. He left active duty and worked in his family's business for twenty-five years. He retired from the Marine Corps Reserve as a colonel in 1970. ★

David F. Thwaites

LIEUTENANT COLONEL, USAF

September 8, 1921–December 15, 2015

SOME OF THE PEOPLE WHO KNEW DAVID THWAITES well thought that a story from his youth gave a good insight into his character. He was a teenager, fascinated by flight. A barnstormer came to town offering flights in a biplane for a dollar. Thwaites had managed to save the money, but the flyer said that he had to have his parents' permission. Thwaites said that was no problem and waved at a couple of strangers standing nearby. When they waved back he said, "See, that's my mom and dad saying it's okay." The next thing he knew he was taking off.

Thwaites grew up in the borough of Conshohocken in what would become the suburbs of Philadelphia. Historically an industrial and manufacturing center, it was hit hard by the Depression. Rather than laying off most of its employees, the rubber factory where Thwaites' father worked allowed all of them to work one day a week to scrape by. Wanting to improve his prospects, Thwaites' mother got the principal of the local high school to place him in a secretarial course. But when he graduated, the ability to type and do book-keeping didn't seem to offer a life course. An Eagle Scout, Thwaites asked his scoutmaster for advice and was urged to join the military.

Enlisting in the Army Air Corps, Thwaites initially chose to be a radio operator, but he failed the math test. After taking courses at the all-black Hampton Institute, near where he was stationed in Virginia, he passed the exam and was sent to Seattle to serve as a radio man in a B-17. The pilot of the bomber thought that Thwaites should be flying planes and urged him to apply for flight school. He was accepted in the summer of 1942, received his wings in July 1943, and was deployed to England a few months later on board the *Queen Elizabeth* as part of the 356th Fighter Group.

The 356th, stationed at Martlesham Heath Airfield, just outside Ipswich, flew bomber escort missions. It had the highest loss-to-kill ratio of any group in the Eighth Air Force, and Thwaites said that he had taken serious hits from

Chandler Crowell/Chandler Crowell Photography

enemy flak on thirteen occasions. He believed that if he had been flying any plane other than the heavy and durable P-47—named "Polly," after his wife Pauline—he would probably have been shot down more than once. He came back from one mission and noticed when getting out of "Polly" that a bullet had entered the cockpit and clipped a neat hole in his pants leg without breaking the skin. After another engagement with German fighters, his engine quit over the English Channel. As the plane dropped closer and closer to the water, Thwaites had one foot out on the wing and was ready to jump when the engine—almost magically, it seemed—started up again.

Thwaites' first kill came on February 13, 1944, when he brought down a Focke-Wulf 190 over Cambrai, in northern France. On May 13 he destroyed another Fw 190 over Hamburg and six days later he was credited with another kill, along with three probables. On May 25, he shot down a Messerschmitt Me 109 in a high-speed dogfight over Neufchâteau.

After flying in support of D-day, Thwaites became an Ace on August 4, when he shot down an Me 109 near Bremen. After this mission he reported that he had seen the German pilot bail out. When another pilot said that he should have strafed him because he would just fight again in another plane, Thwaites shrugged in disgust and walked away.

David Thwaites had six kills when he came back to the United States in September 1944. He worked as a flight instructor for the duration of the war at Dover Air Force Base in Delaware. He served in the Army Air Forces and the USAF for the next twenty-six years, serving as head of the 15th Tactical Reconnaissance Squadron and other commands. In between his assignments he earned an engineering degree at the University of Washington. After retiring as a lieutenant colonel in 1965, he worked at the National Security Agency in his first love of radio technology. ★

Alexander Vraciu

COMMANDER, USN

November 2, 1918–January 29, 2015

IN ONE OF THOSE ICONIC BLACK AND WHITE photographs of World War II, Hellcat Ace Alex Vraciu stands on the deck of the USS *Intrepid* after just landing from one of the air battles in the Battle of the Philippine Sea, on June 19, 1944. He has a huge grin on his face as he holds up all five fingers on one hand and one on his other to signify what he had just accomplished—flying through flak from friendly ships and fire from enemy aircraft to take down six Japanese planes in the space of eight minutes with a mere 360 shots fired. The brash Vraciu had vowed to "clean the skies" of enemy aircraft that morning before taking off, and that ecstatic smile indicates that he feels he has made good on his promise.

Growing up in East Chicago, Indiana, Vraciu got used to having to explain that his name was pronounced like "cashew." He also had to explain to his friends that his parents, who had emigrated from the Transylvania region of Romania at the turn of the century, were nonetheless "eight centuries away from Dracula."

When he entered DePauw University in 1937, Vraciu thought he might take a pre-med course. But with war on the horizon, preparing for a profession seemed a luxury. He took a Civilian Pilot Training Program course and in effect majored in flying. When he graduated in 1941 he volunteered for naval aviation but wasn't called for training until October. He got his wings in August 1942 and was assigned to VR-3 (later changed to VF-6).

The new squadron was under the command of Lt. Cdr. Edward "Butch" O'Hare. The charismatic O'Hare was a national hero as a result of an action on February 20, 1942, when he single-handedly repelled a group of nine Japanese bombers headed for his aircraft carrier, the USS *Lexington*. He shot down five of them while breaking up the attack in an action that won him the Navy's first Medal of Honor in World War II, a meeting with President Franklin Roosevelt, and adoring coverage by the American press.

Frank Olynyk

Vraciu and O'Hare became close friends during the squadron's training period in Hawaii. When VF-6 was assigned to the USS *Independence* in the late summer of 1943 (and soon transferred to the USS *Intrepid*), O'Hare had made Vraciu his wingman.

Vraciu got his first enemy plane on October 5 when he and O'Hare chased a couple of Zeros preparing to land at Wake Island and each shot one down. When he landed Vraciu was thrilled to see that someone had written his kill in chalk on the superstructure of the *Intrepid* so that crew members could share vicariously in the victory.

On November 20, he was returning from a patrol over Tarawa when he saw a Japanese "Betty"

bomber skimming low over the water in an effort to escape notice. Vraciu dived down and, as he later said, "burned" the plane. But his sense of triumph turned to ashes six days later when Butch O'Hare was shot down by another "Betty" on a hazardous night mission. Feeling a deep sense of loss, Vraciu vowed revenge: "I'm going to get ten of those bastard Bettys!"

He had an opportunity to begin to make good on his promise on January 29, 1944, when he launched from the *Intrepid* for a morning raid against Japanese airfields on the Kwajalein atoll. He was about to set up for a strafing run on some enemy planes he had spotted on the ground when he saw a string of "Bettys" swooping down in a landing pattern. Thinking of O'Hare, he said to himself, "My prayers are being answered." He picked out one of the "Bettys" and dove on it, unleashing a short burst that sent it down. Then he went after another that was trying to evade him and hit it with a burst in the wing root, which caused it to explode. And then he hit a third and saw bodies dropping out of the plane into the water, as crew tried to get out of the burning bomber when it was too low for a parachute to open.

Vraciu had twelve kills by June 19, the day on which he experienced what he later described to oral historian Ronald Marcello as a "once-in-a-lifetime pilot's dream" when his squadron came upon fifty enemy dive-bombers the Japanese had sent in a desperation maneuver against the U.S. task force. Taking part in the feeding frenzy that would become known as the Great Marianas Turkey Shoot, the Hellcats attacked. Vraciu got the six enemy planes that led to the photo of his celebration back on the *Intrepid*, which was printed in papers back home. He shot down another Zero the next day, which gave him a total of nineteen kills. Because he was now the leading Navy Ace of the war, he was brought home to the United States and put on a war bond tour.

Vraciu hated it and didn't bother to be diplomatic in expressing his feelings either then or many years later when he told Marcello, "I didn't want to go around talking to a bunch of draft dodgers." After constantly pressuring his superiors, he was sent back to the USS *Lexington* in December 1944 to participate in "rolling back the carpet to Japan." On his second mission against the Philippines on December 14, he was hit by antiaircraft fire and forced to bail out over the jungle. Having heard of U.S. pilots whose eyes were gouged out and whose ears were snipped off by the Japanese, he made up his mind not to be captured. When some men approached he drew his .38 pistol, but they yelled "Filipino! Filipino!" When Vraciu realized they were anti-Japanese guerrillas he allowed them to dispose of his parachute and dress him in peasant clothes. As they set off for the jungle, one member of the band, a good English speaker who was starstruck by Hollywood personalities, pressed Vraciu for gossip. Had Madeleine Carroll gotten remarried? Did Deanna Durbin have any kids yet?

Vraciu was on the run with the guerrillas for the next five weeks. He was often irritated at being out of the action. He got a wake-up call one day when he was told that twenty-two Filipino men living in a nearby village had been executed by Japanese soldiers, in an effort to force them to give information about his whereabouts.

Finally the guerrilla band linked up with the forces of Douglas MacArthur, who had just made his famous return landing in the Philippines. Vraciu was repatriated and sent to Pearl Harbor, where he asked to be sent back to the *Lexington*. His request was granted, but when he got there he was told that he couldn't return to air combat because if he were shot down and captured he might be tortured into revealing what he knew about guerrilla operations.

Alex Vraciu served in the Navy until 1964, retiring as a commander. The Hellcat he flew on many of his missions was later restored and became part of an English collection housing the largest number of airworthy World War II warbirds in Europe. ⭐

Ralph H. Wandrey

MAJOR, USAAF

November 15, 1921–

WHEN RALPH WANDREY, THEN A LANKY twenty-three-year old, flew into a jungle airstrip in Dobodura, New Guinea, as part of the 9th Fighter Squadron of the 49th Fighter Group early in 1943, he felt that he was entering a parallel universe. Back home in Iowa where he had grown up, cattle grazed placidly on grasslands that seemed to stretch almost infinitely into the horizon on an inert plane. By contrast, the undergrowth in the New Guinean rainforest was thick and impenetrable, with a looming mountain range in the background. "It was inhabited by twenty-foot-long crocodiles and twenty-two-foot pythons," Wandrey remembered, "and two miles ahead of where we parked our airplanes was the Japs' front line."

One day not long after his arrival at Dobodura, he was standing on the wing of his P-38 when he saw a puff of dust in the ground nearby. Then another, closer to the plane. And finally a shot that hit between his feet and penetrated the wing of his plane. He jumped into the cockpit and took off. When he landed later on an Australian officer presented him with the rifle of the sniper who had tried to kill him. Wandrey would take it home after the war and mount it on the wall of his living room as a reminder of what he had survived.

At this point in the war, the United States was finally on the offensive, but the outcome was still very much in the balance. American forces had just managed to defeat the Japanese on Guadalcanal after months of battle. Gen. Douglas MacArthur still believed it was possible that the enemy would invade Australia. Wandrey's squadron of P-38s was tasked with defending U.S. troops and positions. "It was months before I saw one offensive mission," he later said.

On July 23, 1943, Wandrey was on a strafing mission when he saw that one of the P-38s from his squadron was being chased by three Japanese Zeros. He dove to intercept them and opened fire. "There was a satisfying flash as the Zero burst into flames and plummeted downward," he later said. "I gave the next one in line a burst and saw my bullets exploding on his engine and

canopy. 'This is easy,' I thought to myself." Then he saw four other Zeros behind him and had to run for his life, realizing that surviving aerial combat was more difficult than he thought.

Wandrey got his next victory five days later, along with a probable. At this point he was flying as wingman for Medal of Honor recipient Richard "Bing" Bong, who became America's "Ace of Aces" during the war by downing forty Japanese aircraft. With less acute eyesight than most pilots, Bong scored his victories by getting very close before opening fire, often flying through the debris of the planes he destroyed, with Wandrey often alongside him. On one occasion, as he described in an oral history for the Library of Congress, Wandrey later switched planes with Bong for one flight. When he landed, an enlisted man, noticing the twenty-seven Japanese flags painted on the side of his plane, came running up to ask for an autograph. Wandrey was about to sign when he mentioned that he was not Bong. The enlisted man grabbed the autograph book back and ran off.

On a raid against the Japanese fortress on Rabaul, Wandrey's plane was badly damaged by ground fire and he was forced to bail out. After he was rescued, a jeep brought him back to the base. As he entered the mess hall where the other pilots were having lunch, Bong blurted out, "Wandrey, what the heck are you doing back here?" Wandrey replied, "I came to eat. What do you think?" Bong feigned annoyance: "Well, I suppose you'll want your jacket back then." Wandrey realized that the other pilots, giving him up for dead, had already divided up his belongings.

Wandrey got his fourth kill on October 24, 1943, and his fifth five days later, becoming an Ace. Shortly afterwards, the squadron switched to the P-47 Thunderbolt, and, after a few missions, the 9th Squadron was ordered to relocate to a place called Gusap. Since they would not be returning to Dobodura, they had to pack all their personal gear into the cockpit of the plane. As Wandrey later told writer James Oleson, every nook and cranny of his plane was crammed full of belongings and he was taxiing for takeoff when the crew chief stopped him, held up the squadron mascot—a white Muscovy duck named Huckleberry—and told Wandrey he had to take him. He wrapped the duck in a sheet and crammed him into a narrow space on the floor of the cockpit.

When he was about five minutes from the new landing field, a call crackled through Wandrey's headset telling him that the area was under attack by about sixty Zeros. He saw them in the distance and, with Huckleberry looking up quizzically, rose to engage. He lined up one of the planes and squeezed the trigger. Nothing happened. The Zeros began to converge on him. Wandrey saw bullets ripping through his left wing and went into an evasive dive so steep that he momentarily blacked out upon pulling up. Coming back to consciousness with the duck honking nervously, he finally managed to land, took a look at dozens of bullet and cannon-shell holes in his wing, grabbed Huckleberry, and headed for the maintenance tent, where he learned that he had been unable to fire because the trigger wire to his guns was somehow not connected.

After 191 combat missions Ralph Wandrey returned to the United States in August 1944 and became a flight instructor for the duration of the war. He was medically discharged in 1947 after contracting tuberculosis of the renal system. When he got his diagnosis, the doctor told him that people with this disease usually died within two years. Wandrey became a guinea pig for a new "wonder drug"—streptomycin—and after taking massive doses during years in and out of hospitals he was cured. He went on to a productive postwar career working for several railroads. ★

Charles E. Watts

LIEUTENANT COMMANDER, USN

November 14, 1921–

CHARLES WATTS, CALLED "BILLY" from the time he was a boy, was getting ready to climb into his F6F Hellcat for a bombing run against the Japanese naval base at Kure, on the inland sea of Japan, when he learned that six out of fourteen Hellcats that had launched from the USS *Hornet* in a prior flight earlier that morning of March 18, 1945, heading for the same target, had been shot down. Forcing himself to concentrate on the mission and not the meaning of such losses, he launched from the carrier as part of a sixteen-plane group, eight of them carrying 500-pound bombs. A few minutes after getting airborne, they were intercepted by a group of enemy fighters. The eight Hellcats not carrying bombs rushed to engage them. Watts and the seven other planes kept going to the target.

In his year of combat Watts had learned to fear antiaircraft fire far more than aerial combat itself. Nearing the target, he saw several Japanese ships below. But he also saw, as he later said, "the thickest, worst flak I'd ever experienced." It was surreal as well as fearsome because the explosions, blooming like flowers of evil all around him, were in different colors, the Japanese gunners' way of trying to gauge the right altitude to score a hit. As his plane was rocked by the concussions, he gritted his teeth and said to himself, "Well, this is it." Then he picked out a Japanese aircraft carrier as his target and began his dive, three other Hellcats following behind him.

Making a low pass over the carrier, Watts pulled up to see what damage his bombs had done. Nothing. Looking at the other three Hellcats, he saw that because of some malfunction, they too had been unable to release their bombs. He lined up to go back into the flak to give it another try. This time the bombs released but Watts missed the enemy ship he was aiming at. Seeking revenge for the miss as well as for the anxiety he had experienced, he led his flight on a search for targets of opportunity, destroying two locomotives, strafing a Japanese airfield, and then shooting up twenty enemy seaplanes anchored just offshore.

Watts had grown up on a North Texas farm established by his great-great-grandfather, a man known as "Sugar" Johnson Watts. He thought that he would probably be a farmer too, but when he graduated from high school his father insisted that he get away and get an education. Watts spent the next two years at East Texas State College, aware that it was only a respite because the war raging in Europe would inevitably involve the United States.

A few months before Pearl Harbor, wanting to "get a head start" in the service, he hitchhiked to Dallas with a close friend to enlist in the Army Air

Corps. But the Army rejected him because he was too young so he took a job until early 1942, after America had been attacked at Pearl Harbor, when he was accepted by naval aviation. After getting his wings in March 1943 and qualifying for carrier landings, he was ordered to San Diego and from there to the naval air station in Alameda, where he became part of a new squadron just then being formed, VF-18. It had a couple of veterans from the Battle of Midway but otherwise was composed of untested pilots like Watts himself.

The squadron was assigned to the USS *Bunker Hill* and left Pearl Harbor in mid-October. Its first raid was on November 11, against the Japanese stronghold at Rabaul in New Britain. "We didn't know a sheepdog from a billy goat about combat," Watts later told journalist Jane Howard. "We were mostly twenty-one-year-olds, a few were twenty-two or twenty-three." The mission was escorting dive-bombers and torpedo planes to attack enemy ships at the island fortress.

As the U.S. aircraft approached the target, Watts saw what looked like an air armada—at least 75 Japanese fighters. He steeled himself. "But they didn't attack us," he later recalled. "They just formed up on either side of us, almost like they were escorting us."

The Zeros stayed about three hundred yards away, putting on an "air show" of slow rolls in an effort to entice the Hellcats into pulling away from the dive-bombers and torpedo planes and come after them. When the Americans arrived at their target and began to attack the ships in the Rabaul harbor, the Zeros finally sprang into action, filling the air with bullets. Watts saw tracers coming over his wings and just as he realized that a Zero was on his tail, his division leader shot it down.

After the bombing mission was completed, the squadron returned to the *Bunker Hill*. Watts was eating a hurried lunch when Japanese planes attacked. All the pilots jumped up from the lunch tables and ran for their planes, which had been refueled and rearmed. "When there was finally a break in the attack," he recalled, "they launched me. A Jap 'Val' [dive-bomber] pulled out of a dive about two hundred yards in front of me. I hadn't even gotten my wheels up. I shot it down with one blast."

A second "Val" flashed in front of him and he poured a burst into its wing root. When the plane started to fall, he came alongside it and saw the rear-seat gunner slumped over dead. He told himself that his objective was killing machines, not people. But it was a sobering moment. In this first day in action he saw more combat than he would on any other day during his two tours.

Watts had 2.25 victories (the .25 coming when he shared credit with three other pilots for the kill of a "Betty" bomber) when his first tour ended in March 1944. His second tour began in Guam as part of a land-based squadron, some of whose men, including Watts himself, patrolled the island with rifles looking for Japanese soldiers when they weren't flying.

Then he was assigned to the USS *Hornet* and was in combat during the first half of 1945. He had a close call on February 23, when he was part of an attack on Chichi Jima. "At about 12,000 feet everything was serene," he later recalled. "I was admiring the beaches below and watching the movement of the waves. Then we dove down and at six thousand feet the antiaircraft batteries opened fire, lighting up the island like a Christmas tree." He was struck under his arm by a piece of shrapnel, which might have killed him if it hadn't first been slowed by hitting the protective metal around his seat.

It was a little less than a month later, as the *Hornet* pressed the attack on the Japanese mainland, when Watts survived the deadly Technicolor flak of Kure Naval Base on a mission that made him think his number might be up.

He was an Ace with 8.75 kills on June 16 when he flew what he was told in advance would be his last mission, a bombing run against Kyushu. He couldn't help thinking how ironic it would be to get shot down on his final flight, after surviving so many, but his orders were to stay above ten thousand feet and the mission turned out to be uneventful.

Watts was in San Francisco by July. He stopped for a leave at his home in Texas on the way to his next assignment in Pensacola, and was suffering through an attack of malaria there when news came over the radio of the bombing of Hiroshima.

After the war Billy Watts got married, graduated from Southern Methodist University, and had a successful career in the oil industry. ★

Darrell G. Welch

COLONEL, USAF

March 13, 1918–January 13, 2015

ONE SUMMER MORNING IN 1942, residents of Midland, Texas, jittery because the nation was at war, were alarmed by the sound of an aircraft roaring over the city. But as they looked out their living room windows they saw that it was not a Japanese Zero like those that had a few months earlier led the attack on Pearl Harbor, but rather a gleaming new twin-engine P-38. It was piloted by Darrell Welch, and he was buzzing the twelve-story T. S. Hagan Petroleum Building, the city's architectural pride and joy just completed the previous year. Others were baffled by the spectacle, but Estelle Linebarger, who had been a schoolmate of Welch's since the first grade, knew exactly what was happening. "Darrell was telling everyone goodbye," she later told journalist Ed Todd, "because he was going off to war."

Welch had a rough time growing up, being thrown from a horse, bitten by a rattlesnake, suffering diphtheria, and losing his mother—all before the age of ten. Raised with the assistance of relatives, he graduated from Midland High in the trough of the Depression and went off to the University of Texas to study engineering. On his own financially, he mopped floors in the journalism building every day at 5:45 a.m. to pay his board, and worked bussing dishes at a small local restaurant every evening in exchange for his dinner. He felt he was losing ground, and had dropped out to get a full-time job in the fall of 1940, when FDR signed legislation establishing the Selective Service Act. Welch had never been in a plane before but didn't see himself slogging through a ground war. Since he had the required college credits, he went to Randolph Field outside San Antonio and joined the Army Air Corps on October 14, 1940, the day before the draft went into effect.

He was ordered to Glendale, California, for training. At the airfield there he often saw Wallace Berry, Jimmy Stewart, and other stars who owned private planes. He once drove by the Lockheed plant in nearby Burbank, caught a glimpse of two gleaming prototypes of the twin-engine P-38 developed there, and decided that this was the plane he wanted to fly.

After being commissioned in May 1941, Welch was assigned to the 27th Squadron of the 1st Fighter Group at Selfridge field in Michigan. He and the other pilots flew P-35s and P-46s for a couple of months before his dream came true when the 27th was selected as the first Army Air Corps squadron to be supplied with P-38s.

In August 1942, a month or so after Welch's goodbye buzz at Midland, the 27th was ordered to England and ferried their planes to the RAF base near the town of High Ercall in Shropshire. A few weeks later the unit was sent to the Nouvion Air Base in Algeria. Newly promoted to captain, Welch knew that they would be fighting seasoned German pilots, some of whom had been in continuous combat since the Spanish Civil War. His squadron lost three P-38s on its first mission, escorting U.S. bombers hitting targets in Libya.

His first kill came on January 18, 1943, when he shot down one of the Messerschmitt Me 109s attacking a group of B-17 bombers his squadron was escorting on a mission over Tripoli. On March 23 he got another German fighter during a patrol over Bizerte, at the northernmost tip of Tunisia, and the following day was promoted to squadron commander.

By late spring, the Allied push in North Africa had given them command of the sea lanes in the Mediterranean, which meant that Rommel's forces, now on the defensive, had to be resupplied from Sicily primarily by air. On April 15, Welch was the leader of a mission looking for German Ju 52 transport aircraft. There was no radar and scant intelligence, so the U.S. flyers had to guess where the enemy might show up by dead reckoning.

About forty-five minutes after passing over Tunis, he saw what looked like a swarm of locusts taking shape on the horizon. Soon the sky was filled with more than seventy Ju 52s flying in a "V" formation about fifty feet above the ocean, with about thirty Me 109s flying cover above. The P-38s began a feeding frenzy on the Ju 52s as the German fighters dived down to try to ward them off.

Welch went after the lead transport and knocked it down into the water with a single burst. He had zeroed in on a second victim when he saw tracer bullets coming up at it from below and realized that another P-38 was on the attack. "That guy just beat me out of a victory," he murmured to himself in annoyance. But there were more than enough

enemy planes to go around and he turned his attention to another Ju 52. He knew that the way to quickly bring down the German aircraft was to target the engines. He flew as close as possible to the nose of the plane and fired short bursts from his four .50-caliber machine guns and the 20-mm cannon.

In the next fifteen minutes Welch was credited with killing two more Ju 52s, and he always believed that he got at least one more that wasn't confirmed. He was so focused on the transports during the wild melee that he didn't see the two Me 109s on his tail until machine-gun fire shredded his cockpit, sending a dagger-like piece of Plexiglas shrapnel into his shoulder.

His plane was badly damaged and drifting away from the other P-38s, which continued to pursue the Ju 52s. With one of his engines partly disabled, Welch dived, turned, and skidded in an effort to evade the two 109s closing in on him. He knew that it was only a matter of time until his plane was destroyed and he felt irked that he would not be able to celebrate becoming an Ace back at the base. Then, miraculously, it seemed at the time, two P-38s from another squadron suddenly appeared, diving right over him to open fire on the Me 109s and drive them off, allowing Welch to limp back to base.

This engagement was the biggest American air victory of the war at this point, and Welch made the front page of the newspaper back in Midland. A month later, he completed his tour and was sent home. He thought that he might be reassigned to the Pacific, but it never happened.

When the war ended, Darrell Welch returned to college and completed his degree, then returned to active duty with the Air Force and moved home to Midland, where his raucous goodbye to the town a few years earlier was still a local legend. He was stationed in Japan and the Philippines, served at the Pentagon, and taught at the Air War College, before retiring as a colonel in 1970. ★

William H. Wescott

LIEUTENANT COLONEL, USAFR

September 1, 1922–February 25, 2016

WILLIAM WESCOTT GREW UP IN WISCONSIN RAPIDS, Wisconsin, the son of a railroad conductor who had steady work through the Depression and helped feed the family with produce from the small farm he had outside of town.

As a boy, Wescott's imagination was ignited by books about Eddie Rickenbacker and the other World War I Aces, knights of the air engaged in wheeling dogfights in biplanes with bulky machine guns mounted on their noses. He enlisted in the Army Air Corps right after Pearl Harbor was attacked, his two years at Ripon College helping him meet the qualifications for pilot. By January 1942 he was in pre-flight training. Over the next few months he flew a variety of warplanes—dive-bombers, fighters, seaplanes. After getting his wings at Lake Charles Field in Louisiana, he served in the 24th Bomber Group (BG) flying A-24 Banshee dive-bombers in the Aleutians, and in the 417th BG flying A-20 Havoc light bomber intruders in New Guinea.

After the war, he flew P-51 Mustangs with occupation forces stationed in Japan, doing surveillance of ocean traffic between Korea, China, and Japan, and patrolling the 38th parallel dividing North and South Korea. Then he came home to work as a gunnery instructor at Nellis Air Force Base in Nevada, an experience that would serve him well when he was assigned to the 51st Fighter Interceptor Wing and sent to Korea in late February 1952.

He got into the thick of the air fight almost immediately after being "wet-nursed" through a few missions by his squadron operations officer. Wescott's baptism by fire, as he later told writer James Oleson, came during a patrol on April 1. He was flying wingman to the element leader when several cannon shots that seemed to him the size and color of oranges whizzed by his canopy. He looked back and saw a pair of MiG-15s about six hundred feet behind them. His flight leader called for a split-S and a hard six g maneuver downward, followed by a rolling pull up. They shook the MiGs, convincing Wescott that MiG pilots "didn't know gunnery."

Mark Skalny/Mark Skalny Photography

It was also on this patrol that "Westcoast," as the men in his squadron sometimes called him, got his first kills flying as wingman for a skilled pilot named Bill Craig, with whom he had earlier served at Nellis. They had just broken off from an attack when Wescott saw two MiGs closing on Craig and told him to "*Break Right!*" When that MiG and another followed, Wescott told Craig to "*Break Left!*" This brought the MiGs right across Wescott's path, and he shot them both down.

On April 13, he got two more kills when he and another F-86 Sabre jet were "jumped" by four MiGs that overshot them, putting two of them directly in Wescott's gun sights. One went down immediately. After pouring fire into the second MiG, Wescott came up alongside him for a moment and saw what he thought was a Russian pilot dead in the cockpit.

By this time Wescott had thought carefully about the differences between the F-86 and MiG-15. The Soviet plane climbed faster, but the Sabre jet could go supersonic in a dive, which allowed American pilots to feel confident that they could dive away from tight spots and pull up to reengage the enemy on their terms. This is what happened on April 26 when Wescott got his fifth victory.

Initially Wescott did not claim the victory—not having seen the MiG he hit with several bursts actually go down. But Col. Francis "Gabby" Gabreski, the legendary fighter Ace from World War II and Korea who was at that time commanding the 51st Fighter Interceptor Wing, reviewed films of the encounter closely and saw the enemy pilot bail out. Told that he had gotten his fifth kill and was an Ace, Wescott was less excited than his ground crew, who considered it, in part, their achievement as well.

In June, Wescott became commanding officer of the 39th Fighter Interceptor Squadron and flew missions in this capacity until late August 1952, when he returned home. After serving at Nellis AFB as an instructor, he was transferred to Edwards AFB and headed the weapons test program of the F-100A Super Sabre. He left active duty in September 1955 and joined the Air Force Reserve, eventually attaining the rank of lieutenant colonel.

Wescott later worked for North American Aviation as a test pilot and finished his career at the Sabreliner division of Rockwell International. ★

David C. Wilhelm

CAPTAIN, USAAF

May 15, 1919–

DAVID WILHELM WAS BORN IN 1919 into a world that seemed to be his oyster. He grew up in a classic redbrick house in an upper-class area of North Chicago, where one of their neighbors was the family of Richard Loeb, who, along with Nathan Leopold, murdered a teenager named Bobby Franks in 1924 in what was then called "the crime of the century." Wilhelm's father was an executive with the Cudahy Company, the meatpacking giant that wielded political clout throughout the Midwest and that became one of the targets of Upton Sinclair's muckraking classic *The Jungle*. His mother was a Cudahy by birth and inherited the wealth and privilege associated with that dynasty.

As a boy, Wilhelm was sent to a boarding school in Tucson, where he learned to play polo, then on to Andover and finally to Yale. While there he entered ROTC, primarily because its cavalry horses made good mounts for extracurricular polo matches, in which he starred. Upon graduation in 1942 he entered the field artillery as a second lieutenant because of his ROTC background. As an officer he was allowed to transfer to other branches of the Army and after serving several months at Fort Sill in Oklahoma he decided to request the Army Air Forces, not only because he didn't see himself in ground combat, but also, as he later said, "simply because of the glamour and thrill of flying."

Wilhelm began flight training in a Stearman biplane trainer in Bainbridge, Florida, then graduated to the P-40 Warhawks at the Pinellas Army Air Base in Clearwater Beach. After completing fighter training he became part of the 31st Fighter Group and was assigned to a staging area at Newport News, Virginia. On June 7, 1943, his squadron boarded *The Empress of Australia*, a former ocean liner pressed into wartime service as a troop transport, and headed for Casablanca. Near its destination, the ship went into evasive zigzagging maneuvers when it was reported that a German submarine was waiting in ambush, but the submarine was destroyed by a U.S. warship.

Wilhelm entered combat in Morocco flying a British Spitfire, an aircraft that was a world away from the lumbering and outmoded P-40s in which he had trained. ("It was short range, could climb like a bird to intercept the German Messerschmitts and Focke-Wulfs," he later said.) Later, after the Allied beachhead was established in Salerno, his squadron was sent to Monte Corvino, a location south of Naples, where the pilots were billeted in a bombed-out building near the airstrip.

Wilhelm got valuable "on-the-job training" from the enemy. On one mission, for instance, he was chasing a Focke-Wulf Fw 190 when the German pilot (Wilhelm later learned he was a member of the elite Hermann Goering squadron) did a "hammerhead stall" in front of him, dropping down, and then as Wilhelm went by, coming up behind him in a firing position. It was only by what he called "violent evasive action" of his own that he was able to keep from being shot down.

As the Allies were liberating Rome, the high command replaced the Spitfires of Wilhelm's squadron with P-51 Mustangs (which he felt was "like going from a Model T to a Cadillac"), relocated the squadron to the San Severo base in eastern Italy, and gave it the new mission of escorting B-17 and B-24 bombers on attacks against oil fields, munitions factories, and other targets in Germany, Yugoslavia, and southern France.

Wilhelm would never forget the 5 a.m. briefings that preceded these missions. They were "tense and solemn," he later wrote in his book *Cowboy Ace.* Officers highlighting targets "always brought a groan from the pilots." The planes were ready for takeoff by 7 a.m. Then came a quiet two-hour flight to rendezvous with the B-17s, and "a hairy 20 to 40 minutes of careening around the sky at full power" as they tried to keep the enemy from knocking the bombers down. The first week after they began flying the Mustang, his squadron lost twelve of its twenty-five pilots to the enemy.

But there were sometimes moments of comic relief amidst the tragedy. In one mission over Ploesti, Romania, a Mustang pilot who had just relieved himself into the "pilot relief tube" they all used on these long flights suddenly found himself in a violent battle with several German fighters. He yelled out over the radio, "I've been hit and I have glycol all over my windshield. Going to have to bail out!" But the other Americans convinced him that the yellow fluid on his windshield was actually urine, not fluid from a damaged radiator, and got him back in the fight.

Wilhelm shot down his first Messerschmitt over Ploesti on April 21, 1944, got his second two weeks later over Zagreb, and his third over Ploesti again on May 24. By June 27 he was an Ace and got his sixth and final kill over Bucharest on July 3.

Soon after this he was brought back to the United States, where he served as a flight instructor for the remainder of the war and was furloughed out of the Army Air Forces in May 1945. After working briefly for Cudahy, the family business, Wilhelm bought a cattle ranch in Fraser, Colorado, which he operated himself. He couldn't completely eradicate the heritage of family privilege—his sister once showed up in a fur coat at one of his cattle brandings—but he became a success on his own terms, at one point in his long and varied career in the cattle business owning a feedlot with an annual volume of 200,000 head. He was proud to have done it his way. Summing up his life in *Cowboy Ace,* he wrote, "I have been my own 'pilot' rather than associating myself with other commands." ★

Bruce W. Williams

LIEUTENANT, USNR

January 19, 1919–

GROWING UP IN SALEM, OREGON, during the Great Depression, Bruce Williams felt that he had outgrown the world he had been born into. He always recalled how his father, a local attorney, had taken him as a boy to see the Ku Klux Klan, which the elder Williams loathed, stage its annual ride through the city. And when Bruce himself entered Willamette University in 1937, the school still forbade drinking and smoking on campus and had just recently relaxed a ban on dancing.

While finishing his bachelor's degree and spending a year at the Willamette Law School, Williams followed the war spreading through Europe and felt that it was certain that the United States would become involved, and that this involvement would change the country forever. FDR had signed legislation that established the first peacetime draft in 1940, and Williams felt he could control at least a piece of his destiny if he volunteered before he was called. Convinced that the cockpit of an airplane would be a better place to spend the war than a foxhole, he quit law school and entered the Navy as an aviation cadet in the fall of 1941.

A husky six-footer who had played football and basketball in college, Williams was in training at Corpus Christi, Texas, when Pearl Harbor was attacked. He received his wings in the late spring of 1942. Driven to excel, he saw combat as an arena where he could prove himself. But although he was ready to fight early in the war, he was not given a chance for a year and a half, serving as a flight instructor instead of a combat pilot. Finally, in June 1944, he was assigned to the newly formed VF-19 ("Satan's Kittens") serving on board the USS *Lexington*, and set out to make up for lost time.

In his first days of combat, Williams had what he later called one of his "first big scares of the war" during an attack on Japanese installations on the island of Chichi Jima. "The antiaircraft batteries were murderous," he recalled. "It was like flying down a gun barrel. It was hard to get in and get out." He was right to be apprehensive. One of his squadron mates, Joseph Kelly, was

Anna Reed/Anna Reed Photography

one of several American pilots brought down in the fighting. He was taken prisoner by the Japanese, subsequently killed, and his heart eaten at the officers' mess, an act for which the Japanese officer in charge was hanged at the end of the war.

But Williams was willing to push his Hellcat to the limit. On a September 22 engagement near Luzon, his flight of ten Hellcats was jumped by upwards of fifty enemy fighters. Williams recalled what followed as "a dogfight to save ourselves." He shot down two of the sleek Ki-61 "Tony" fighters, which U.S. intelligence had mistaken for Messerschmitts at the beginning of the war. Then he got another "Tony" on October 12, and two days later took down a Zero in a tree-skimming fight that took place twenty feet above the ground.

Williams' disregard for his own safety almost led to disaster on October 21. He was leading a flight of eight Hellcats on a bombing run against two Japanese ships when he spotted three ammunition barges and dove low to go after them. "I saw my tracers going into the barges and starting a fire," he said later on. "I decided to get out of there!"

But not soon enough. The enemy barges below Williams suddenly evaporated in a giant explosion that destroyed all the instruments of his Hellcat, shredded its right wing, lodged a foot-long chunk of wood in its engine, ripped off its belly tanks, and suddenly catapulted the bucking plane two hundred feet upward, flipping it, as a Navy press release about the incident made a point of stating, "on its back."

But the Hellcat was one of the most rugged fighters in the American arsenal. (*Air & Space* writer Cory Graff later wrote that if the Japanese Zero resembled a samurai warrior, the Hellcat was more like a "burly Brooklyn bouncer.") Williams somehow managed to get it back under control. Not knowing the location of the *Lexington*, he was mentally preparing for a water landing when the carrier suddenly came into view. His commanding officer

got Adm. Marc Mitscher to turn the entire task force into the wind so that Williams could land. The deck crew of the *Lexington* took one look at the Hellcat, decided it was beyond repair, and immediately pushed it overboard. *Air & Space* magazine in 2001 designated Williams' plane as one of the ten most damaged aircraft in the war.

Williams was taken to the commanding officer of the *Lexington*, who asked him how high he had been flying during his strafing run on the ammunition barges. "Ten feet, sir," Williams answered. The officer gave him an incredulous look, shook his head, and walked off muttering, "You damn kids!"

Three days later Williams was back in the air again in a new plane and shot down three enemy Ki-21 bombers trying to attack the U.S. task force, making him an Ace and giving him seven kills in just over a month of intense combat.

Bruce Williams came home to Salem at the end of the war, finished law school at Willamette, and became as hard-charging a trial attorney—one of the best in the state—as he had been a pilot.

In May 2015, Williams, then ninety-six, was flown to Washington, D.C., in a private plane to participate in the ceremonies that surrounded the Congressional Gold Medal awarded to all 1,447 American Fighter Aces from World War I to the present. Upon his return to Salem, Williams was asked what he thought of the flight. "Terrifying," he replied. ★

John T. Wolf

LIEUTENANT (JG), USNR

February 4, 1921–

JOHN T. "MIKE" WOLF HAD SEVEN VICTORIES during the war in the Pacific, but one of his strongest memories was of a day during the Battle of the Philippine Sea when he had no kills but helped save lives. After taking off with his squadron from the USS *Hornet*, as he later told journalist Terri Gleich, his F6F Hellcat experienced trouble—a broken seal that sprayed oil all over the windshield. Wolf managed to make it back to the carrier for an emergency landing and then followed the progress of the battle as a noncombatant. When it became obvious that the distance to the target had been miscalculated and many of the Hellcats returning after the attack were running out of fuel and being forced to ditch, Wolf asked the captain of the *Hornet* if he and other pilots could drop surplus rubber rafts to mark the position of the downed pilots. As a result all of his squadron's flyers who ditched in the battle were saved.

Wolf grew up in Long Beach, California. He was attending Long Beach City College (and serving as student body president) when Pearl Harbor was bombed. He remembered that the night of December 7, 1941, antiaircraft guns started shooting at what they thought, incorrectly, were Japanese planes, and the next morning the city's streets were littered with shrapnel and shell casings.

With some friends and fellow "beach bums," Wolf tried to enlist in the Coast Guard, but he was rejected because he was too skinny—about 138 pounds. He then went to naval aviation but thought he had no chance because he wore glasses. He didn't wear them at his physical. The doctor examining him was called away for a moment and when he returned asked Wolf absentmindedly if he had already done an eye check. Wolf deadpanned, "Yes, SIR." He passed the exam and didn't wear his glasses for the next four years. As he commented years later, "I saw well enough to get the plane off the ground."

After entering the Navy in May 1942, Wolf did flight training at Naval Air Station Los Alamitos in California and at Corpus Christi, Texas, and completed carrier qualifications in Norfolk, Virginia. He was assigned to the new VF-2,

Alan Abramowitz/Abramowitz Studio

which had been formed at Naval Air Station Atlantic City in June 1943. VF-15, under the command of the charismatic David McCampbell, would have more kills. VF-17, the "Jolly Rogers," was more in the public eye. But VF-2 would have more Aces—twenty-seven—than any other naval squadron. Known as the "Rippers," VF-2 also had a dragon logo designed by Walt Disney Studios.

Sent to Hawaii to participate in exercises, VF-2 so impressed Lt. Cdr. Butch O'Hare that he asked that it replace the fighters in his own air group on board the USS *Enterprise* for the upcoming campaign in the Gilbert Islands. Wolf went into combat on board the carrier in November 1943.

In March 1944, VF-2 transferred to the USS *Hornet*. Wolf shot down a Zero on March 30. On June 11, he had his biggest day of combat flying as part of a strike force of more than one hundred Hellcats against Guam. When one F6F was hit by antiaircraft fire and went down, the squadron commander, with Wolf on his wing, went down to try to pinpoint where it hit. Within seconds, Wolf saw thirty "bandits" above them. The two Hellcats did a "chandelle" turn and climb and got an altitude advantage on the Zeros. In the furious action that followed, Wolf shot down three of them. In this engagement, he also saw the strange sight of a Japanese pilot in a parachute coming down almost directly on top of a Hellcat pilot, who had also bailed out of his plane. Since Wolf had no more ammunition, he flew through the top part of the Japanese pilot's parachute to try to get him away from the American. (A large part of the chute trailed behind him as he landed on the carrier.) He later heard that despite his efforts the American flyer had been captured and executed.

In comparison to the adrenaline-fueled time in the air, pilots' daily lives on board the carrier seemed to unfold in slow motion. Wolf told his daughter Diane that he found some of the unwritten "rules" a little disconcerting, particularly the taboos against making "best" friends because you never knew who was coming back from a mission, and against "frat-ernizing" with enlisted crew members. (Wolf was once reprimanded by the captain for spending too much time with the Hellcats' mechanics.) But some of these rules made perfect sense to him—especially the ban on criticizing fellow pilots who felt that they simply couldn't handle combat any longer and requested reassigned duties.

When Wolf shot down a Zero near Iwo Jima on July 3, it was his seventh and last kill. On September 29, 1944, his squadron was dropped ashore on Ponam Island to await transport back to Honolulu and from there to the United States. One of his assignments in the months that followed was as a "guinea pig" in centrifuge testing at the University of Southern California for a new flight suit, which increased the number of g's the wearer could withstand without passing out.

After the war, Mike Wolf left the Navy and built a successful financial planning business back home in Long Beach. ⋆

John A. Zink

LIEUTENANT (JG), USN

August 8, 1921–

UNLIKE OTHER BOYS OF HIS ERA, JOHN ZINK was not particularly interested in flight while growing up in St. Mary's, Ohio. Twenty years old when he entered the Navy in June 1942, he chose aviation for two reasons. One was that his older brother, whom he admired, was a naval aviator. Second and more important, he was not inclined to spend the war "walking in the mud" as an infantryman.

Zink's father had purchased a beer distributorship when Prohibition ended in 1933, and after graduating from high school in 1939 John worked for him driving a delivery truck. He decided to study engineering at Ohio Northern University in the fall of 1941, and was studying in his dorm room on the afternoon of December 7 when news of the attack on Pearl Harbor made him realize that his college days were numbered. After talking to his brother, who was then working as a flight instructor, Zink enlisted in the Navy just as he was about to be drafted into the Army. He was allowed to finish his first year at Ohio Northern and reported for duty in mid-June 1942.

Zink did his primary training in Livermore, California, learning to fly in one of the yellow N2S Stearman biplane trainers other cadets called "the Yellow Peril," but Zink always defended as "the best airplane I ever flew." After advanced training in Corpus Christi, Texas, he received his wings on August 1, 1943, and then qualified for carrier landings on the Great Lakes. Soon after, he was assigned to VF-11 training at Naval Air Station Alameda in the San Francisco Bay Area. A few of the other pilots couldn't resist violating the strictly enforced rule against flying under the Golden Gate Bridge. But Zink, knowing that it was a brig offense, wasn't tempted. The only time he went under the bridge was in mid-1944, on a "jeep" carrier headed toward Hawaii.

After a few weeks in Hilo, VF-11 was assigned to the USS *Hornet*. About this time Zink's father died and after a week's compassionate leave to attend his funeral, Zink returned to Hawaii in time to ship out with the squadron on a transport ship headed for the *Hornet*.

Tom Dubanowich

He went into combat at the beginning of October 1944, on missions to "soften up" enemy bases in and around the Philippines. On October 14, he was flying on a patrol mission as wingman for the leader of a flight of eight Hellcats when they intercepted a large number of Japanese "Judy" dive-bombers headed for U.S. ships. As the Americans made their first pass on the "Judys," they were "ambushed" by Japanese Zeros. Zink had just shot down one of the dive-bombers when he saw that the flight leader's plane had been hit. As the Hellcat fell toward the ocean, Zink followed to try to help the pilot. But his flight leader was dead when the plane hit the water.

Zink says, "Just then I looked into my rearview mirror and saw a Zero on my tail. It shocked me. And I got out of there." But before the engagement was over he had shot down a Zero to get even for his flight leader.

Thinking back on this fight and the ones that followed, he mused: "I was never scared during, but I was practically paralyzed with fear afterward. I always felt very lucky. It was not easy to answer why

I was always able to come back to the ship while other guys didn't."

By mid-December, Zink had four more kills, including two of the fast new Yokosuka P1Y light bombers, known as the "Frances" by Allied intelligence. An Ace now, he was back on the *Hornet* after having been "loaned out" to the *Intrepid* and *Hancock* for brief periods.

Early in 1945, the *Hornet* was ordered back to the U.S. base at Ulithi, in the Caroline Islands, for reprovisioning. When it arrived, Zink was ordered back to the United States. He always regretted being taken out of the action just at the moment when enemy kamikaze attacks were becoming heavier: "I would have liked to have been there and played a role in knocking them down before they hit our ships."

Back at Naval Air Station Alameda, Zink trained with another squadron for a few months. By the time he returned to action on board the *Hornet*, the war was over. One of his strong memories was, when returning home for good on a troop ship in the fall of 1945, the commanding officer of his last squadron spent the voyage trying to convince Zink to make the Navy his career. Day in and day out, Zink listened politely to the officer's arguments, but his answer was always the same: "No dice."

After leaving the Navy, John Zink finished his degree at Ohio Northern University and then went to Ohio State to study dentistry. After advanced training in oral surgery he began a practice in Lima, Ohio, which became his new hometown. ★

William H. Allen

MAJOR, USAF

April 22, 1924–August 17, 2014

ACE WILLIAM ALLEN was photographed for *Wings of Valor* but passed away before completing his interview. He is credited with five aerial victories in World War II.

Robert A. Karr

LIEUTENANT COLONEL, USAF

January 11, 1924–January 17, 2015

ACE ROBERT KARR was photographed for *Wings of Valor* but passed away before completing his interview. He is credited with six aerial victories in World War II.

Author's Note

I EITHER SPOKE WITH OR COMMUNICATED IN WRITING with almost all of the Aces profiled in this book or with their families in the cases of the few who were too aged or infirm to be interviewed or to review what I wrote about them. I was amazed by how many of the Aces, although well into their nineties, have near total recall of their air battles and flying careers. Their memories are a national treasure.

Another major resource were the memoirs that some of the Aces have written about their combat experiences. Some of these works are exuberant tales of flying and fighting; some are more sober accounts of the human costs of battle. Taken together they tell the epic of America's air wars in Europe, the Pacific, and later in Korea. I have cited some of these memoirs in the profiles of the Aces who wrote them. I would recommend them to readers looking for a more detailed account of a given Ace's life and times.

I also looked at biographies other authors had written about some of these men and at the important military histories of the campaigns in which they fought.

I have already acknowledged my reliance on Frank Olynyk's monumental work *Stars and Bars* (1995), which contains detailed entries on the units in which the Aces served, the planes they flew, and the dates and places of their victories along with the types of enemy aircraft they destroyed. I leaned heavily on this matchless and encyclopedic work for basic empirical data about the Aces' combat careers.

I also consulted two invaluable books by James Oleson: *In Their Own Words: True Stories and Adventures of the American Fighter Ace* and *In Their Own Words: The Final Chapter*. In these works, Oleson gathers personal remembrances by the Aces—some brief and others quite extensive—that open a unique window onto the camaraderie, occasional comedy, and tense drama of the fighter pilot experience.

I referred to military historian Eric Hammel's excellent trilogy *Aces in Combat: The American Aces Speak*; *Aces Against Germany: The American Aces Speak*; and *Aces Against Japan: The American Aces Speak*. These books also present the Aces' own candid descriptions of their actions.

And of course I relied on the internet for instant information that would have taken months to acquire in the analog age. I found a wealth of incidental details about the Aces' air battles and lives; even the most casual of these details helped give body to the profiles. Also on the web I found interviews the Aces have given to their hometown newspapers over the years, oral histories housed in the Library of Congress and in the virtual libraries maintained by fighter pilot associations, and other useful material that I have cited, when appropriate, in the text.

But finally *Wings of Valor* is a collection of narratives, not a research project. My intention is descriptive as well as documentary—to tell how the amazing individuals in this book became pilots and Aces and a little about what the experience meant to them and how it affected their lives. I was always aware in writing about these men—and I hope the reader will be as well—that they are Eminent Americans, and we will not see their like again. ★

—PETER COLLIER

PHOTOGRAPHIC SOURCES

Nick Del Calzo, lead photographer
William H. Allen; Clarence E. Anderson; Abner M. Aust Jr.; Clarence A. Borley; James L. Brooks; Henry Buttelmann; Richard G. Candelaria; Dean Caswell; Lawrence A. Clark; Charles G. Cleveland; John T. Crosby; Jefferson J. DeBlanc; James E. Duffy; Fred L. Dungan; Billy G. Edens; Arthur C. Fiedler; Joseph J. Foss; Frank L. Gailer Jr.; Robert E. Galer; Clayton K. Gross; Willis E. Hardy; Frank D. Hurlbut; Arthur F. Jeffrey; Robert A. Karr; Dean S. Laird; James F. Luma; Joseph D. McGraw; Robert C. Milliken; Sanford K. Moats; Steve N. Pisanos; Tilman E. Pool; Luther D. Prater; R. Stephen Ritchie; James E. Swett; Ralph H. Wandrey; Charles E. Watts; Darrell G. Welch; David C. Wilhelm

Alan Abramowitz/Abramowitz Studio
John T. Wolf

Andrew Achong/Andrew Achong Photography
Jeremiah J. O'Keefe Sr.

Amber Barker/Looking Glass Photography
Richard H. Fleischer

Mark R. Bertelson
Richard L. Bertelson

Chandler Crowell/Chandler Crowell Photography
Robert A. Clark; George G. Loving; David F. Thwaites

Michael Davis
Barrie S. Davis

Tom Dubanowich
Raymond M. Bank; Robert P. Fash; Edward L. Feightner; John A. Zink

Ariel Fried/Ariel Fried Photography
Donald M. McPherson

Marco Garcia/Marco Garcia Photography
Winton W. Marshall

Marc Glassman/Marc Glassman Photography
Frederick R. Payne

Roy Grinnell
Richard H. Fleischer (painting)

Gabe Hernandez
Lynn F. Jones

Dominik Huber
Robert B. Carlson

David Jaffe/Lift-Off Studios
Ralston M. Pound

Athena Lonsdale/Athena Photography
Cecil G. Foster; Kenneth B. Lake; Frank E. McCauley

Alex McKnight/AM Photo, Inc.
Benjamin C. Amsden; Richard S. Becker; Perry J. Dahl; Charles D. Hauver;
Philip L. Kirkwood; Jack Lenox; James F. Low; George P. Novotny

August Miller/August Miller Photo LLC
Alden P. Rigby

Eric Muetterties/Studio 52-Eric Muetterties Photography
Leslie C. Smith

Frank Olynyk/AFAA
Clyde B. East; Henry Meigs II; Ralph S. Parr; Alexander Vraciu

Peter Panayiotou/Panayiotou Photography, Inc.
Fred F. Ohr

Anna Reed/Anna Reed Photography
Bruce W. Williams

Rich Saal/Rich Saal Photography
Stephen J. Bonner Jr.

Mark Skalny/Mark Skalny Photography
William H. Wescott

Michael Schoenholtz/Michael Schoenholtz, LLC
George I. Ruddell

John Slemp/Aerographs Aviation Photography
W. Robert Maxwell; Leroy W. Robinson

Gregg Wagner/AFAA
photographs of young Aces

Jimmy Williams/Jimmy Williams Productions
Donald J. Strait

Todd A. Yarrington/Yarrington Studio
Donald R. Quigley

Selected Bibliography

Anderson, Clarence E., and Joseph P. Hamelin. *To Fly and To Fight: Memoirs of a Triple Ace*. Pacifica, CA: Pacifica Military History, 1999.

Cleaver, Thomas McKelvey. *Fabled Fifteen: The Pacific War Saga of Carrier Air Group Fifteen*. Pacifica, CA: Pacifica Military History, 2014.

Davis, Larry. *The 4th Fighter Wing in the Korean War*. Atglen, PA: Schiffer Publishing, 2001.

Foster, Cecil G., and David K. Vaughn. *MiG Alley to Mu Ghia Pass: Memoirs of a Korean War Ace*. Jefferson, NC: McFarland, 2001.

Hammel, Eric. *Aces Against Japan II: The American Aces Speak*. Pacifica, CA: Pacifica Military History, 2007.

Lopez, Donald. *Into the Teeth of the Tiger*. Washington, DC: Smithsonian Books, 1997.

Loving, George. *Woodbine Red Leader: A P-51 Mustang Ace in the Mediterranean Theater*. New York: Presidio Press, 2003.

Mersky, Peter B. *Whitey: The Story of Rear Admiral E. L. Feightner, A Navy Fighter Ace*. Annapolis, MD: Naval Institute Press, 2014.

Oleson, James A. *In Their Own Words: The Final Chapter: True Stories from American Fighter Aces*. Bloomington, IN: iUniverse, 2011.

Olynyk, Frank. *Stars and Bars: A Tribute to the American Fighter Ace 1920–1973*. London: Grub Street, 1995.

Pisanos, Steve N. *The Flying Greek: An Immigrant Fighter Ace's WWII Odyssey with the RAF, USAAF, and French Resistance*. With a foreword by Walter Cronkite. Sterling, VA: Potomac Books, 2008.

Sears, David. *The Last Epic Naval Battle: Voices from Leyte Gulf*. New York: NAL, 2007.

Trest, Warren A. *Once a Fighter Pilot: The Story of Korean Ace Lt. General Charles "Chick" Cleveland*. Montgomery, AL: River City Publishing, 2012.

Varhola, Michael. *Fire and Ice: The Korean War, 1950–1953*. Boston: Da Capo Press, 2000.

Vraciu, Alex. Oral history project, interview with Ronald E. Marcello, October 9, 1994: "Vraciu, Alex (b. 1918)." Vol. OH1037, Pearl Harbor Survivors Project, Oral History Program, University of North Texas.

Wilhelm, David. *Cowboy Ace: The Life Adventures of David Wilhelm.* Parker, CO: Thornton Publishing, 2010.

About the Authors

NICK DEL CALZO is an award-winning photojournalist who conceives and produces photographic projects that advance human values. He created the book concept and photographed our nation's heroes for *Medal of Honor: Portraits of Valor Beyond the Call of Duty*, which has sold more than 300,000 copies. In 1997 he photographed and produced *The Triumphant Spirit: Portraits & Stories of Holocaust Survivors,* another highly acclaimed book that features portraits of then-living survivors of the Holocaust. He lives in Denver, Colorado.

PETER COLLIER is the author of several best-selling dynastic biographies, among them *The Rockefellers: An American Dynasty*; *The Kennedys: An American Dream*; and *The Fords: An American Epic.* His most recent books are *Medal of Honor: Portraits of Valor Beyond the Call of Duty* and *Choosing Courage: What It Means to Be a Hero.*